"SCOTT WERBELOW'S ADVENTURES** as a game warden will keep you on the edge of your seat. It's a must read."

-Jim Zumbo, Former Hunting Editor,
Outdoor Life Magazine

"GAME WARDEN SCOTT WERBELOW** in many ways reminds me of C.J. Box's Joe Pickett, only in his instance a real person and a much better storyteller!

- Larry Weishuhn - "Mr. Whitetail"

"THE TALES IN *SON OF A POACHER II*** are as raw and potent as a shot of whiskey. If you've ever wondered what it would be like to walk in the shoes of a Wyoming game warden, this book is for you.

- John B. Snow, Shooting Editor,
Outdoor Life Magazine

SON OF A POACHER II

BLAST FROM MY PAST

Scott C. Werbelow

CONTENTS

PROLOGUE

As readers know, Scott C. Werbelow's first book, *Son of a Poacher–Wyoming Warden in the Making*, chronicles his growing up with a poaching father and being raised on a sheep/cattle ranch in northern Wyoming by his mother and stepfather, Diana and Martin Mayland. Not much in Scott's young life could get in the way of his wild, fun-loving outlook on life and his determination to find a way around any obstacle that stood in his way.

Some interesting facts about the place where Scott grew up, might help the reader enjoy his story even more. Wyoming is the 10th largest state in the U.S. It is approximately 372 miles wide and 279 miles long. Elevation ranges between 3101 and 13,809 feet. A traveler encounters mountains, grasslands, streams, and desert-like topography covered with sagebrush, cacti, and sandy soil. Wyoming roads connect ranchland and towns whose distances apart vary from 5 to 100 miles. Road travel is complicated by weather conditions including blizzards, mud and rockslides which at times warrant temporary road closure.

Wildlife in Wyoming is abundant and thrives under the management of the Game and Fish Department. There are over 800 non-game species along with Wyoming's premier wildlife which are protected by less than 65 district game wardens in the entire state. The Department's state logo is "Conserving Wildlife and Serving People". Besides managing wildlife, an equally important part of a warden's job is building and maintaining strong working relationships between landowners, outfitters, and sportsmen. A game warden's duties and responsibilities include wildlife management, data collection and analysis, enforcement of game, fish, trapping and boating laws and regulations. A warden's time is also spent preventing damage to crops and livestock by wildlife and responding to nuisance wildlife calls from the public. Only approximately 30% of a game warden's time is actually spent performing law enforcement duties.

Through all these efforts, the Wyoming Game and Fish Department ensures that the public continues to enjoy Wyoming's fish and wildlife resources through hunting, fishing, trapping, wildlife watching and other forms of outdoor recreation. Hunters, anglers and wildlife watchers contribute over a billion dollars to Wyoming's economy each year. Wyoming game wardens play an important role in protecting all of Wyoming's treasured wildlife.

Chapter 1

CASPER WYOMING

I could feel warm blood trickling down my face as the large Hispanic man held his double-bladed ax against my forehead. He stared into my eyes and said, "You need to get the F--- out of our camp right now!" I looked directly into the man's eyes and replied, "No, you and your ax need to go sit back down in your chair by the fire or you are both going to jail for interference with a police officer!" The large Hispanic man looked over at my partner Cleeve who still had his pistol drawn and aimed at the man's head. The man looked at me and said, "OK!" He then walked back to the fire and sat down in his chair. Whew, I thought to myself as I took a deep breath. I noticed my hands were trembling. I couldn't believe that I had just used my authority and the man actually complied with me. Cleeve holstered his pistol and kept an eye on me while I issued a citation to the second man for fishing without a license. My hands were still trembling as I wrote out the citation in the cab of my patrol truck under the glow of my dome light. Blood continued to drip off my face and onto the front of my red shirt.

I was glad that I had Cleeve for backup, if not things may have gone very differently. I had the man sign his citation and got the heck out of there as quick as I could! We drove back up to the Cortes patrol cabin in the dark and parked in front of the cabin. Cleve said, "Congratulations, you handled that situation well, except you forgot to give the man back his driver's license and it's still lying on the dash!" Crap! I thought to myself, I could have been killed and now I have to bring the man back his driver's license! Cleeve said, "Why don't you run back down there and I'll pour you a drink for when you get back," as he exited the passenger side of the patrol truck. I said, "Hopefully I make it back to enjoy that drink!" as I tore out of the driveway to return back to their camp. I didn't want to return to their camp because now they have had some time to think about things and get really mad! I soon returned to their camp and they were all drinking tequila next to their campfire, I'm sure they did not want to see me again! I jumped out of my patrol truck and quickly placed the man's driver's license under his windshield wiper on his truck. I yelled at the camp from a distance and said, "Sorry, I forgot to give you your driver's license back, it's underneath your windshield wiper!!" I heard a man yell "F--K YOU FISH COP!!" I quickly jumped into my truck and got the heck out of there!

Cleeve and I spent the night in the Cortes patrol cabin and got an early start checking fishermen the next morning. It was Memorial Day weekend. Many fishermen would be out fly fishing the blue-ribbon fishery known as the "Miracle Mile." The senior game warden for that area was a female at the time and not many people cared much for her. Cleeve and I had met with the female senior game warden for that area earlier that morning. She said, "Good luck guys, you'll check a lot of fishermen but you won't come across many violations because they are all purist fly fishermen from Colorado. They catch and release all their fish, and rarely will you check someone fishing without a license!" We thanked her for her words of encouragement and went to work checking fishermen.

After two full days of checking fishermen, we hadn't come across a single violation on the 4-5 miles of river that we were patrolling. We pulled in to spend Sunday night at the Cortes patrol cabin. Cleeve said, "I think she was right. Nobody violates the law on this stretch of the river!" I was still pretty new at being a game warden but I told Cleeve, "No, we just need to work harder at detecting violations!" He said, "What do you mean Swerbe?" I said, "Come in the cabin and sit down while I pour you a whiskey. Cleeve lit the propane lantern in the cabin with a wooden match and cleared all the vintage Playboy magazine's off of the small kitchen table as I poured him a whiskey.

I said, "Cleeve, tomorrow is Monday. Most fishermen bought their "Daily" fishing licenses for the weekend and probably not for Monday. We don't know who is keeping fish or how many they are keeping unless we stop by their camp in the morning and document who has fish in their camp. Let's check all the camps in the morning and document who already has a limit of fish and who doesn't have a valid fishing license for tomorrow!" I then said, "Once we document who already has a limit of fish in camp and who doesn't have a valid fishing license for tomorrow, we will watch those individuals tomorrow and see if they continue to fish!" Cleeve started laughing as he was reading a cartoon in the 1970's Playboy magazine. He looked up at me, took a sip of whiskey and said, "That sounds like a good idea, Swerbe!"

When we got ready for bed Cleeve said, "Oh crap, we need to reset all those damn mouse traps before we go to bed!" We had set seven traps the night before, all seven traps had a dead mouse in them! I grabbed the jar of peanut butter and reset my trap line. As Cleeve reached up and shut the propane lantern off, I heard the sound "POP" as the light went off. I laid there in bed for a few minutes. It was dead quiet when Cleeve said, "Swerbe can you tell me a bedtime story!" I said, "Screw You Cleeve!!" Cleeve responded, "Thank you, that's my favorite story! I just want to listen to you talk so I can fall asleep before you do and don't have to listen to your damn snoring all night!" I said, "If the mice have to listen to me, so do you, goodnight, Cleeve!" As I lay there quiet in the dark nestled in my warm sleeping bag, I heard the sound "SNAP" I think another mouse just took his last breath of fresh air.

We woke up early the next morning and lit the lantern. Cleeve cooked bacon and eggs for breakfast while I threw out seven more dead mice and reset the trap line. Other senior wardens had called the Cortes patrol cabin the "Hantavirus Hotel." I can see why now!! I had never seen so dang many mice in my life! We finished breakfast. I, of course, washed all the dishes because Cleeve was allergic to dish soap! We jumped in our patrol truck and went down to the river and checked every camp along the river for about 4-5 miles. We talked to a lot of fishermen and looked at many fishing licenses if they had fish in camp. After about two hours we had checked every camp along the river and documented three people that didn't have a valid fishing license for Monday. We also checked two camps that had a limit of large trout in their coolers. Interesting enough, the camps that already had limits of fish and no valid fishing licenses were all in close proximity to one another making it easier for us to watch all of those individuals if they decided to fish that day.

We parked our patrol truck on top of a big hill about one mile from the river where we could watch that stretch of river through our spotting scopes. Cleeve was watching 4-5 fishermen on his left and I was watching 4-5 fishermen on my right. Three of the fishermen that I was watching were wearing hip waders and fly vests. They looked very professional and all were fishing with a fly rod. The fourth guy was wearing bib overalls and had waded out into the river with no hip waders just his tennis shoes and bib overalls. This man was fishing with a lure and not a fly pole. I decided this would be a good person to watch. As I zoomed in my crappy department-issued spotting scope, I soon recognized this was one of the people that Cleeve and I checked earlier that morning who had no valid fishing license for Monday and a limit of trout already in his cooler back at camp. This was going to be good!

I watched this man fish for nearly four hours. He had a metal fish stringer attached to his shoe laces that he kept under water next to his feet. Whenever he would catch a fish, he would reach down in the water and place the fish on his stringer. The limit for fish on this stretch of water was 3 fish and only one could be over 20 inches. This man kept every fish that he had caught. If the fish was bigger than the one on his stringer, he would simply release the fish on his stringer and add the bigger fish. Wardens call this "High Grading" and this is illegal on this stretch of river. Fishermen must either immediately release a fish once caught or immediately kill the fish and add it to their possession limit. I thought it was interesting that this man never raised a fish out of the water! I did not know how big his fish were or exactly how many fish he had on the stringer. After over four hours of watching this man, I watched him wade across the river back to shore where his truck was parked. I was excited to watch him lift his stringer of fish out of the water so that I could finally see how many he had and how big they were. Except, this didn't happen. He walked out of the river and never raised up his stringer of fish! I thought to myself, "Where in the heck is the stringer of fish, did he lose it while wading through the fast water?"

Cleeve said, "Hey, Swerbe, I got two people fishing over on my side that we checked this morning and they didn't have fishing licenses!" I said, "Good deal, I have a guy with no license and a possible over limit of fish over here on my side!" I continued watching my guy and noticed that when he got back to shore, he ran to his truck and was limping! I yelled at Cleve and said, "WE HAVE TO GO AND CHECK THIS GUY RIGHT NOW, I THINK HE HAS A LIMIT OF LARGE TROUT IN THE PANTLEG OF HIS BIB OVERALLS!!" We would need to get down there very quickly because this guy was already leaving in his red Chevy pick-up and could disappear on us if we lost sight of him. Cleeve fired up the patrol truck and hauled ass down a rough two-track road to get down to the river as quickly as possible.

Cleeve had been training his new golden retriever pup that he named "Iggy" to bird hunt and had forgotten that the puppy had been lying on the lid of the large black tool box in the bed of our patrol truck while we were watching fishermen. We hit a large rock in the road and I saw a flash of Iggy as she flew through the air and out into the sagebrush. I heard the dog yelp and Cleeve said, "What the heck was that?" I said, "That was the sound of your new puppy, Iggy, flying out of the back of the truck, you DUMBASS!!" Cleeve mashed on the brakes and said, "SHIT, I hope she is all right, I forgot she was back there!" It took several seconds for all the dust to pass us as we stopped suddenly in the road! We both jumped out of the truck to check on Iggy and she turned out to be fine, just a few minor scratches! We quickly loaded her in her kennel and back down the road we went to catch up with the fisherman who was just about to reach the main highway back to his camp.

We soon met the fisherman as he was stopped and getting ready to pull out on the main highway in his 1979 red Chevy pick-up. Cleeve pulled the truck up alongside his truck and I exited the vehicle and walked over to the driver's side door of the fisherman's truck. I said, "How are you doing today, sir?" The driver of the truck nervously replied, "I'm doing pretty good I guess!" At that moment I could see the end of the fish stringer hooked to the top button of the man's bib overalls. I thought to myself, "Holy crap, this man has a stringer full of fish inside of the pant leg of his bib overalls!" I said, "How is the fishing today?" The man replied, "Oh, I haven't been fishing, just took my dog for a little walk down by the river, my license has expired and I already have a limit of trout back at camp, as you already know! I looked into the cab of the truck at the man's lap and said, "Yes, I know that, but how come you are all wet up to your waist and you have a fishing pole in the back of your truck?" The man replied, "I always have a fishing pole in the back of my truck and I slipped and fell into the river while throwing my dog a stick to fetch!" I then looked in the back of the truck and I said, "Well, your dog is dry and your fishing line is still wet!" The man didn't say anything to that. I then said, "Sir, could you please step out of the truck!"

The man's cheeks tightened up and his face became red. I observed him clutch the steering wheel with both hands, tight enough that his knuckles were turning white.

I said again, "Sir, could you please step out of the truck!" I could tell that the man was very angry so I stepped back away from his door so that I could react quickly if need be. He threw the door open very fast and slowly slithered out of the truck. He said, "What do you want me out of the truck for?" I looked at his left leg and it was twice the size of his right leg. I stood there for a couple seconds staring at the man's leg and finally saw a fish moving inside his pant leg. I said, "Sir, when you fell into the river, did those fish swim up your pant leg and put themselves on your stringer?" The man was very angry and replied, "Something like that!!" I then asked the man to please un-hook the stringer of fish from the strap on his bib overalls and show them to me. He couldn't get the fish to drop back down his pant leg because his pants were so tight from all the fish shoved inside of them. He struggled for several minutes and finally said, "Oh f--ck it!!" He then un-hooked the buttons on his bib overalls and stood on the bottom edge of his pant cuff with the other foot and pulled his leg out of the bibs with the stringer of large trout. While doing so, he started hopping around on one leg and lost his balance and fell down onto the ground with one leg halfway stuck in his bib overalls.

Cleeve had just let his pup Iggy out to pee, and she saw an opportunity to lick the man's face while he was down on the ground. He finally got his leg pulled out and he had five trout all over twenty inches in length on his stringer. Iggy knew he was upset and she was just trying to give him a puppy kiss! After all, who could resist the fresh smell of a puppy's Breath. To say the least the man was very upset and humbled at this moment. He apologized for fishing without a license and keeping an over-limit of trout. He was issued a $210.00 citation for fishing without a license and also issued a citation for "Over Limit" of fish which cost him another $110.00 plus $20 per fish over his limit. The whole fishing escapade cost him $400.00 and his fish were seized.

As Cleeve and I left the area in our patrol truck, I looked in my mirror and could see the guy standing next to his truck with nothing on but his white T-shirt holding an empty stringer of fish. Cleve looked over at me and said, "Good one, Swerbe, now let's go write my guys some tickets for fishing without a license! By the end of the day, we wrote three citations for fishing without a license and two citations for "Over Limit" of fish. As were leaving the area Monday evening we ran into the senior female game warden for the area. She asked, "How did it go?" Cleeve handed her over $1000.00 in cash and said, "Oh, not bad! Could you please take this cash and all these citations and hand them in at the court house next time you are in town!" She grabbed the money and citations and said, "Sure," as she drove off with a scowl on her face!

Cleve and I would, spend the next several weekends checking fishermen and boaters for compliance on area lakes in the Casper area. I soon learned that I preferred to check fishermen and not recreationalists that were just out having a good time with their new high dollar boats. Fishermen were generally polite, but the folks out recreating with water skis, jet skis, and jet boats did not want to be checked by game wardens wearing red shirts. Many of them had just bought a $50,000-$100,000 boat that they were going to get to use maybe three times in a summer, and they wanted to be left alone to drink beer and raise hell on their new boats, with their new girlfriends! When we checked a boat, we would ask for boat registration, approved type 3 PFD (Personal Floatation Device) for each person on board, fire extinguisher, throw-able cushion, and fishing licenses if they were fishing. I started out wanting to check every boat on the lake. Cleeve said, "Just settle down, Swerbe, we have all summer to check boats, don't burn yourself out in the first week!" He then told me that based on his experience from working the lakes with a year of experience under his belt that it was sometimes better to just sit back and watch every boat on the lake and you would quickly know which boats need checked. I didn't agree with Cleeve, I had a blue flame shooting out of my rear end and wanted to check every boat and fisherman on the lake every day.

Cleeve throttled up the 21-foot Lund patrol boat with the really cool red and blue light bar overhead and headed for Fremont canyon on Alcova Reservoir. We rounded a sharp corner in the canyon and I noticed a chocolate brown-colored boat tied off to the canyon wall with about eight passengers on board. We came around the corner quickly and were in close proximity to the boat. From a quick glance it appeared to me that at least five people were fishing from the boat. I quickly smacked my partner Cleeve with my right hand on his left shoulder as he was driving the boat and said, "STOP, let's check that boat quick!" Cleeve quickly pulled back on the throttle and the nose of our patrol boat dipped forward as the boat came to a quick stop and water rushed forward by us. Cleeve maneuvered our patrol boat towards their boat at a very low speed. Once we got about 20 yards from the boat a very unattractive women in her mid-fifties stood up and took her one-piece swim suit completely off right in front of us. Cleeve said, "OH MY GOD!!" and jerked the boat to his right and gunned the throttle nearly hitting their boat. We sped off and went around the next corner in the canyon before coming to a stop. Cleeve pulled back on the throttle and we came to a quick stop.

Cleeve looked at me and said, "What in the hell was that all about? She had to have known we were game wardens with our red shirts and patrol boat with the red and blue light bar." I laughed and said, "Yea, she did know we were game wardens alright. That's why she took her swimsuit off and gave us a show, because I'm guessing none of the men had fishing licenses and her husband told her to get naked so that the game wardens wouldn't stop and check for fishing licenses!" Cleeve said, "CRAP, I bet you are exactly right!" Cleeve quickly turned the patrol boat around and mashed on the throttle headed back to locate the chocolate brown boat and check for fishing licenses. We quickly came around the corner, the boat was gone! We had only been gone a few short minutes and they were flat gone! We searched the entire lake and never found that boat again anywhere. We even went back to the boat ramp hoping to catch them taking their boat out of the water, and again no boat in sight. I looked at Cleeve and said, "Well, I hope you just learned something right-there buddy, don't ever shy away from checking a boat just because there is a naked woman on board!" Cleeve said, "Yea, I won't fall for that trick again!"

We started out our forty-hour work week on Friday and had our forty hours in by Sunday evening. Cleeve told me to go home and spend some time with my wife, Lana, and kids Wendy and Wes, and get some rest because next weekend was the fourth of July weekend. The lakes would be absolutely crazy with boaters, fishermen and recreationalists. Cleeve said, "If you think this summer has been busy so far, wait until next weekend, it's going to be absolutely crazy out there on the water!"

I went home to Shell and enjoyed several days with my family. I missed them all very much. It was so good to see my kids and get to play with them for a few days. Wes was now six years old and growing up fast on the guest ranch. My wife Lana had both kids already riding horses at a very young age. Thursday came too soon I had to pack up my car and head back to Casper for the busy 4th of July weekend.

Wesley riding his favorite horse, Champ.

Scott C. Werbelow

It was 8:00 A.M. on the fourth of July. My partner Cleeve and I were already out on the water on Alcova Reservoir patrolling. I had never seen so many jet skis, jet boats, and recreational boaters in all my life. Cleeve and I were sitting there in our patrol boat watching all the madness. I said to Cleeve, "Look how the entire lake is white capping, and the wind isn't even blowing. This is from hundreds of boats creating "wake" all at the same time!" Cleeve looked at me and said, "You haven't seen anything yet, Swerbe, wait until tonight when there will literally be hundreds of boats sitting out on the lake to watch the fireworks display, and over ninety percent of them will have alcohol on board!" Cleeve also told me that the local marina was planning on having a "live" band play all day and night and there would be hundreds of spectators at the marina drinking and enjoying the Fourth of July. Cleeve looked at me and said, "I hope you brought an extra-large lunch and a spare pair of handcuffs today, Swerbe, because you are going to need both!"

At about noon we were patrolling along Sandy Beach. I had never observed so many good-looking women wearing bikinis in all my life. Everyone was sun tanning, drinking alcohol and listening to loud music all up and down the sandy beach. Cleeve and I would wave at them and they would wave back. This was to let everyone know that we were in the area patrolling and you better not jump on your boat and operate it while intoxicated. I personally was all about checking fishermen and not arresting people for BUI (Boating Under the Influence) If we came across an intoxicated operator of a boat, we would have to run them through certain field maneuvers and give them a PBT (Portable Breathalyzer Test) This gets kind of tricky when you are on the water because it's not like you just observed someone cross the yellow or white line on a highway. A BUI would typically result in a boating accident where people were seriously injured or even killed or some sort of careless/reckless operation of their watercraft had been observed by others and reported. I absolutely hated dealing with drunk boaters. Because once you arrested someone your day was pretty much shot transporting them to jail and filling out paperwork! On top of that, our patrol trucks were only a single cab truck with no room to transport drunk passengers in handcuffs. Once you arrested someone, it pretty much meant your partner and your dog had to ride in the back of the truck because there simply was no room for anyone else. It was also a safety issue because you could not lock them behind a protective glass in the backseat away from you and all the other guns in your truck. I always kept my 12-gauge shotgun and M-14 rifle in a gun rack mounted to the ceiling of my truck above my head. My side door panels were always packed with spare ammunition, knives, axes, camera, GPS unit, evidence collection kits and biological kits for collecting blood samples from sick wildlife, etc. We simply just didn't have enough room in our trucks to safely transport poachers, drunks or anyone for that matter. Because of this we generally would request another law enforcement agency to transport arrested persons to jail for us. They always enjoyed this call because often times the person that was arrested would be belligerent and end up puking in their patrol vehicle while being transported to jail.

About that time the mobile radio in our boat sounded, "Any available game and fish unit available on Alcova Reservoir?" I grabbed the mic and replied, "Casper Gf-97 go ahead with your traffic" The dispatcher replied, "We just received a report of someone on a jet ski in the Fremont canyon area driving carelessly and nearly had a head on collision with another boat." I responded, "10-4, copy that. What is the physical description of the jet-ski and do you have a phone number of the RP?" (Reporting Party) Dispatch responded, "GF-97, the individual is a white middle-aged man, operating a yellow jet ski and wearing a red life jacket last seen headed towards Fremont canyon, no RP information, the call came in anonymous." I responded, "10-4, we will be 10-76 (in-route)." Cleeve mashed down on the throttle of the Lund patrol boat and flipped the switch to turn on the really cool overhead red and blue lights! As Cleeve raced across the rough water at a high rate of speed, I was sitting in the back of the boat trying to put cheese on a cracker to eat for lunch.

The water was so rough that my cheese and crackers flew out of my hands and went overboard into the lake. I yelled at Cleeve, "SLOW YOUR ASS DOWN, I CAN'T EVEN EAT MY DAMN LUNCH BACK HERE!!" Cleeve smiled and yelled, "SWERB IF YOU'RE EVER GOING TO BE A HIGH-COUNTRY RANGER YOU NEED TO LEARN HOW TO EAT ON THE RUN!!" I yelled back, "I WILL BE A HIGH-COUNTRY RANGER SOMEDAY AND NOT A BABY WATER WARDEN FOR THE REST OF MY CAREER!!"

We headed up Fremont canyon and soon observed a lady on a boat waving her arms at us to get our attention. Cleeve throttled the boat down and headed over to her location. The lady appeared really shaken up and angry. As we pulled up along-side her boat she yelled, "SOME ASSHOLE ON AN JET-SKI JUST ABOUT HIT MY BOAT HEAD ON, HE SWERVED AT THE LAST SECOND AND SOAKED MY HUSBAND AND I WITH A ROOSTER TAIL OF WATER!" She went on to say that her black lab dog became so scared that it jumped off the boat and into the lake. The lady also told us that he was riding a yellow jet ski and wearing a red life jacket and was headed up Fremont canyon. Cleeve and I thanked her for the information and told her that we would look into the matter. The lady said, "GOOD, these damn jet skiers think they own the damn lake, I wish they would outlaw the damn things all together!!"

Cleeve and I headed up Fremont canyon. We did not meet another boat or jet ski all the way up the canyon. As we were getting near the end of the canyon a yellow jet-ski with a man wearing a red life jacket came hauling ass around the corner and nearly hit our boat head on. I yelled at the guy as he went by and said "GET YOUR ASS OVER HERE RIGHT NOW!" The man shut the jet-ski down and circled around to the side of our boat. He stayed about twenty yards from our boat sitting on the jet-ski with the engine running. I yelled at the man and said, "Please come over here I need to visit with you about a few things." The man replied, "Nope, we are having a perfectly good conversation right where I'm at!" I said, "Please shut the jet-ski off so that I can visit with you about nearly hitting another boat head on a few minutes ago!" The man replied, "F—k YOU, YOU'RE JUST OUT HARASSING PEOPLE ON JET SKIS, IT WASN'T ME THAT YOU ARE LOOKING FOR!" I said, "Sir, bring your jet ski over here right now!!" He said, "F—k you," and tore off on the jet ski running wide open and headed back across the lake towards the marina. Cleeve looked at me and said, "I think that guy has been drinking!" I said, "Whatever the case, he's an asshole and needs an attitude adjustment!" Cleeve said, "I agree, but did you see the size of his fricken muscles?"

Cleeve throttled up the boat and we headed across the lake towards the marina. We soon arrived at the marina and pulled into a large boat dock and tied off our boat. There was a live band playing and probably nearly three hundred spectators listening to music and drinking copious amounts of alcohol. I quickly looked the crowd over for a man wearing a red life jacket. I did not see anyone that fit the man's description but I did see a yellow jet ski parked in a nearby boat slip. Cleeve and I decided to gas our boat up at the marina and just hang out for a while to see if we could locate the man that we were looking for. The music sounded good and the girls were pretty. A few minutes had passed when the owner of the marina, a guy named Kyle approached us and said, "See that guy over there, I just kicked him out of my bar for fighting!" I said, "That's interesting, that is the guy we are looking for!" The man worked his way through the large crowd and was headed back down towards the boat dock. About that time, he took off running and jumped on the jet-ski, started it up and "gave it the onion" in the "No Wake Zone."

He stood up on the seat with both of his feet and started spinning the jet-ski in tight circles to create a large amount of wake. Once he created "wake" he would circle around and jump the jet-ski off the wake that he created. All of this happening right in front of the marina in a "No Wake Zone" I walked to the end of the boat dock, waved my arms and yelled, "GET YOUR ASS OVER HERE RIGHT NOW!!" The man saw me and shut the jet-ski off. I yelled, "SIR, PLEASE COME TO SHORE SO THAT I CAN VISIT WITH YOU ABOUT A FEW THINGS!" He replied,

"NO, WE CAN HAVE A PERFECTLY GOOD CONVERSATION RIGHT WHERE I'M AT!" I yelled at him to come to shore and he flipped me off and yelled "F—k you Fish Cop!" The music had now quit playing and all three hundred spectators had their eye on Cleeve and me yelling at the drunk on the jet-ski. About that time someone patted me on the shoulder and said, "Sorry Sir, is this man giving you a hard time?" I turned around and could not believe who had just spoken to me. It was a guy that I played college football with and he was also a running back for the Chadron Eagles. I said, "Holy shit Dave, good to see you!" as I shook his hand. I told Dave that yes, the man was giving me a hard time and that I was losing my patience with him. Dave said, "Well I will get him to come to shore because that's my damn jet ski!" Dave yelled at the man and said, "BART, BRING MY DAMN JET SKI TO SHORE RIGHT NOW!"

I felt relieved that I had both Cleeve and Dave for back-up. I'm pretty sure you didn't want to mess with Dave. The guy was in very good shape and tough as nails. I used to work out with Dave in the weight room at college and knew what he was physically capable of. The crowd was now very quiet and all attention was focused on me and Bart. I thought to myself, Good Lord, what have I got myself into in front of three hundred spectators! Bart fired up the jet-ski and gunned the throttle. He was coming right towards us at a high rate of speed. He ran the jet-ski up on the beach and came running towards me very fast. I was standing on the end of the boat dock, not a good place to get into a fight if you want to stay dry! Bart came running down the boat dock towards me. When he got closer, I held my hand out and said, "STOP, right there, I need to visit with you!" Bart yelled, "NO, WE DON'T NEED TO VISIT, YOU AND I NEED TO GO TO THE END OF THE DOCK AND SETTLE THIS RIGHT NOW JUST YOU AND ME!!" WOW, this guy evidently wanted to kick my ass in front of all the spectators. I quickly glanced at my partner Cleeve. He had one hand on his baton and the other on his OC spray. Bart was built like a brick shithouse and had a tattoo on his right shoulder of a skull and cross bones that read (Born to Kill) on his left shoulder, he had a tattoo of a Pirate that read (Born to Fight.) This man had been drinking heavily and it was very possible that he was on drugs as well.

I calmly took my $5.00 Hollywood sunglasses off, unhooked my portable radio mic from the collar of my redshirt and handed them to Dave. I looked at Bart and said, "Please remove your sunglasses so I can determine how much you have had to drink today!" Actually, I knew there was a pretty good chance that I was going to end up head-butting this guy, and I just didn't want broken glass stuck in my forehead! Bart said, "F--- YOU!" and took a swing at me. I quickly ducked and grabbed his arm as it went by my head and performed one of the most beautiful "Arm Bar" take downs that you have ever seen in your life.

Bart's face hit the metal boat dock hard and I immediately had one of his arms behind his back and my knee firmly planted on the back of his neck. Before I knew it my partner Cleeve and two deputy Sheriffs were assisting me with the scuffle. Bart didn't have a chance. Both of his hands were cuffed in seconds with a knee on the back of his neck. My partner Cleeve helped Bart up and quickly ran him through some field sobriety tests and gave him a PBT (portable breathalyzer test) to determine the level of alcohol in his system. I got up, tucked my redshirt back in and put my really cool sunglasses back on as Dave handed me my portable radio. I thought to myself, this is going to be a long damn day!! Cleeve asked the deputies if they thought the man was drunk enough to go to jail. I think the deputies knew that they would be the ones transporting him, because they both quickly said, "No, no I think he is fine, he just needs to calm down and sober up a bit. They just didn't want him puking in their patrol truck I'm pretty sure!!

After knowing that the deputies didn't think he was drunk enough to go to jail I approached Bart alone and whispered in his ear while he was handcuffed. I said, "All three of those guys over there want to see you go to jail today on the Fourth of July, do you want to go to jail on the Fourth of July?" Bart replied, "No, Sir, and I'm sorry for everything and I won't get on that jet ski again today or cause any more problems for anyone."

I said, "Ok, if you can promise me that you will knock your shit off and cooperate while I write you a few citations I think I can talk them out of taking you to jail today." Bart responded "Yes, Sir" I took the handcuffs off Bart and asked him for his driver's license. Bart told me that he didn't have his driver's license on him but he could verbally give me all the information that I needed to know about him to write the citations. I ended up writing him a citation for creating wake in a "No Wake Zone," a citation for careless operation, and a citation for interference with a peace officer. I also "Must Appeared" him so that he could get an opportunity to tell the judge what had happened that day and maybe get some jail time and probation out of it.

Cleeve came walking up just as Bart had signed all three of his citations and shook my hand and said, "Thank You, Sir!" I shook his hand back and said, "Anytime, Bart!" with a smile on my face. The large crowd had begun to disperse with only about forty people still standing around watching us. As Cleeve and I left Bart, Cleeve looked at me and said, "Holy shit Swerbe, what did you say to that guy to get him calmed down, sign three citations, shake your hand, and say Thank You Sir?" I winked at Cleeve and said, "People skills Cleeve, people skills, you will learn that some day!!" Cleeve just smiled and kind of scratched his head. Cleeve replied, "That was the best arm bar takedown that I have ever seen before and you haven't even been through the Wyoming Law Enforcement Academy yet!" I responded, "Fourteen years of wrestling practice, Cleeve!"

It was now about lunch time and very hot outside. Cleeve and I decided to head up to the restaurant in the marina and eat a cheeseburger. They had really good food at the marina and we ate lunch there often. As we were walking up the stairs, we met two very cute women wearing bikinis coming down the stairs towards us. One of the women said, "You guys look really hot in those red shirts." The other women grabbed my crotch as she walked by me and whispered, "And you look extremely hot!!" I couldn't believe this just happened. A woman had just grabbed my crotch while I was in uniform! Cleeve looked at me and said, "Holy shit Swerbe, did she just grab your junk?" I said, "Yes sir, and if she isn't careful, I'll write her a citation for interference with a police officer as well!" Cleeve just laughed and shook his head and said, "What are we going to do with you, Swerbe!"

We got back down to the boat Cleeve said, "Hey Swerbe, did you ever run an IR (Incident Report) on that Bart guy?" I said, "No, I forgot to but all of his information is right there on the citation if you want to run him quick!" Cleeve replied, "I think we should run that guy and see what he has for prior offenses because that guy was an asshole. It wouldn't surprise me if he doesn't have a warrant for his arrest!" Cleeve grabbed the mic on the boat mobile radio and said, "Casper GF-96" Dispatch responded, "GF-96 Casper go ahead with your traffic." "I need an IR on a Bart Brookner, common spelling D.O.B. (Date of birth) 07/04/1974." "10-4 GF-96, 10-12 (Stand-by) GF-96 Casper that comes back not on file." Cleeve responded, "10-4, thank you." Cleeve looked at me and said, "Did you get his driver's license, Swerb, it came back not on file?" I said, "No, I didn't because he didn't have one, he just provided all the info to me!" Cleeve said, "Do you really think today was his birthday? I think you have just been had, Swerb, he gave you all fake information!" "Son of a bitch," I blurted out! "He was an asshole, a drunk asshole at that. He didn't have to go to jail and now he doesn't even have to pay his fines because we don't know who in the hell that guy really is!!" I was furious and felt really stupid! Cleeve said, "That's ok, we will run into him again or surely someone in the marina knows who he is and what his real name is and we will figure it out. But if you keep doing stupid shit like that you will be a baby water warden for a long damn time!" Dammit, I was so naïve and didn't think somebody would blatantly lie to a game warden's face like that!! Man, did I have some learning to do!

The day was long and hot. I ended up with a horrible headache from lack of water and dealing with naughty people of the public. We still had many hours to work not to mention we would be on the water

Scott C. Werbelow

until well after dark and after the fireworks display was over with. I was not looking forward to the thought of hundreds of people operating their high-powered motor boats at night under the influence of alcohol, with no headlights to even be able to see where they were going.

It was about 10:00 P.M. Hundreds of boats sat out on the lake waiting for the annual fireworks show to begin. The evening was absolutely beautiful, just about every boat had music cranked up and people dancing, laughing, and drinking. The show finally began and it was a beautiful display of fireworks over the glare of the water at night. I thought to myself, this is really cool, wish I wasn't working on the holiday and my wife and kids could be here with me listening to music and watching the show. About that time a series of very loud cannon balls went off that was so loud it shook our patrol boat. Various boats started their engines and sped off in the night. All you could see was the small navigation light on the front and rear of the boats as they sped across the lake. I looked at Cleeve and said, "Now what do we do?" He replied, "Just listen carefully and wait, just wait for it!" I said "Wait for what Cleeve?" he replied, "With all these boats racing around in the middle of the night with people drinking someone will have an accident in the next 5-10 minutes!" We both just sat there in our patrol boat with the engine shut off and listened carefully. About that time, we could hear the loud sound of a jet boat blasting across the lake at a high rate of speed. I quickly grabbed my shitty pair of department-issue binoculars and could barely see the front navigation light of the jet boat as it traveled over fifty miles an hour across the lake. I watched the boat in my binoculars until it disappeared into the night. I could no longer see the lights of the boat but I could still hear the sound of the high-powered engine racing across the lake. About that time, I heard this god-awful crashing noise and could no longer hear the sound of the boat's engine running. Cleeve looked at me and said, "I told ya so Swerb, that boat just crashed into something, it's time for us to go back to work and it may not be very pretty!"

We headed towards the sound of the crash and the location of where we had last seen the boat's lights in the night. Cleeve looked at me and said, "I wonder if they hit another boat or ran into Goose Island?" As we got closer, I could see fire flames shooting into the air. I picked up my binoculars as Cleeve was racing across the water with red and blue lights flashing and observed a boat on fire. I said, "Over there Cleeve, looks like they ran into the damn island!" Cleeve maneuvered the boat over to the location of the flames shooting into the air. He quickly beached the boat and yelled, "Swerbe grab the fire extinguisher and put that fire out if you can!" I grabbed the fire extinguisher and raced over to the jet boat that was engulfed in flames. I thought to myself, Lord please be with me and please don't let me find any dead bodies on board of this burning boat! The flames were burning high and the fire was hot, it was difficult to get near the boat without getting burnt myself. I got as close to the boat as I could safely get without getting burnt. It was hard to see but I could not see any people on the boat, I thought to myself thank god!! I sprayed the fire extinguisher until it was empty, I controlled the fire but didn't get it put out completely.

About that time another boat came by the scene and backed their boat up to the burning jet boat. The boat's operator raised the engine slightly out of the water and threw a huge rooster tail of water onto the burning boat. Cleeve grabbed his cordless handheld spotlight and yelled "Swerb, come quick, we have to find the bodies!" Cleeve and I raced through the tall grass and willows shining the handheld light back and forth. The first thing I saw was an empty large Gott cooler and many Coors Light cans lying on the ground everywhere. We traveled further, shining our light, and found life jackets, sun screen, water skis, fluorescent orange skier down flag, sunglasses, but still no people. Finally, I heard a moaning noise off to my right. I said, "Cleeve, quick shine your light over here!" Cleeve quickly came over my direction and shined his light in the tall grass. Two people were lying face down in the grass moaning. I walked up to the man face down in the grass and tapped him on the shoulder and said, "Sir, are you alright, we are with the Wyoming Game and Fish Department!" The man slowly rolled over his face was covered in blood. He looked at me with one eye open and said with a slurred speech, "When did you Sonsabitches put that rock there!" I said, "Sir we didn't place a rock anywhere you just ran into Goose Island with your jet boat!" About that time the other person started slowly moving around. I was happy to see that she was alive as well. She looked over at her husband and said, "Honey are you alright?" He replied, "Yes honey I think I'm alright, just a little stiff!" She rolled onto her back, put her hands over her bleeding face and said, "Glad to hear you are finally stiff! You, big sack of dumbass!!" Cleeve radioed the Sheriff's office for assistance and called for an ambulance. Thank God there were only two people on the jet boat and nobody was seriously injured. The jet boat received an extensive amount of damage but the other boat was successful in getting the fire extinguished. Both people on board the boat received extensive injuries, but were still alive with no broken bones. The male was extremely intoxicated when I interviewed him. His wife had not been drinking at all. I asked the man who was operating the boat when they crashed into the island? He said, "My damn wife, she told me that I was too drunk to drive, that's the last time I will listen to her bullshit!!" I'm pretty sure the man was operating the boat, but after interviewing both of them separately I could not prove otherwise and was just exhausted and wanted to call it a night! Another sixteen-hour day in the books performing watercraft enforcement.

With no serious injuries involved, Cleeve and I ended up loading the couple up on our boat and gave them a ride back to their camp site at Black Beach. Once we dropped them off safely at their camp site, I looked over and observed a large party barge anchored in a near-by cove. This appeared to be a home-made pontoon boat. The boat was built out of metal garbage cans that were all welded together for the "pontoons" The large party barge had two stories, a top deck and a bottom deck. They had a bonfire built on the top deck and they were playing heavy metal music very loudly. Cleeve and I idled our patrol boat over to the cove to get a closer look. I picked up my shitty department binoculars and observed several naked women drinking moonshine on the top deck of the boat. They had a large home-made water slide that the women were sliding down one after another. I shined our handheld spotlight on the home-made pontoons that were made out of old garbage cans, while I searched for their boat registration numbers. The boat registration numbers had been spray painted on the old garbage cans with black paint. The men started dancing with the women and firing their pistols in the air as they danced and yelled "YEEHAA!!" I looked at my partner Cleeve and said,

Game and Fish personnel extinguishing a boat on fire.

"Let's save this one for in the morning, if we make contact with this boat tonight somebody will end up going to jail or possibly shot!" Cleeve agreed and we decided to call it a night.

The next morning, I met Cleeve at the office early and we hooked onto our patrol boat and headed for Pathfinder Reservoir for hopefully a slow day of checking fishermen. We had just launched our patrol boat on Pathfinder Reservoir when dispatch called me on my portable radio.

"Casper GF-97." I looked at Cleeve like NOW WHAT! We just got on the damn water! I grabbed my mic off my shirt collar and responded, "Casper GF-97 go ahead" Dispatch responded, GF-97, we have a report of a homemade pontoon boat with individuals firing rifles at baby geese on Alcova Reservoir near Black Beach." "Casper GF-97, copy that traffic we are currently on Pathfinder reservoir but will be 10-76 to that location." I looked at Cleeve and said, "Oh yea, forgot about that boat, we may have our hands full with this one! We quickly loaded our patrol boat and headed for Alcova Reservoir. We knew they had been drinking heavily the night before and had plenty of firearms on their homemade boat. It was illegal to have any firearms on your person while in the State Parks area. Cleeve asked me if we should call State Parks law enforcement for backup on this one. I told Cleeve, "Too many law enforcement personnel on this call may only escalate the situation with these hillbillies, let's contact them first and see how it goes!" We quickly unloaded our patrol boat and headed for Black Beach. As we went by the marina, I noticed the homemade pontoon boat pulling up to the marina fueling area to get gas. I told Cleeve, "There's our boat right over there" Cleeve said, "Oh good, I would rather make contact with them at a public place rather than out on the water somewhere." Cleeve turned sharply to his left and idled the boat up and headed towards the marina. I started to get butterflies in my stomach as we approached the homemade pontoon boat. I thought to myself, hope this contact doesn't turn into a shootout!! As we pulled in behind the pontoon boat, I noticed a male subject with long hair and many tattoos get off the boat and head up the hill towards the marina. I also noticed another large male individual with a pony tail standing in the doorway of the enclosed first floor area of the pontoon boat. He was tall and well-built with a long beard and a diamond earring in each ear, he kind of looked like a pirate to me!

I quickly grabbed my portable radio mic and said, "Casper GF-97 for your 10-43 we have located the pontoon boat on Alcova Reservoir and will be making contact with this boat at the marina, please give us a status check in five minutes." Dispatch replied, GF-97 Casper, copy that and will do!" I looked at Cleeve and said, "You ready" Cleeve responded, "YUP, let's do it!" Cleeve and I approached the man standing in the doorway of the pontoon boat. The man looked nervous as we approached him, he quickly said, "Is there something I can help you with?" I said, "Yes sir, there is, I need to know why you are shooting baby geese and I need to have a look at all your firearms on the boat!" I thought to myself, let's just cut to the chase here, accuse this man of something and act like we seen it all happen! Even though I had only been a game warden for a couple of months, I was tired of being lied to and was not in the mood for any bullshit! The man quickly responded, "I didn't shoot any geese, it was that guy walking up the hill to the marina right over there! As he pointed towards the guy with long hair and tattoos walking away from us towards the marina. I said, "Ok, do you own this boat?" He said "Yes Sir" I said, "I need to see all the firearms on the boat and the firearm that was used to shoot baby geese," He said, "Ok, come on in." Cleeve and I followed him onto the boat. It was the creepiest thing that I had ever seen in my life. The boat had a strong odor of marijuana with clear mason jars filled with moonshine sitting on the kitchen table. The man said, "There is a loaded AR-15 in that closet and a loaded .44 magnum pistol underneath the hand towel by the sink. There is also a loaded .223 rifle behind the door by the bedroom, the one that was used to kill the baby geese" As Cleeve and I walked through the first floor of the pontoon boat gathering loaded firearms we had to step over a naked lady who was passed out on the floor and another naked lady who was passed out in a recliner chair that looked like it had been salvaged from a dump site. The man said, "Never mind the naked women, they partied a little hard last night!" I thought to myself, sometimes you just can't explain what you are actually seeing in a situation like this!! Cleeve and I unloaded all the firearms and advised the man that it was illegal to have firearms in a State Park. He apologized and told us that he was not aware of that regulation. The man was very cooperative and gave us his name and his driver's license for identification purposes. He also gave us the name of the guy that shot the baby geese, but he couldn't remember the details of what had happened as he was too drunk to remember.

My portable radio blared "Casper GF-97 status check?" I responded "Casper GF-97, everything is 10-4 at the moment, please give another status check in ten minutes." Dispatch responded "10-4, be safe!!" I learned that status checks were important, especially when the suspects could hear that someone was checking on me and knew my location and who I was out with. This told them, don't try anything stupid because back-up will soon be on the way! Cleeve and I left the boat and went down to our boat to wait for the man to come back from the marina. The man soon returned carrying a bag of Doritos and a bottle of Mountain Dew. As he approached the boat, I confronted him and said, "Gilbert you need to tell me about the geese that you shot earlier this morning!" The man seemed surprised that I knew his name and what he had done. He lied to me at first and denied everything until I told him that his buddy had told me the whole story. I actually didn't know any of the story but was trying to get there. He finally admitted that he was shooting at something that could have been baby geese but he was too intoxicated, and wasn't sure what he was actually shooting at. I asked him how many geese he killed and if he collected any of the baby geese. He told me that he didn't collect any baby geese and he wasn't sure how many he had killed. I asked him for his driver's license and stepped into my boat nearby to run an IR (Incident Report) this would tell me if this guy had ever been in trouble before. I also called the RP (Reporting Person) and asked her for the details of what she had observed. She didn't observe any dead geese but said he was damn sure shooting at a (flock) of baby geese and she could see the water splashing around the baby geese as the bullets hit the water. She told me that after the shooting ended, she couldn't see any geese around because they all went under water to hide. She told me all the men were being loud as if they had been drinking heavily, and that they were listening to heavy metal music.

Dispatch came back "GF-97 Casper 10-0!" 10-0 means "Caution" man wanted!! I thought to myself Shit this man is wanted and he just heard the radio traffic!! Gilbert heard the radio traffic and put his hands behind his back, bent over slightly at the waist, and turned his head to the left. He said, "That's correct, I do have a warrant for my arrest, so I guess I'm headed to jail!" I thought to myself, well, shit Swerb, you better arrest your first suspect as he is standing here in front of you with his hands behind his back! I always thought arresting someone would carry a little more hype than this! I arrested Gilbert and issued him a citation for "Attempt" to take waterfowl out of season and without a license, even though I had no evidence of any dead baby geese! Cleeve called a deputy sheriff that agreed to transport Gilbert to jail. The deputy actually knew Gilbert well from all the other times that he had been arrested. Cleeve and I contacted the local State Parks law enforcement officer and let him know about the man with firearms on his boat in the State Park. We hung around for back-up as that officer issued citations to the owner of the boat. Everything went as smooth as it could have, smoother than I would have ever anticipated.

Cleeve and I showed up at court for Gilbert's IA (Initial Appearance.) Gilbert read his rights and pled guilty to shooting baby geese out of season without a license. Gilbert told the judge that he wasn't sure what he was shooting at because he was so drunk that day! The judge looked at me and said, "Officer, did you see this happen?" I said, "No Sir, but I have an RP that witnessed everything and I have a written confession from the suspect." Gilbert turned around and looked at me, he gave me a very evil look and said, "Your Honor I would like to change my plea to "Not Guilty, I would like to request a jury trial and I request to be let out on OR. OR means (Own Recognizance) I thought to myself, Man, this guy knows the system, once he learned that I didn't see any of this happen he changed his plea! The judge said, "Well sir, I guess that is your right, I will schedule a jury trial and let you out on OR. Gilbert smiled at me as he walked down the isle of the courthouse and said, "See you at the jury trial man!" I was speechless, I just wanted to choke him! I later got a call from our District Attorney, she asked me if I had any dead geese as evidence? I told her no, that I did not and she recommended that I dismiss the case due to lack of evidence. I thought to myself, Holy shit, this guy admitted to shooting at baby geese, he wrote out a written confession admitting to shooting at baby geese, I have an RP who observed it all and is willing to testify and this guy just got away with everything because I have no evidence! I learned a valuable lesson that day, this is how our justice system works and there are many who know exactly how it works! I will be a better game warden next time! I thought to myself!!

As the summer went on, we checked hundreds of fishermen and boaters for compliance. I worked many long days and nights. At that time there were no permanent jobs available and I was competing with nine other wardens around the state for a permanent job. I knew working for Terry Cleveland was either going to go really well, or not well at all. I had a few regrets that summer. My best friend Pat invited me to attend his wedding that summer. It was over a busy weekend. I didn't dare take a weekend off in the busy part of summer because I felt Mr. Cleveland wouldn't approve of this and might think I was a slacker. I ended up missing that wedding and regretted that for the rest of my life. At the time I just knew that I had to work hard to get a permanent job as a Wyoming game warden and the competition with other wardens performing watercraft enforcement was very high.

The date was August 23, 1996. I received a call from my brother Wade that my grandpa Lester had a massive heart attack and had died. He was 78 years old. Grandma Helen had lunch ready for him at their home in Emblem. Grandpa Lester was always on time for lunch at 12:00 PM each day. When he didn't come in for lunch Grandma Helen stuck her head out the front door of their home and yelled his name. She waited several minutes and he still didn't show up for lunch. She went outside looking for him and found him lying on the ground dead next to the combine in the parking lot next to their house. Grandpa had been getting the combine ready to do some thrashing and apparently had a massive heart attack while working on the combine. This was devastating for my grandma Helen. They had been together for so many years and now she just lost the love of her life. I would have to leave Casper and attend the funeral in Emblem. I made a hurried trip to Emblem to attend Grandpa's funeral and quickly headed back to Casper and right back to work again. Another regret that I still hold, not spending more time with Grandma after the passing of my grandpa Lester. I was so driven to work hard and get a permanent job to take care of my family that sometimes I didn't slow down for the really important things in life.

The next thing I knew the summer was coming to an end and I was tired of checking fishermen and boaters. I just wanted to be out in the field during the fall checking hunters, I had not officially done this yet as a Wyoming game warden. I had a performance appraisal scheduled with Mr. Cleveland on Monday morning at 8:00 AM. I was nervous that my appraisal would not go well because I had heard from other wardens that Mr. Cleveland would fire you at the drop of a hat if you were not performing at a very high level. My other worry was that the department may be out of money and my time with the Game & Fish department may be over with at the end of August, if another region couldn't find enough money to keep me on through the fall hunting seasons. I thought to myself, what if they run out of money and I have no job until April 1st next year. What would I do for work! I was also concerned that if I didn't get a full-time job within one year that I would have to again take the very competitive game warden's exam and go through that whole process again. I'm sure the psychologist Dr. Whyme would remember me and make it tough for me to pass the psychological exam again. I also thought what if they move me to another district, where will it be and what will my wife Lana think about me being gone from home again? She had told me earlier that once I became a permanent employee and stationed somewhere that she would then move and be with me, but not until then. So many thoughts raced through my head, but first I must make it through the appraisal on Monday with Mr. Cleveland.

Monday morning came and I nervously walked into Mr. Cleveland office in Casper. I shook his hand tight and looked him directly in the eyes and said, "Good morning, Mr. Cleveland how are you?" He replied, "I'm doing well, thank you. Now please be seated and let's get started with your appraisal." Mr. Cleveland wasn't much for small talk. His first question was, "So Scott, now that you have a summer under your belt how did you like being on the Reservoir Crew checking boaters and fishermen this summer?" I replied, "Mr. Cleveland, I really enjoyed it sir and I gained a wealth of knowledge and experience, but I don't think I would like that job the rest of my career." Mr. Cleveland looked up at me and smiled over his narrow eye glasses that were sitting on the tip of his nose. He knew exactly what I was telling him. I then said, "I really enjoyed the summer, Mr. Cleveland, but I'm ready to be riding a horse and singing cowboy songs in the mountains somewhere in northwest Wyoming. I thought to myself HINT, HINT!! Mr. Cleveland again looked over the top of his reading glasses and smiled.

Everything had been going pretty good in the appraisal so far when Mr. Cleveland looked at his copy of the appraisal and kind of scrunched up his face. He said, "I have a question for you Scott. I see on June 8th you coded 8 hours to stripping all the equipment off GF-67 to get it ready for trade. Did it really take you eight hours to strip one patrol truck? I said, "Mr. Cleveland, I actually stripped three trucks that day and only listed one truck because I couldn't remember the license plate number on the other two trucks." He looked up over his reading glasses and said, "Fair enough, thank you!" I thought to myself WHEW, I should have listed those other trucks in my DAR (Daily Activity Report), Mr. Cleveland doesn't miss anything! We finally got through the appraisal and Mr. Cleveland looked over his glasses and said, "Scott, I don't generally give a good appraisal to someone just starting out like yourself, but I have been impressed with all your hard work and strong work ethic this summer, congratulations!" He then said, "I know working the reservoirs can get a little tiresome at times, but just keep a good track record and you will do fine." I stood up, gave Mr. Cleveland a firm handshake and said, "Thank you very much Sir!" I will never forget that day. I made it through a Terry Cleveland performance appraisal. Maybe there was some hope for me getting a permanent job someday.

After the appraisal I walked back to my office to work on our final year-end report for all our work efforts that summer. I walked into the office and Cleeve said, "Well, how did it go Swerbe?" I replied, "It was a real Son of a Bitch Cleeve, I might be a baby water warden the rest of my life!" Cleeve laughed and said, "I might be right there with you buddy!" I laughed and said, "No actually it went pretty well, I might actually be a high-country ranger singing cowboy songs that I don't know the words to off my horse someday in northwest Wyoming." Cleeve said, "Yea, I can see it now- Swerbe, you will be wearing chaps with golden in-laid badges up and down each leg and white gloves with fringes on them. That's kind of a Jackson Hole thing up there in the high country!" He then giggled and said, "Except you Swerb, you don't know the words to any cowboy songs, you can't tie a damn game warden knot and all you will do is spit Copenhagen down your chin all over your new high country ranger chinks in front of all those pretty people that live in Jackson Hole!" I laughed at Cleeve and said, "I would rather end up in Medicine Bow than Jackson Hole, that's more my speed!"

We ended our work on the Reservoir Crew that summer towards the end of August. I traveled back to Shell to be with my family. I was really worried that I would be out of work with the Game & Fish Department until April 1, the next year. Would they send me back to Casper or station me somewhere else in the state? I was home for about one week when the phone rang one day. Mr. Cleveland called and asked me if I would be interested in working the fall hunting seasons in the Lander region starting September 1 and running through the end of October. I was so excited I was going to have a job for another two months and I was finally going to be able to check hunters during the fall hunting seasons. Mr. Cleveland then told me that the Regional Wildlife Supervisor Kent Schmidlin in Lander would be getting in touch with me soon. Just before he hung up the phone Mr. Cleveland said, "Oh and by the way, I told them to take good care of you down there, so they are going to allow you to live in the Ocean Lake house on our WHMA (Wildlife Habitat Management Area) It's a nice place and I think you will enjoy living there for a few months." I thanked Mr. Cleveland from the bottom of my heart and couldn't wait to tell my wife Lana the good news. Mr. Cleveland knew that I didn't have much money and also knew that I had been living in the basement of my old high school football coach's house rent free. So, I think he did everything he could to accommodate me and save me some money which I greatly appreciated.

My good friend Greybull game warden Bob Trebelcock had just recently transferred from Greybull to Lander. Bob was now the Lander game warden. The Lander game warden district was considered one of the premiere game warden districts in the state of Wyoming. If anyone ever ended up with a game warden position in Lander it was because you had done an excellent job as a game warden wherever you were stationed prior to transferring to Lander. Wildlife Administration was rewarding you for all your great work and chances are you were competing with many other top game wardens in the state to get that position. I thought to myself, I wonder if Bob Trebelcock had any say in me getting a chance to work the fall hunting seasons in Lander? I was excited to call Bob and tell him that I was headed to Lander in a few days. My guess was, Bob already knew and had something to do with it.

I quickly told my wife Lana the great news. I think she was happy for me, but again she was not going to make the move to Lander with me for only a two-month assignment. She again said, "When you get a permanent job, I will make the move." I was excited that I would get to work with Bob again, but I was going to miss being with my young kids Wesley and Wendy. Sometimes life didn't seem fair, but I knew I had to accept this position and do very well at it.

Chapter 2

LANDER

I soon received a call from Kent Schmidlin, wildlife supervisor for the Lander region. Kent's voice on the phone was very upbeat and positive. He was very excited to meet me and have me working in the Lander region. We set up a time to meet in his office on Monday morning at 8:00 AM. I was really excited to work for Mr. Schmidlin. I had heard from several others that he was an awesome supervisor.

I walked into Mr. Schmidlin's office in Lander, he greeted me with a hearty smile as he reached out and shook my hand firmly. Kent was a tall, skinny man. He stood about 6 foot 4 inches tall and weighed about 200 pounds. His hair and mustache were white in color and he wore a pair of round wire- rimmed glasses and a dusty gray cowboy hat. After visiting for a few minutes, he introduced me to everyone in the office and gave me two large brown cardboard boxes full of law enforcement supplies. I quickly looked into one box and it appeared that I had just been issued another shitty pair of department-binoculars. One eye piece was missing and the other eye piece had black electrical tape wrapped around it to hold it into place. I was glad that I had purchased a new pair of Brunton binoculars earlier that summer with my own money. He also handed me a laptop computer and said, "Here, take this with you out to the Ocean Lake house. You are going to need this to do your monthly reports, CMS reports and check your email." I had never seen a laptop computer before and I was pretty sure I was probably not smart enough to make it work but I took it with a smile and thanked him.

Kent loaded me up in his 1995 "game warden green" Ford Bronco. The bronco was very clean and had a set of small red and blue lights in the lower left corner of the rear window. The front bumper had a heavy-duty push bar mounted to it with small red and blue lights also mounted to it. I felt really honored to get to ride with Mr. Schmidlin out to Ocean Lake to check out the new house that I would be temporarily living in for a few months. We soon arrived at the yellow house that was located in a grove of cottonwood trees on the north side of Ocean Lake. The location of the house was beautiful with Ocean Lake right out the back door. The white fence around the house was in need of repair. The leaves on the large cottonwood trees that circled the house and yard were just starting to turn yellow and a beautiful bright orange in color. Fall was in the air. This place reminded me of our huge yard lined with cottonwood trees back at Bear Creek Ranch. I felt very blessed that I still had a job with the department and a nice place to live, even though I probably wouldn't be staying there very much with hunting seasons going on.

Kent gave me a tour of the inside of the house and the garage. The garage was dirty and full of old boxes with only enough room to maybe park one truck in. The walls in the house were in need of new paint and there was little to no furniture in the house. I told Mr. Schmidlin that I was thankful for the house and I offered to paint the inside of the house if the department would only purchase the paint. Mr. Schmidlin replied, "That's very kind of you to offer Scott, but I don't think the department wants to spend any more money on this house as they are planning to tear it down sometime in the near future." I told Mr. Schmidlin that seemed like a damn shame to me because it was a nice house and located in a beautiful area next to the lake.

I jumped back into the Ford Bronco and we headed back to Lander so that I could get my patrol truck checked out. I was very excited to see what my new patrol truck was going to look like. I thought to myself, will I be getting a new truck like I had in Casper? Or will I be getting some old ridge runner that's on its last leg? I was hoping my patrol truck looked better than my department binoculars! We soon returned to Lander and Mr. Schmidlin showed me where he lived and introduced me to his wife. She was a very pretty and sweet lady and invited me and my family over for dinner some night once we got settled in. I explained to her that my wife Lana would not be moving over and living with me at the Ocean Lake house, but we would definitely take her up on the dinner invite sometime soon. I left their house feeling very welcome to the Lander region. I felt like the Schmidlin's really did care for me and my family. This was a feeling that I never had with any of my previous supervisors.

We soon returned back to the regional office. Mr. Schmidlin made sure that I had all the equipment that I needed. He then took me out back to the equipment compound and showed me my patrol vehicle. It was a 1992 ford F-250 truck with faded green paint. The tires didn't have much tread left on them and the truck had a few minor dings, dents, and scratches. Definitely not the nice truck that I had left in Casper. But none the less this was my new patrol truck, I was very excited to finally have a chance to check hunters in the fall and not have to deal with anymore boaters for a while. Mr. Schmidlin handed me the keys and I thanked him for all his hospitality. I loaded up two cardboard boxes full of law enforcement equipment and my silly laptop computer and headed for Ocean Lake. I remember feeling very happy at this point in my life. Tomorrow would be September 1st, opening day of the antelope hunting seasons in the area. This would be my first official day as a Wyoming game warden checking hunters in the field.

I decided to stop by Bob Trebelcock's warden station in Lander and say hi. I hadn't seen Bob in several months while I had been working on the Reservoir Crew in Casper and felt like we needed to catch up. Bob invited me into the warden station and offered me a Bud Light. I wasn't much of a beer drinker but a cold beer did sound good. We caught up on stories and Bob grilled me a nice juicy hamburger on his grill in the backyard. After our meal Bob asked me where I had planned on patrolling in the morning for the antelope opener. I told him that I was planning on patrolling antelope hunt area 74 between Shoshoni and Casper on the south side of Highway 20. This was not part of Bob's district, but was located in the Lander region. I found that it's always good to let neighboring wardens know where you planned on patrolling, just in case you ever needed back-up. The next thing I knew it was about 9:00 PM and I needed to get headed home to Ocean Lake and get a good night's sleep for the big day I had ahead of me tomorrow.

I soon headed for Ocean Lake. It was very dark out. I was driving about 70 miles per hour on a rural secondary highway north of Kinnear. I came across a car driving very slow ahead of me. The car was traveling about 30 miles per hour with no tail lights. I came up on the car fast and nearly ran into the rear of the car due to the fact that they had no tail lights. I slammed on the brakes to keep from hitting them and then quickly swerved hard to my left to pass them before I ran into them. I blew by the car fast and looked into my rear-view mirror as I made a lane change after passing. The car only had one working headlight. I sped back up to about 60 miles an hour and noticed the car had sped up and was right on my tail end. I could hear a horn honking and the car was swerving left to right and on my tail. This kind of concerned me because we were on the Indian reservation and it was quite possible that I had a car full of intoxicated Native Americans on my ass! I sped up to 70 miles per hour to see if they would back off, nope they stayed right on my ass!

I had never traveled this road before and didn't know it at all, especially at night. I knew I needed to make a right- hand turn up ahead but wasn't quite sure where it was at. I sped up to 94 miles an hour and discovered my truck had a governor on it and would not allow me to go any faster. However, the car's headlights slowly disappeared in my rear-view mirror and I was now outrunning the car. I quickly looked up and saw that my turn to the right was coming up very quickly and I was traveling way too fast to make the turn. I mashed on my brakes knowing that I needed to make that turn, or I may have to deal with the car full of intoxicated Native Americans in a remote area late at night. I felt pressure on the brakes and the truck started to slow when all of a sudden, I heard a pop and my brake pedal went straight to the floorboard with no pressure. SHIT!! I HAVE NO BRAKES, NONE, NOTHING, NADA!! I went roaring by the turn and couldn't do anything about it! I thought to myself, Shit, I can't stop along the highway, I may get shot! I don't even have my 9mm pistol, it's in a cardboard box on the passenger side floorboard and I don't even know if it's loaded! My truck slowed to about 25 miles per hour and I noticed a road coming up to my left that went between two cornfields. I thought to myself, I will quick hide my truck between the two cornfields. I made a hard left turn and was praying that there was not a closed gate or anything parked in the road as I had no brakes. My patrol truck slid sideways and nearly hit the gate post on the right-hand side of the road.

Thankfully there was nothing parked in the road, I finally came to a stop about 100 yards up the road between the two cornfields. I quickly shut my lights off and watched for the car to go by in my rearview mirror. I thought to myself, what if they saw me turn off the highway between the cornfields and turn down this lane and come towards me? I have no idea where I'm at, now me and my truck are in a really remote area and nobody would ever find me if I needed back-up. I don't even have time to find my pistol. Maybe I could hide in the cornfield if things really go to shit! I looked up in my rearview mirror and observed a car with one headlight drive by my location. I thought to myself, WHEW!! I waited a few minutes and turned my truck around and traveled back towards the highway with my lights out and absolutely no brakes. The last time I had driven something with absolutely no brakes is when I was a child and blew through the aluminum gate at Beaver Creek Ranch on the farmhand three-wheeled tractor that my stepfather Martin had told me not to take out of low gear. But driving a truck down the highway with no brakes certainly makes one look a little further ahead. The car was gone, I quickly turned on my headlights and turned back onto the highway and headed south. I wanted to haul ass and get out of the area but I simply couldn't drive fast with no brakes. I finally arrived back at the Ocean Lake house about 11:00 PM. I was tired and needed to get prepared for the opening day of antelope season. I would need to get up at 4:00 AM and worry about checking hunters all day with no brakes. There was no way I could spend opening day of antelope season getting my brakes fixed, that was simply unacceptable. I thought to myself, maybe I could repair the brakes before I go to bed, shit I don't know if I have a flashlight in my box of equipment and I don't know if the truck has any tools in the large black metal tool box that was bolted to the bed of the truck! I was starting to stress a little bit and I thought to myself, Swerb, everything is going to be alright, quit stressing over nothing, hell you can probably fix those brakes quicker than you can get on your new laptop and check your damn email.

I left the truck running with the headlights on to shine on the front door of the house so that I could see to get in. I grabbed a large box of law enforcement equipment and headed for the front door of the house. I went to turn the handle, SHIT the door was locked and Mr. Schmidlin never told me where the key was located or hidden! I couldn't just call Mr. Schmidlin because we didn't have cell phones back then. I could have dispatch call him but I didn't want to wake he and his wife at this hour of the night. I really needed a damn flashlight! I hauled the heavy box of law enforcement equipment back over to my truck and set it down in front of my headlights so that I could see in the box. No flashlight in that box, shit, hopefully the other box has a damn flashlight! I rooted through the second box looking into the shadows casted from my headlights and low and behold I felt a flashlight in the bottom of the box. The flashlight was about twelve inches long and made of medal. I quickly grabbed it out of the box and held it up in front of my headlights. The flashlight had been engraved with some lettering along the handle. The lettering read GF-1 JAY LAWSON. Holy Shit, I have the Chief Game Warden's flashlight! I thought to myself, surely it doesn't work, it probably hasn't been used in years! And when does a flashlight ever work when you really need one! I clicked the little black button on the flashlight and I'll be damned if it didn't work! Something, finally going my way! Now I just need to find a key for the house!

I searched high and low for a key to open the house and never found one. Thank God the bathroom window wasn't locked, and I was able to crawl through the small window and land on my head next to the filthy toilet bowl. I shined my flashlight around looking for a light switch on the wall. I flipped the switch and nothing, no lights in the bathroom. I moved to the living room and flipped another light switch, nothing, no lights! I finally determined that there was no power to the house, nor was there any water! This was evident when I shined my flashlight into the toilet bowl and it looked like a rusty five-gallon bucket full of petrified hog nuts! Apparently, someone had used the toilet possibly several years ago and had forgot to flush. WHEW, what a mess!! I made my way to the garage and found a breaker box. I flipped the main breaker and "WALLA" we now have power to the house. I also found the main water valve to the house and noticed it had been turned off. I turned it on and "WALLA" we now have water as well! Things are now starting to look up. I went back out to my truck to turn off the motor and lights. Now that I had a flashlight, I popped the hood to check the brakes. The master cylinder was completely empty and I could see where brake fluid had shot all over the place. I thought to myself, Man, if I could just find some brake fluid, I might be able to get these brakes working again! I jumped in the back of the truck and popped open the large metal tool box lid and propped it open with a broom handle stick that was lying in the tool box. The first thing I noticed was two empty quart containers of brake fluid. I picked both of them up and shook them, they were both completely empty. This told me that someone else had problems with the brakes and they had used a great deal of brake fluid. I rooted around the toolbox some more and low and behold I found another quart size container about half full of brake fluid.

I quickly filled the master cylinder full of brake fluid and said a quick prayer that the truck would repair itself over night and be ready to roll in the morning.

Finally, it's about midnight. I'm back in the house with electricity, water and two cardboard boxes full of law enforcement equipment sitting on the kitchen counter top. I went through the boxes and found a 9mm pistol, four boxes of ammo, leather holster, handcuffs, baton, bullet proof vest, shitty pair of binoculars, beat up spotting scope, and a citation book full of tickets. I think I'm ready for tomorrow. I just need to get my department-issue 12-gauge shotgun and my M-14 rifle back in Casper. Maybe I can pick those items up over the next few days when I'm checking antelope hunters near Casper. I looked over and saw that damn laptop computer lying on the counter top. I plugged it in to charge and decided to open it up so that I could check my email. I messed with it for over an hour and never did get logged on, as I didn't have a correct password! I slammed it shut tired and frustrated. It was now 1:00 AM and I was tired. I dug my alarm clock out of my suitcase and set it for 4:00 AM and walked into the bedroom. This is when I discovered some really important information. There was no bed in the bedroom and I had forgot my sleeping bag in the back of my personal truck that was parked back at the Lander office. I grabbed my department- issue coat and used it for a pillow, curled up on the floor with my clothes still on, and slept in the fetal position. The next thing I knew my little wind-up alarm clock was racing across the floor, it was 4:00 AM and time to get to work!

I headed into the bathroom and flipped on the light switch. This is when I soon remembered the mess in the toilet. I had no cleaning supplies or a cleaning brush. I went straight to the kitchen and located a broom leaning against the wall between the refrigerator and the stove. I thought to myself, Ah Ha! This will work for a cleaning brush to clean the toilet! Several flushes later things were starting to show improvement.

I headed out the door in the dark, hoping that I had not forgotten any needed supplies for my first official day checking hunters in the field.

Scott C. Werbelow

Somewhere today I would have to buy some food for several days, find some cleaning supplies, and purchase some brake fluid. I jumped into the back of my patrol truck to load the heavy metal tool box with supplies. I bent over to put a box in the tool box and bumped the broom stick that was holding the lid open. My head was in the tool box and the heavy metal lid came smashing down right on top of my head. "BAM," was the sound of metal to bone as the lid smacked me on top of my head. I just wanted to cry it hurt so badly! I lifted the heavy tool box lid off of my head and propped the broom stick up again to hold it open. I reached up and felt a warm moist knot on top of my head with my right hand. I was bleeding badly from a large gash in the top of my head. SHIT, I thought to myself. Do I need stiches!! I ran back into the house and stuck my bleeding head underneath the shower head and rinsed the blood off the best that I could. I grabbed my only towel and placed it on top of my head with pressure to stop the bleeding, ran out the door and jumped into my patrol truck with no brakes. Hopefully the truck "fixed" itself over night and would be fine.

I was starting to stress a bit because I wanted to be somewhere between Casper and Shoshoni checking antelope hunters by day break. I fired up the truck and headed down the highway constantly pumping my brakes to see if they would work. After about fifteen miles of pumping my brakes the brake pedal started to stiffen up and "Walla" my breaks started working again. By now the bleeding had nearly stopped and I had brakes. "Thank You Lord" I said in relief. I started thinking to myself, do I have everything that I need to be a successful game warden today? Do I have game tags, donation coupons, extra conservation stamps, warning citations, seizure tags, tape measure to measure length of antelope horns? Do I have an evidence kit, DNA kit, metal detector, rubber gloves, scalpel? Do I have a pen that works in case I need to write a citation do I have an extra pen in case I lose my pen or it runs out of ink? Do I have proper court information and bond schedule? Do I have water to wash my hands and drink and clean the gash in my head? I looked down at my speedometer

46

and I was doing 85 mph. Shit, I need to slow down before I get a speeding ticket or hit a deer.

I rolled through Shoshoni Wyoming a little after 5:00 AM. Thank God the small convenience store on the corner was open. I was able to buy some cleaning supplies, brake fluid and some food. I had an empty cooler in the back of my patrol truck. I filled it with a bag of flour tortillas, Velveeta cheese slices, beef jerky, sausage sticks, Cheetos and a bag of small assorted candy bars. I also bought a role of Copenhagen, some Swisher Sweet cigars, and a large bag of sunflower seeds. I thought to myself, this should get me through the next several days.

I was now somewhere between Casper and Shoshoni the morning sun was just starting to peek over the hills to the east. It looked like it was going to be a clear and nice day. The wind was not even blowing yet. I noticed a well-maintained county road to my right so I decided that I would head south and get out into the hills and try and find some antelope hunters. I was actually excited about checking antelope hunters because you can actually see the antelope and the hunters from a distance with all the wide-open space. This allows a game warden to watch hunters from a long distance. You can see if they are wearing fluorescent orange and you can actually see who shoots the antelope, and how many antelope may have been shot. I decided that if I was going to catch a poacher like my Ole Man, I would need to get way out in the hills into a very remote area because this is generally how the hardcore poachers would operate. They didn't want anybody to ever see them poaching, so they would find remote areas to hunt.

I soon found a rough two-track road that headed east down a power line. These roads were used for workers to maintain large power lines. I drove and drove and drove and never came across a single hunter. I looked at the clock on my dash and it read 12:14 PM. I could not believe that I had not checked a single antelope hunter on the opening day of hunting season and it was already past noon. Maybe I got a little too far out into the hills, I thought to myself. I pulled my patrol truck underneath the large power line and decided to eat some lunch. I pulled out a flour tortilla and placed a piece of Velveeta cheese inside of it, rolled it up tight and placed it on my defroster inside of my truck. I turned the heater on high until the cheese would melt and run out of the ends of the tortilla shell. By the time the cheese melted the tortilla would get crusty hard. I was pretty proud of myself for cooking such a nice warm meal. Once the quesadilla was ready, I pulled out a fold-up lawn chair and set it up in the back of my patrol truck. I stretched my legs out and rested them on the top of my toolbox and leaned back in my chair. It was so peaceful and quiet out there that you could have heard a pin drop. The sun was high and shining bright, temperature was about 75 degrees. The knot on my head was still throbbing.

As I was finishing my absolutely wonderful quesadilla, I looked to the east down the power line road and could see something reflecting in the sun about one mile away. I jumped out of the bed of my truck and located my shitty spotting scope underneath my seat. I quickly mounted the spotting scope to my driver's side window and zeroed in on the shiny object. It was a white pick-up truck with a four-wheeler in the back. Two guys were unloading the four-wheeler, one of them wearing white pants. Neither one of them had any orange clothing on, it looked like one of them had a rifle. It was difficult to see them very well because of all the heat rays bouncing through my spotting scope. The men quickly sped off on the four-wheeler, they were headed north going cross country and not traveling on any kind of a road. I thought to myself, who goes antelope hunting wearing white pants!! As they went out of my sight, I zoomed the spotting scope back onto the white truck. After looking very closely it appeared to me that someone was sitting in the driver's side seat of the white truck. I decided I better get headed that way and visit with the driver of the truck. I was pretty excited as this would be my first official big game hunter field check as an official Wyoming game warden.

I approached the white Chevy truck head-on and stopped in the middle of the two-track road facing directly towards the individual sitting in the driver's seat. I exited my patrol truck and walked up to the driver's side door of the white Chevy. A young man rolled down the window and said, "How are you today, sir?" I didn't respond and walked past the driver's side window and quickly looked in the bed of the truck to see if they had any dead antelope in the back of the truck. I did not observe any dead antelope but I did observe two tiny drops of red blood on the wheel-well of the truck and 2-3 tiny antelope hairs lying in the bed of the truck indicating to me that someone had already killed an antelope earlier that morning.

I walked back over to the driver's side window and said, "I'm doing pretty good young man, who killed the antelope earlier today?" The young man swallowed hard a couple of times and said, "Umm, one of the guys that just left on the four-wheeler." I said, "The guy wearing the white pants or the other guy?" The young man responded, "The guy wearing the white pants." I responded, "The guy wearing the white pants and no fluorescent orange carrying a rifle that already killed an antelope this morning?" The young man responded, "Yes Sir" in a very quiet and weak voice. I asked the young man what the guy's name was who was wearing white pants. He replied "Sam." I then asked him if Sam had killed a buck or a doe and where the animal was located. He replied, "Sam killed a nice buck antelope and they stashed it in an old abandoned cabin to keep it cool and keep the flies off the carcass. About that time, I heard two shots go off north of me that sounded like they came from a high-powered rifle. From my location I could not see the four-wheeler or the other two men. I thanked the young man and went back to my patrol vehicle and ran a 10-28 (license plate check) on the truck and advised dispatch of my location the best that I could. I actually didn't know where in the hell I was other than it was a very remote location out in the middle of nowhere. I was somewhere out in antelope area 74.

I sat in my patrol truck for nearly an hour when I finally observed two male individuals riding a four-wheeler towards my location. I picked up my very-used department binoculars and observed a buck antelope on the front of the four-wheeler and what looked like a doe antelope on the back of the four-wheeler. I then waited for the two hunters to arrive at their truck. When they pulled up, they seemed a little surprised to see the game warden parked on the other side of their truck. I stepped out of my truck and said, "How are you today Sam?" He nervously responded, "I'm doing great how about you?" I said, "I'm doing great, looks like you got yourself a nice buck there." Sam responded, "Yeah not too bad, he's only fourteen inches I was hoping to get something a little bigger, but I got excited!" I said, "Good deal, congratulations, can I see your license for this antelope?" Sam responded, "Oh you bet, I have it right here in the glove box." Sam then pulled an unopened envelope out of the glove box of the white Chevy pickup. This was his antelope license that headquarters in Cheyenne had mailed to him. He hadn't even opened the envelope to verify he was hunting with the correct license. I said, "Thank you Sam, however we have a couple small problems going on here!" Sam said, "What's that?" I responded, "First off you need to wear fluorescent orange while you are hunting big game animals. Second, you need to keep your four-wheeler on an established road. Third, you need to fill this antelope license out before you leave the site of kill. And fourth, where is the antelope that you already killed earlier this morning?"

Sam's eyes became very large, he replied, "We stashed that antelope in an old abandoned cabin so that the meat wouldn't spoil!" I responded, "Sam, you are only allowed one buck license for this area, so now you are also over your legal limit." Sam looked down at the ground and put his hands over his face as if to say "Holy Shit, I'm in a bunch of trouble right now!" I then looked at the doe antelope on the back of the four-wheeler and I asked the other man for his license. He replied, "I'm sorry sir, I don't have a license at all!" I then asked him if he killed the doe for the meat or accidently killed the doe trying to hit a buck. He responded, "I killed her for the meat, sir!" It became evident to me that these guys were out in the middle of nowhere trying to kill as many antelope as they could and not put a license on any of them. I seized both antelope and told the men to load the antelope in the back of my patrol truck and be careful not to get blood all over my blue cooler. I decided it was really important for me to follow them back to the abandoned cabin to verify another dead antelope, or possibly several more dead antelope?

I followed these guys for nearly an hour on a very rough two-track road in the middle of nowhere. I started asking myself questions like is there really a cabin or are they lying to me? Are they taking me out in the middle of nowhere to ambush me in a remote cabin? Who owns the cabin? Is it on private or public land? My quesadilla was beginning to wear off so I pulled out some antelope jerky sticks and a couple cheese sticks that I had stashed in the side door pocket of my truck, gobbled them down as I continued to eat their dust down the bumpy two-track road. We finally arrived at an old abandoned cabin next to a creek that had very high greasewood growing on the banks of the creek. The cabin was old and in very rough shape with parts of the roof missing from high winds in the area. I told the three men to wait in the truck while I checked out the cabin. I was going to call dispatch and give them my location, but I didn't know where I was for sure. I didn't have a map of the area and this was before GPS units and cell phones. As a matter of fact, I had remembered seeing a pay phone sitting alongside the highway near Moneta as I passed through that area just before daylight earlier that morning.

I slowly walked over to the cabin keeping my eyes on the three men in the white Chevy truck. I attempted to push open the dilapidated sagging door on the south side of the cabin. This was the only door on the cabin and it faced towards the creek. After several failed attempts to push the door open, I stepped back and gave the door a swift kick with my cowboy boot and the door opened to the inside with small splinters of busted wood flying through the air. I slowly poked my head in the cabin and could not see anything because the windows had been boarded up and no sunlight could shine through. SHIT, I thought to myself, I can't see a damn thing and I'm not walking in this cabin alone when I can't see anything except a perfectly round spider web in the corner of the door about the same height as my forehead.

I quickly went back to my patrol truck and grabbed my department-issue flashlight that had Jay Lawson GF-1 inscribed on the handle. I thought to myself Alright dammit, you worked for me last night, please turn on and work for me again!! I clicked the little black button and the light came on, thank God!! I thought to myself, I should actually get some spare batteries. This flashlight is becoming a pretty important part of my life since last night not being able to get into the house and find a spare key and now needing to look in this dark dilapidated cabin! The three men started to get out of the truck and head for the cabin. I yelled at them to please stay in the truck until I told them otherwise. I didn't know them and I sure as hell didn't trust them. I wanted all of them where I could see them all together.

I lowered my head to walk through the small doorway into the cabin. I felt a spider web stick to the top of my forehead as I moved forward into the cabin. The web was so strong and big that it nearly tore my hat off as I entered into the cabin. I shined my flashlight around in the cabin and observed old rusty tin cans on the floor, an old bed spring with no mattress, and an old rusty wood stove in the northeast corner of the cabin. I could tell nobody has lived in the cabin for years. Probably an old sheep herder or cowboy camp back in the day. I shined my flashlight throughout the one-room cabin and observed no dead antelope anywhere. I stepped back out of the cabin and cleaned the spider web off my face and hat. I looked over at the truck with the three men sitting in it. Sam yelled, "THE ANTELOPE IS IN THE ROOT CELLAR ON THE NORTH SIDE OF THE CABIN!" I waved my hand and yelled, "THANK YOU!"

I walked around the north side of the cabin and observed another dilapidated door lying flat against the ground with three rusty hinges on one side. I bent over and slowly lifted up on the large heavy door. Once I got the door open wide enough for the sun to shine in, I observed a freshly-killed buck antelope lying down in the bottom of the root cellar. Root cellars were used back in the day before refrigerators were invented to keep food and water cool during the hot summer days. This particular root cellar was very cool as I could feel the cool air hit my face as I opened the door. I also got blasted with a strong odor of buck antelope in the rut when I poked my head into the root cellar. "WHEW, I thought to myself! I walked back to the Chevy pickup and requested that the men get the buck antelope out of the root cellar and load it in the back of my patrol truck. This buck only had horns about twelve inches long. Sam was either high grading bucks and found a larger buck to shoot or they were just out shooting as many antelope as possible before they got caught.

I ended up seizing all three antelope and issued Sam citations for taking antelope w/o license, over limit of antelope, fail to properly tag antelope, and fail to wear fluorescent orange while hunting big game. I issued his buddy citations for taking antelope w/o license, and failure to wear fluorescent orange. I asked them all to get back in their truck while I issued all the citations and filled out seizure tags. I parked my patrol truck behind them while issuing the paperwork. I wanted to be able to see

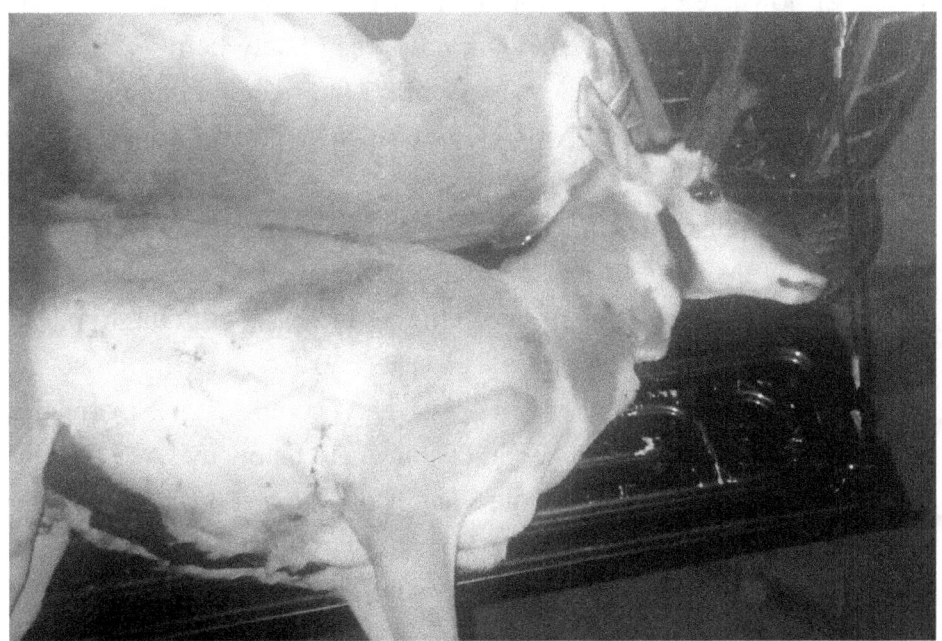

Seized antelope in back of patrol truck.

them at all times. It took me nearly an hour to write out all the citations. This is a very dangerous part of the job, because it's hard to focus on writing citations and watch others. They are generally pretty upset when they know they are getting a citation. I exited my patrol truck and walked over to their pickup. I explained to them how to take care of the citations or show up on the court date and had them sign all their citations. I also told them that if they didn't show up on the court date or pay the fine that a bench warrant would be issued and they would be arrested and possibly lose their hunting privileges in the future. I walked back to my patrol truck and put my citation book back in the side door pocket and jumped in my truck. I took a deep breath and thought to myself, that was a pretty good case for my first contact with a big game hunter. I was happy that animals were seized, citations issued and I was still alive. I just didn't know where I was. I looked up and a Dodge dually truck went racing by me on the rough two-track road in front of me. The truck had Texas plates. I thought to myself, what in the hell is someone from Texas doing out here in the middle of nowhere? I need to follow this truck because if they are from Texas and in a remote area, they are more than likely doing something wrong!! I don't think they saw me parked off the side of the road next to the old cabin as they were driving pretty fast when they went speeding by me.

After their dust settled, I started down the road slowly. My plan was to follow them until I could find a high spot and sit back and watch them hunt or do whatever they were going to do. I could see a high spot in the road ahead. This would be a good place to stop and glass. I approached the high spot in the road very slowly so that I could just peek over the edge and hopefully see them hunting somewhere below me. As I crested the hill, I almost hit them head-on. They had gone a short distance over the hill and turned around and came back down the road towards me. I swerved hard to my right and they swerved hard to their left. The driver mashed on the brakes and came to a sliding stop just past my driver's side window. He threw the loud diesel dually in reverse and romped on the throttle. A large cloud of black exhaust blew up in the air as he mashed on the throttle in reverse to visit with me. I didn't know if he wanted to visit with me or yell at me for being parked almost in the middle of the road when he came flying over the hill. He soon was even with my truck and he rolled down his tinted window.

The man yelled in a deep voice, "WHAT IN THE HELL ARE YOU DOING OUT HERE?" He looked absolutely huge sitting in that Dodge dually truck. His curly brown hair stood on end and he had a reddish colored shaggy beard. His head nearly touched the roof of his truck. He was so big he looked like he had to shove himself in the truck just to fit. I also noticed he was wearing Carhartt bib overalls and smoking a stubby cigar about two inches long and round as a small dog turd. I told myself, don't show any fear, this man is from Texas and probably a big ole blow hard that will try to intimidate me with his size and gruff personality. I slowly rolled down my window to talk to the man. He had electric windows, I did not. He asked me what I was doing out here in the middle of nowhere parked in the middle of the damn road on a blind hill. I apologized to the man for being in the middle of the road and asked him if he was hunting antelope. He stated that he wasn't hunting antelope, but that he owned a large ranch in the area and had received landowner licenses each year from Cheyenne headquarters to hunt antelope. I was having a hard time hearing the man talk over the loud sound of the diesel engine running, so I exited my truck and walked up to his driver's side window.

There was another man sitting in the passenger seat next to him. He had a straggly beard as well and was a very skinny man who wore a greasy ball cap. This man was smoking unfiltered Camel cigarettes and missing a couple front teeth. He had a nervous laugh and just sat over there and smiled at me while smoking his cigarette. I introduced myself to the driver and shook his hand. The driver said his name was Jon Kay. As we exchanged small talk, I noticed a couple small drops of blood on Jon's Carhartt pants. I also noticed a double barrel shotgun lying on the seat between the driver and passenger. The barrel of the shotgun was pointed towards the floor board of the truck. I asked Jon if he had been hunting anything today. Jon responded, "No, why do you ask?" I said "Because I see you have a shotgun and you have blood on your pants." Jon said, "Oh, I was afraid you were going to ask me about that. I killed a cottontail rabbit in my yard last night." I said, "Where is your yard" He replied, "At my ranch" I then asked him where the dead rabbit was and he replied, "In my stomach, I ate it for dinner last night." I said, "Good for you, I guess I need to see your small game license!" Jon was getting agitated, he pulled his stubby cigar out of his mouth, squinted his eyes at me and said with a deep voice, "MY WHAT?" I said, "I need to see your small game license. If you killed a cottontail rabbit you need a small game license!"

Jon quickly pushed me out of the way with his door as he exited the vehicle. I remember this man being very tall and big. I remember looking right at his grey chest hairs that were sticking about three inches out of his unbuttoned shirt above his Carhartt bib overalls. Jon was looking down on top of my head and I'm 5'-11". He said, "I don't have a small game license, I didn't realize that I needed one to kill a damn cottontail rabbit!" I was very nervous that "Big Jon" might shove me in a posthole! I very calmly said, "Yes sir you need a small game license, do you have a driver's license on you?" He replied angrily, "WHY, ARE YOU GOING TO WRITE ME A TICKET?" I said, "Yes, Sir, I am." Jon angrily handed me his driver's license. I stepped in my patrol truck and nervously wrote out a citation to Jon for taking a cottontail rabbit without a license. Both men were walking around my truck at this point in time wanting me to roll down my window so they could both yell at me! I thought about calling dispatch just to let them know where I was at, but I didn't know how to tell them where I was, because I really didn't know!

I heard the other man yell to Jon, "LOOKS LIKE HE HAS BEEN HARASSING SOMEONE ELSE AND CONFISCATED ALL THEIR DAMN ANTELOPE!" I looked at the bond amount on the ticket and it was going to cost Jon $110.00 for taking that rabbit without a license.

I thought to myself, that's a pretty expensive meal!! And I hope he has $110.00 in cash or I'm going to have to arrest him and take him to jail since he is a non-resident and needs to pay the fine in the field or go to jail.

I stepped out of my patrol truck and requested that both men get back into their truck. They both complied thankfully. Once they were in the truck, I explained the citation to Jon and advised him that he needed to pay the $110.00 fine amount. Jon screeched, "CHRIST, I don't have that kind of money on me right now!" I replied, "Well maybe your buddy can help you out or I'm going to have to arrest you and take you into town to post bond since you're from Texas. They both got their wallets out and came up with $104.00. I said, "That's close enough, I'll make up the rest and maybe you can owe me a drink sometime!" I, of course was being sarcastic but Jon didn't find any humor in that statement whatsoever. He pulled his cigar out of his mouth and said, "The only drink I'll ever owe you will be a shot of my piss!" He then fired up his diesel truck and tore out of there with a big plume of black exhaust pouring out of the large chrome exhaust pipes mounted in the back of his truck and sticking up over his cab.

I walked back and climbed into my patrol truck and put my ticket book away in the lower door pocket of my truck. I sat there for a minute and noticed my hands were trembling. I thought to myself, that guy could have just killed me, dispatch has no idea where I am at and neither do I. I just wrote a guy a citation for taking a damn rabbit without license and I don't even have any evidence because it's in his damn belly!! The more I thought about what had just happened I soon realized that I had just been had! This man didn't kill no cottontail rabbit!! He got caught with blood on his pants so he lied and told me that he had killed a cottontail rabbit not knowing that he needed a license to shoot a rabbit. If I would have searched his toolbox, I probably would have found an over-limit of sage grouse, that's why he had a shotgun!! DAMMIT, I thought to myself.

I couldn't believe it. I had written six tickets in less than an hour out in the middle of nowhere. The day was getting warm, I would need to head back to Lander and get the seized antelope in a cooler before the meat wasted and get them donated out to needy people. I would also need to stop by the courthouse in Riverton and turn in the cash and other copies of citations before closing time. It seemed like a waste of time to me, I had just gotten out to this area, checked two vehicles and now I needed to leave the area. There had to be hundreds of other hunters in the area that I never even got to contact. I would plan on coming back to this spot first thing in the morning. Besides I needed to get my sleeping bag out of my personal truck in Lander and start carrying it with me so I could sleep in the back of my truck and not be driving so many miles every day. I should also get the large gash in my head looked at from the fight I had with the toolbox lid and make sure I didn't need any stiches. I probably better grab another bottle of brake fluid as well.

My alarm went off at 4:00 AM the next morning. I was eager to get back out to the area that I had been in the day before and learn some more new country and hopefully check a bunch of antelope hunters. I slept great that night because I finally had my sleeping bag and a pillow. I never did get logged on that damn laptop computer to check my email. By the end of the night some Spanish speaking-lady was talking to me over the laptop. I had no idea who she was or where she came from. I got nervous after that and shut the computer off. Hopefully she didn't give my computer some damn virus or something.

The morning sun was just coming up. I was headed east on the same power line road that I had been on the previous day when I had come across the white Chevy pickup and the guy wearing white jeans poaching antelope. I grabbed a couple more antelope jerky sticks and some cheese sticks and chased them down with some luke warm coffee. I thought to myself, this is going to be a great day! I threw a big dip of Copenhagen into my lower lip, because I always enjoyed that first morning chew after breakfast. I soon went back to the area where I had met "Big Jon." I looked around for some evidence of dead sage grouse where he had turned his truck around the previous day. I did not find anything and was glad that I hadn't run into "Big Jon" anywhere after he had some time to think about things and probably get really mad at me. I decided to take a new two-track road that headed to the south. I loved taking new roads and learning new country. I traveled on this road for miles and miles and it kept getting rougher and rougher. It was at the point that I just wanted out of there, because I didn't know where I was and nobody would ever find me if I was to break down or get stuck. I wouldn't even know how to tell someone how to find me if I needed help with something.

I finally found another "power-line" road and headed west thinking this road would eventually take me out to a better road. After traveling this road for a while, it soon became very rough. I was at the point that I didn't want to turn around and have to go all the way back the same way that I had come because it was so rough! I was driving underneath the power lines when I popped over a steep hill and came across a woven wire gate that was across the road in front of me. There was a brand-new florescent orange sign on the gate post that read NO TRESPASSING!! I thought to myself, who in the world would own any land clear out here in the middle of nowhere? I looked a little closer and the gate had a brand-new chain and lock around it. I thought to myself, SHIT, there is no way that I'm going all the way back the same way that I just came. It would take me the rest of the day and there were no hunters in the area, so this would be a complete waste of my time! Against my better judgement I decided to take the gate apart and travel on looking for a better road to get back into civilization.

This was a very difficult decision for me, as I greatly respected private landowners and their private property rights. I would figure out who owned this property and contact them when I got back home and tell them what I had done. I continued down the steep rough road that curved towards the right with a steep canyon off to my left side. As I was going around the corner I looked to my left and spotted what looked like a camp trailer and pickup parked down at the bottom of the canyon. I quickly hit my brakes and came to a stop, grabbed my binoculars and looked below to see if it was a hunter. As my binoculars came into focus, I recognized the large black diesel truck with chrome exhaust pipes sticking out of the back of it. OH F____CK I SAID TO MYSELF, THIS IS WHERE "BIG JON" LIVES AND I'M TRESPASSING ON HIS RANCH!!

Just as quick as I figured out who it was, "Big Jon" came walking out of his trailer and grabbed his binoculars and looked back at me and started screaming and waving his arms. I couldn't tell what he was yelling but it sounded like "GET YOUR ASS OUT OF HERE RIGHT NOW!! I thought to myself, "OH MAN, I have really screwed up this time, I better get down there and apologize to him for trespassing on his ranch. I slowly worked my way down off the rough hill and pulled into his front yard. Jon came running towards me running and screaming with a shovel in his hands. I quickly rolled my window down and said "Good morning Sir, you told me you had a ranch out here and I just wanted to drop by and see it for myself and make sure you weren't shooting any more of them damn cottontail rabbits! I'm sorry for trespassing please forgive me!" As soon as Jon could see that it was me, he calmed down and shook my hand and thanked me for stopping by. He laughed and said that he hadn't been shooting anymore rabbits. We had a good visit and he told me all about his ranch. He actually seemed like a really good guy the more that I visited with him. When I left him, I asked him if he liked hunting sage grouse. He just smiled and said, "Yes, but it has been a long damn time!" I smiled and winked at "Big Jon" and said, "Just make sure you buy a license and the limit is three per day. Big Jon took a puff of his cigar and winked back and replied "I appreciate the advice!"

I jumped back into my patrol vehicle and headed north. I still didn't know where I was at, but I knew the main highway was north of me. I soon ended up on another gravel road that was fairly smooth. It was almost noon and I hadn't checked a single antelope hunter yet that day. I grabbed a few more jerky sticks and a cheese stick for lunch. I swear I could live off that stuff!! I was traveling down the gravel road doing about

45 miles per hour. The wind had started to blow and I could feel it blowing my truck from side to side once in a while. I thought to myself, Man, the wind can sure blow out in this country! About that time, I rolled my window down and spit some Copenhagen out of the driver's side window. I noticed my spit went forward instead of backward and landed on the hood of my truck. For my spit to travel forward, that meant I had a tail wind that was blowing more than 45 miles per hour because that was how fast I was traveling.

As I continued traveling down the road, the high sun reflected off of something shiny down in an old creek bed surrounded by high sagebrush. I quickly stopped and looked through my binoculars. It looked like a two-tone brown Ford pickup about two miles away. The sun was reflecting off the chrome mirror on the truck or I would have never noticed. It looked like someone may be trying to hide their truck in the tall sagebrush along the old creek bed. I thought to myself, could this be my first antelope hunter today? I soon found a two-track road to my right with a closed gate. The road looked like it may eventually lead me to the brown Ford truck hidden in the sagebrush. I stopped to get the gate. The wind was blowing so hard that I couldn't hardly get my truck door open. I pushed with both hands as I stepped out of the truck. My cap with the game and fish logo blew off so quick and fast that I never even saw where it went? I finally got the gate open and never did see that cap again. I hate the wind it puts me in a foul mood I thought to myself. It was all I could do to get the door of my truck open again and get back into my truck. I finally got in out of the wind and looked in the rear-view mirror. My hair was standing straight up and my cap was gone. I was hoping that I didn't run into any hunters to check because I probably looked pretty scary with my hair standing on end.

I finally got near the old brown Ford truck and stopped about fifty yards away. I looked at the truck through my binoculars. There was nobody in the truck that I could see, maybe they were out hunting? I decided to walk up to the truck and look into the back of the truck to see if they may have a dead antelope in the back or something indicating that they were hunters out hunting. The wind was still blowing very hard as I approached the truck. I noticed the truck had a gun rack in the rear window with a lariat hanging off the gun rack. The truck was pretty beat up and had four bald tires. I thought to myself, this may be a rancher's truck or a cowboy out looking for cows or something?

I looked in the back of the truck and there was nothing except a fence stretcher, roll of barbwire, and a rusty coffee can full of fence staples. This made it pretty obvious to me that this truck belonged to a cowboy or rancher type of person. I then heard a noise that sounded like a woman's giggle or laugh. I thought, what the hell was that? I slowly walked over and looked through the driver's side window of the truck and could not believe what I had just witnessed. There were two women naked as jaybirds making out in the front seat of that old Ford! And I recognized one of them!! She was a very beautiful woman. I didn't get a very good look, but the other gal was very attractive as well and I didn't recognize her. I don't think either one of them ever saw me. I was extremely embarrassed for what I had just observed. I slowly backed away from the vehicle and walked back to my truck. As I drove off neither one of them came up for air, and I don't think they had a clue that I was ever there. It took me several miles to comprehend what I had just witnessed. Now it made perfect sense why I had never seen this woman date a man before. I smiled to myself and wrote it off as just another one of those things that happens in the hills. What happens in the hills, stays in the hills!! Sometimes game wardens see and know certain things that they wished they didn't.

I ended up traveling clear over north of Rawlins that day looking for antelope hunters. I pulled into an oil field and observed a brown Chevy truck with a topper sitting in the middle of the road. I pulled up behind the truck and walked around to the driver's side of the vehicle to see if there was anyone in the truck. There was a man with a long dark beard sitting in the driver's seat of the truck with his window down. The man was sound asleep and he had a Peregrine Falcon sitting on his steering wheel. The falcon raised its wings in the air and screeched at me very loudly. I nearly crapped my pants and the man woke up scared to death to see his falcon screeching at a game warden in a red shirt. I stepped back from the truck until the man got his falcon under control. He ended up tethering the bird to his arm and stepped out of the truck. It was at this moment that I realized this man may be using this bird to hunt sage grouse or rabbits.

I asked the man if he was hunting with the falcon. He replied, "Yes sir I am, we just got done hunting some sage grouse and got our limit. He had the bird on his arm and walked around to the back of the truck and opened the rear door of his topper to show me his limit of sage grouse. The bird was still screeching at me and I kept my distance. This contact totally caught me off guard. I had never checked a Falconer in the field before and didn't have a clue what kind of licenses or permits the man even needed. I looked at the sage grouse and the man asked, "Would you like to see my permits?" I said, "Yes sir, I would like to see all of them" The man pulled out a three-ring binder from the back seat of his truck and showed me at least a dozen different permits and licenses that he needed to legally hunt with a Peregrine Falcon. I looked them all over carefully as if I was very concerned. I actually didn't have a clue what he needed to be legal to hunt with his falcon but I'm pretty sure he had all his affairs in order. I tried to have a conversation with this man but he was way out in left field, and nothing this man said made a bit of sense to me. I thanked the man and got the hell out of there. Sometimes you meet some really strange people out in the hills. I would need to go home and read up on my Falconer regulations.

I got back to the main highway and noticed a jeep traveling on a dusty two-track road across the highway from me. I grabbed my binoculars and noticed there were four men in the jeep all wearing a florescent orange hat. By God, I was finally going to get to check an antelope hunter and it was only about 3:00 PM. I finally caught up with them and pulled in behind them and all their dust. They pulled over and I got out to check their licenses. They were all from California hunting antelope. They each handed me their license and conservation stamp. I noticed the landowner coupon was missing from off each of their licenses. I asked them if they had harvested any antelope and they all replied, "No." I then asked "Where did your landowner coupons go?" They said they were camped on private ground at a large ranch and the owner told them to give him all their landowner coupons. I explained to them that they needed to first harvest an antelope on the landowner's private land before they give the landowner the coupon. I also explained to them that they were currently hunting on BLM ground and it would be illegal for them to give the landowner the landowner coupon unless the animal was harvested on their private property. In Wyoming a landowner can turn the coupon into Cheyenne Headquarters at the end of the year and get reimbursed for $8.00 per coupon. This is a program that rewards the landowner for feeding wildlife on their private property. It's not much money but if you collect enough coupons it can add up over time. I have actually seen non-resident hunters trade their landowner coupons for drinks in a local bar before.

I asked them who the landowner was and where he lived. They gave me directions and told me what road to take to get to his house. I told them all not to turn in their landowner coupon unless they harvested the antelope on private property belonging to the landowner. I headed to the ranch headquarters to visit with the landowner. The landowner lived on the south side of Ferris Mountain right at the base of the mountain. I did not know any of the landowners in this area as I was completely new to the area. This can be a touchy situation because game wardens like to maintain good relationships with landowners and the fine amount for this violation was $500.00. I did not want to destroy any good relationships that the senior game warden in Rawlins may have had with this guy.

I pulled into the front yard of the beautiful ranch house. There were large cottonwood trees that surrounded the yard. I also noticed a couple of horseshoe pits in the front yard. I loved to play horseshoes and was actually pretty good at pitching shoes back in my college days. I walked up and banged on the front door of the house. An elderly gentleman answered the door. He came to the front door and yelled at me through the screen, "WHAT THE HELL DO YOU WANT?" I said, "Sir, I would like to introduce myself to you and visit with you about a few things" He said, "If you are here to harass me, you can just get the hell out of here right now!" I said, "Sir, I don't wish to harass you about anything." He opened the door and let me in. He didn't shake my hand and he didn't offer me a cup of coffee or a chair to sit down in. I could tell this man meant business and he wasn't really high on having a game warden in his house.

I cut to the chase and told him that I had run into his California hunters. I was wondering why he had told them all to give him their landowner's licenses when they hadn't killed anything yet and they were all hunting on public lands. He looked at me and yelled, "YOU KNOW HOW MANY DAMN ANTELOPE, DEER AND ELK I FEED ON THIS PROPERTY IN A DAMN YEAR?" I said, "No, Sir, I don't" "A HELL OF A LOT MORE THAN I GET FROM THEM DAMN COUPONS!!" the man replied. He then said, "GO LOOK IN THAT DAMN COOKIE JAR OVER THERE ON THE COUNTER AND YOU WILL FIND EIGHT GODDAMN LANDOWNER COUPONS IN THERE, DO YOU THINK THAT'S GOING TO COMPENSATE ME FOR ALL THE DAMN DAMAGE I PUT UP WITH…$64.00 DAMN DOLLARS!!" The man went over and dug all the coupons out of the cookie jar and slammed them on the countertop. "He said, "TAKE WHATEVER THE HELL YOU WANT, IT DON'T MATTER TO ME!!" I said, "Sir, I understand what you are saying, I'm just here to make sure everything is done legally. I'm not here to take all your landowner coupons, but make sure you give these back to the California guys if they don't end up harvesting an antelope on your private property. The man went on ranting and raving about all of our damn regulations and how the whole world is just coming to an end.

I looked over his shoulder and could see a whole room full of trophies and plaques. It looked like maybe they were all horseshoe pitching trophies. I asked the man if those were all his horseshoe pitching trophies. He said, "Yes, they are." I replied, "WOW, you must be pretty good!" He said, "I won the world championship." I said, "WOW, that's quite an accomplishment, how often can you throw a ringer?" The ole man smiled and said, "About anytime I want to." I told him I really enjoyed playing horseshoes myself. He replied, "You want to throw some shoes?" I replied, "Hell Yeah!!" We hurried out the door and played a game of horseshoes. I thought I was pretty good at the game until this very moment in my life. That ole man never missed a ringer and beat me 21-0. He shook my hand and said, "You throw pretty well for a damn game warden!" I thanked him for the absolute ass whooping that he had just gave me, I told him that I needed that, and I had better get back to work because I hadn't written a ticket all damn day!

I jumped back in my truck and headed south. I couldn't believe how good that ole man was at pitching horseshoes. I had never been beat that bad in my entire life! I would need to practice a great deal to get to that level someday. My stomach started to growl so I grabbed another handful of antelope jerky and cheese sticks and chased it down with some cold coffee. I decided to try and find some hunting camps on my way back home. It was getting late and hunters would be back at their camps, I just needed to find their camps. I ended up driving down a county road north of a very small town named Lysite. Lysite wasn't much of a town just a few buildings sitting alongside the main highway between Casper and Shoshoni. As I was heading north, I came across what looked like a large camp of hunters. It was dark and they had a large bonfire going, with what looked like about eight hunters standing around the fire. I only assumed they were hunters because they were all wearing fluorescent orange hats that I could see in the glare of the flames of the fire.

It looked like they were camped on private property. I decided to pull up in front of their campfire and see if they had harvested any antelope that day that I could check. I felt the need to get some animals checked, because I had already put in over twelve hours that day and hadn't checked a single dead antelope. I stepped out of my patrol vehicle and walked up to their bonfire. I startled the men because they didn't know who I was and they were not expecting any company at that time of the night. I was wearing my bright red shirt with my small gold badge pinned above my heart. The flickering of the bonfire made my badge shine brightly and really stand out in the darkness. One man looked up and said, "Oh shit, the game warden is here!" I responded, "Good evening gentlemen, I'm with the Game and Fish Department, do any of you have any dead antelope in camp that I can check?" One man responded, "Yes sir, we have a whole trailer full of them back in the trees if you would like to see them." I responded, "Thank you, let me grab my flashlight quick." As I walked back to my truck, I could feel my stomach start to grumble severely. I was getting a bad stomachache and it was probably from all the antelope jerky and cheese sticks that I had eaten all day.

I grabbed my flashlight and followed the man back into the woods away from their campfire. The dead antelope were all stacked in a homemade trailer made from the pick-up bed of an old 1972 Chevy truck. The trailer was covered with a bright blue plastic tarp. As the man lifted the blue tarp off the trailer to show me the dead antelope, a very tiny little fart escaped my body as my stomach continued to gurgle. I quickly caught a whiff of the fart. It resembled what a gut shot sage grouse may have smelled like on a hot July day. I thought to myself, OH MY GOD THAT SMELL IS ABSOLUTELY HORRIBLE, I HOPE THIS MAN DOESN'T DETECT THE HORRIBLE STINK THAT JUST RELEASED FROM MY BODY!! About that time the man jerked the blue plastic tarp off the trailer to show me the dead antelope. The man scrunched up his face and said, "Holy Shit, do you smell that smell, I think these antelope have spoiled!" He then poked his face down in the trailer full of dead antelope, sniffed a few more times. He said, "YUP, I think these damn antelope have spoiled in the hot sun!"

I wasn't about to tell the man that what he was smelling was the smell of my tiny little fart. So, I put my face down in the trailer and sniffed a few times and stated, "YUP, I think you may be right. Some of this meat may be spoiled." Dead antelope never smell very good anyways, even if the meat isn't spoiled. I went ahead and checked all the antelope and left their camp with a horrible bellyache. I returned back to Ocean Lake that evening around 11:00 PM. I thought to myself, what a day, I'm tired and need some sleep, I'll check my email another day!

I returned back to the antelope camp north of Lysite several days later only to find a huge pile of dead antelope lying next to their campfire. The hunters had packed up and gone back to Ohio and left all their dead antelope behind. I jumped out of my truck and was furious that they had wasted so much edible meat. In Wyoming you have to take all four quarters of your animal including the back straps and tenderloins. If you leave any of this meat in the field it is considered "Waste of Edible Meat" The fine for wasting meat was $450.00. I had all of the hunters contact information from checking their camp a few days prior. So, I ended up driving to a little town named Moneta which was located about thirty miles away. Moneta had a pay phone next to the main highway and I used it to contact the Ohio hunters.

The first hunter that I called answered his phone. He had remembered me checking their antelope that night several days ago. He said, "Oh Yes, Hi Scott, I remember you checking our camp the other night. How ironic you called because we are just sitting down to eat some antelope steaks." I responded, "Well, you would have much more steak to eat if you hadn't left it all lay on the ground in Wyoming!" He told me that the meat had spoiled and they didn't want to take spoiled meat home with them. I explained the regulation to him and mailed him a citation for $450.00. I told him he better damn sure take care of the citation, or I would find him next time he came to Wyoming hunting and arrest him. I also told him that he had left a horrible mess on the private landowner's property, and that he needed to call the landowner and apologize for leaving the pile of dead antelope carcasses. The man apologized and said he would take care of the citation and apologize to the landowner. It would be several years later that it hit me like a ton of bricks. These hunters dumped their meat because they thought the meat was spoiled. And, the reason they thought it was spoiled was because of that tiny little fart that I had let on that deep dark night.

Chapter 3

JEFFREY CITY

I was able to make it back to Shell for a few days and see my family. I drew an antelope tag for the Red Desert area. This was a very coveted license to have as this area had a number of trophy buck antelope in it. I was excited about taking my family on an antelope hunt for a few days if it worked out. It was also fall of the year and the trout in Boysen Reservoir were really biting and I had a boat that I could hear calling my name. It just seemed I never got much time for family, hunting or fishing. I was so focused on working long hard hours because I felt if I didn't, I may never get a permanent job with the Wyoming Game and Fish Department. I gave my kids and wife a hug and kiss good-bye and headed back to Ocean Lake. I was to meet with my supervisor Kent Schmidlin at 8:00 AM on Monday morning.

I walked into Mr. Schmidlin's office in Lander early Monday morning and was greeted with a big smile and a firm handshake from my supervisor. Mr. Schmidlin always seemed like he was in a good mood and happy to see me. This was a trait that I hadn't witnessed much with other supervisors. Mr. Schmidlin's demeanor just made a person want to work hard for him, I can't explain it in any other way. Mr. Schmidlin asked me if I would be interested in staying in the old warden station in Jeffrey City for a couple of weeks. He explained that a large herd of elk had left Green Mountain and traveled down to private property near the Sweetwater River on Split Rock Ranch. He stated that this elk behavior was not normal. It would be good to have someone babysit those elk for a while as they were very assessable and vulnerable to hunters. He was also concerned about trespassers entering private property without permission to harvest these elk, as there were some really nice bulls in the herd.

Mr. Schmidlin told me where he thought the key to the warden station was hidden. This was good information because he had forgotten to tell me the location on the Ocean Lake house and I ended up diving through the bathroom window, and landing on my head next to a filthy toilet. I learned to ask good questions based on my short experience with the Department. I also asked Mr. Schmidlin if the house had power, water and a bed. He just smiled and said, "I think so!" I was very excited to go on this mission. I had never worked in any of that country before. I thanked Mr. Schmidlin and told him that I would keep in touch as much as I could. That country didn't have very good radio coverage, and back then we didn't yet have cell phones. My supervisor then asked me if I was able to check my e-mail on my new laptop computer. I thought to myself, oh Shit, it's been nearly a month and I haven't checked my email yet! I responded, "Not yet, Sir, but I'm working diligently on getting that done. I drove back to Ocean Lake and quickly loaded up everything that I would need to be gone for a few weeks and headed for Jeffrey City. Halfway to Jeffrey City it dawned on me that I hadn't taken the time to fix the brakes on my patrol truck and I was completely out of brake fluid.

It also dawned on me that my monthly reports were due in two days. Hopefully I could get my laptop up and running to do my reports. If not, I would have to travel over a hundred miles back to the office in Lander just to use a computer. Back then, you could probably get drunk and roll your game and fish truck and still have a job. But if you were one day late on your monthly reports, you may get fired!

I soon arrived at Jeffrey City. The town itself looked like it was a ghost town. Very few people lived in the small town at this time. Jeffrey

City was a booming little place when the oil field was booming in the late 70's. Now, there were houses sitting empty and small dirt two track roads lined with tumbleweeds on both sides of the road. I turned to my right and headed down a narrow dirt road to the south looking for the warden station. The wind was blowing about thirty miles per hour and it was difficult to see the road with all the dust and large tumbleweeds blowing across the road. I looked to my right and observed a few skinny antelope standing behind an old outhouse being used as a windbreak. I thought to myself, Man, this town looks eerie, I wonder if anybody actually lives here. I then noticed a wooden archway to my left that had a woven wire gate stretched across the entrance to an abandoned house. The gate had a chain and padlock lock around the post and a bright orange sign hanging in the middle of the gate that read "NO TRESPASSING, IF YOU ARE CAUGHT ON THIS PROPERTY, YOU WILL BE SHOT." I looked up on the old wooden archway. It had a large draft horse skull nailed to the center of the archway with a large spike driven through the skull to attach it to the old wooden log.

I soon found the Jeffery City warden station. The yard had a chain link fence around it stuffed full of large dead tumble weeds on both sides of the fence. Dust was blowing through the yard as there was no longer any grass left in the yard. The warden station hadn't had anyone living in it for a while. I had heard rumor that the department was in the process of doing away with the warden station, and maybe creating two Riverton game warden positions and changing some warden district boundaries around a bit. As I pulled up to the house, I observed several tee-lock shingles blow off the top of the roof. The house had brown metal siding and there were a couple loose pieces of siding hanging off the north side of the house. The loose pieces of siding would wave around in the wind and occasionally hit the front picture window on the north side of the house.

I found the hide-a-key underneath a red brick just inside of the chain link fence in the front yard. I was surprised that I had actually found the key and it actually opened the front door! As I entered the house, it had a smell of mildew and there was absolutely no furniture whatsoever in the house. I entered the bedroom and realized I would again be sleeping on the floor with my sleeping bag. I soon hauled in all my stuff, including my laptop computer and set it on the kitchen counter. I decided to plug the computer in and charge it. That way it would be fully charged when I try for several hours or maybe even days to get logged into the damn thing. I was also surprised that the power and water actually worked in the house, things were looking up.

It was now about 5:30 PM on a Monday evening. I was getting hungry and wondered if Jeffrey City had a place that I could maybe sit down and order a cheeseburger and watch a Monday night football game. If there was such a place, it would sure be a treat right now. I jumped in my game and fish truck and toured the small town. I noticed the town only had one bar and a post office. The name of the bar was "The Ore House." I decided to park my company truck one block south of the bar down by the fire station. I didn't want the public or anybody in the bar to associate me as a game warden. Sometimes your best poaching stories are overheard in bar conversations. If others know you are a warden, they quit talking pretty quick.

I bellied up to the bar and ordered a crown and coke with a double cheeseburger and fries. The man who waited on me was overly friendly and kept looking at me like, who is this newcomer to the area? He even asked me several questions like, "Are you from here? Where are you headed? Are you staying in town? I just told him that I was passing through and was hoping I could find a place with a good cheeseburger and possibly a Monday night football game. The bartender said, "You want to watch football, let me turn the game on quick!" I thanked him and was pretty excited that I was able to finally watch a Monday night football game. I had always loved watching Monday night football for some reason. It was always hard to take time off from work on a Sunday to watch football when there were hunters who needed checked. So, I

Scott C. Werbelow

really enjoyed relaxing and watching the night games.

I was just about to finish eating my cheeseburger when an attractive young dark-haired woman entered the bar and bellied up to the bar right next to me. She was wearing camouflage pants tucked into her black steel-toed army combat boots. She wore a white tank top and appeared to be pretty tan like she worked a lot in the sun. She had a ball cap pulled down over her eyes with a black pony tail coming out of the back of her cap. A tattoo on her left shoulder read "Rode Hard, Put Away Wet" with a picture of the Wyoming bucking horse below the text. At this point I was somewhat intrigued by this woman but had not yet seen much of her face.

The bartender said, "Good afternoon Bonnie, what can I get you to drink? The usual?" Bonnie nodded her head as if to say 'yes,' 'thank you' as she licked her hand-rolled cigarette and placed the red Prince Albert tin back into her front jean pocket. She pulled out a can of Copenhagen from her other jean pocket and took one of the largest three finger "dips" that I had ever seen in my life. The bartender set a shot of tequila and an opened can of Budweiser in front of her and said, "Enjoy Bonnie!" Bonnie nodded her head as if to say thank you and quickly threw back the shot of tequila and downed it with one big gulp. Then she grabbed the open can of Budweiser and chugged it down until the can was empty. She slammed the empty can of beer on the bar, belched and said, "Another one please, bartender!!" The bartender grabbed the empty shot glass and can of beer, smiled and said, "Absolutely, Bonnie!"

Bonnie again slammed the second shot of tequila and chased it down with several large gulps of Budweiser. She belched again and took a deep drag on her hand-rolled cigarette. I thought to myself, Damn who is this gal? What is her story? I had never seen anything like this before, and I was definitely intrigued.

After a while I noticed that she had slowed her drinking, and she began to watch the football game, or at least act like she was watching it. I still could not see her face as she was sitting right next to me, nor had I heard her actually talk a full sentence. I was dying to see what this whiskey drinking, Copenhagen chewing, beer guzzling, rolled cigarette smoking chick looked like! Finally, I mustered up the nerve and said, "So, Bonnie, what is your favorite football team?" as I took a sip of Jack Daniels on the rocks. I had ordered this drink because I felt like I needed to man up a bit if I was going to fit into this bar. Bonnie turned and looked at me for the first time and smiled. I thought to myself, holy crap she is missing her front tooth, she is kind of cute, but she damn sure is missing a front tooth! She responded in a deep voice, "I don't give a F___K about no damn football game!!" I quickly downed my glass of Jack on the rocks, belched and said, "Yea, me neither, bunch of overpaid Sonsabitches!!"

It was tough to work my way in with Bonnie to actually have a real conversation. I did find out that she worked in the oil field and had recently broken up with her boyfriend. She was nervous that he may show up at the bar and make a scene. She told me that he was very hot-headed and the jealous type. I thought to myself, oh great Swerb, you're about to get shot by some redneck oilfield worker who thinks that I have just stolen his girlfriend in "The Ore House Bar." I almost asked her if he was the one that knocked her front tooth out, but I figured that might be pushing things a bit. About that time 8-10 oilfield workers walked through the front door of the bar and sat at three tables behind us. They were all loud, as if they had previously been drinking. Bonnie looked at me and said, "Oh Shit, he is here!" I really wanted to get to know all these oilfield guys over time, but didn't want things to start out in a fight over a chick that could out-drink me and was missing her front tooth. I decided it was time to "make a mile" and get the hell out of there.

I didn't say goodbye to Bonnie or tell her my name. I simply got up to pay my tab as quickly as possible. As I walked by the table of oilfield workers, I heard one of them say "Hey pussy, want to arm wrestle?" My blood immediately boiled and I turned and said, "Which one of you guys wants your ass kicked?" One of the biggest guys stood up and yelled, "LET'S GO RIGHT NOW FOR $100 DOLLARS!" I said, "I don't have a hundred dollars, but I'll beat your ass for free in front of all your friends. This really upset the man as he flipped the table full of food and drinks over and came charging towards me. Several of his friends jumped up and grabbed his arms to try and hold him back. I said, "Listen, Sir, I don't wish to cause any trouble, but if you want to arm wrestle me, the table is already cleared and it won't cost you a dime when I beat your ass!"

I hadn't arm wrestled in quite some time, but at this point in my life I hadn't ever been beat and I was pretty confident in myself. The other guys got the table set back up and placed a chair on each side of the table. By now I had become the center of attention, and everyone in the bar was crowded around the table to watch the "Event of the Evening." Bonnie was even standing at the end of the table smiling brightly (almost) as if to say "KICK HIS ASS!" Apparently, everybody in the bar knew each other and nobody knew me. I thought to myself, way to go Swerb, now you are the center of attention and if you beat this local hero in front of his cronies, he may kill you!" The big guy stood up and started pounding on his chest and yelled "COME ON MAN! COME ON MAN! I walked over to the opposite side of the table and reached out to shake his hand and introduce myself with some kind of fake name. He wouldn't shake my hand or introduce himself. He said, "I don't give a pinch of shit who you are, but if you beat me right-handed, I'm going to knock your ass out with my left one!!"

I sat down and hooked up with the man. He was quite a bit bigger than me, and he worked in the oilfield so he was probably pretty damn tough. His teeth were nearly rotted out of his mouth. His hair was strawberry red and his eyes were a deep green in color; they almost looked yellow. He was wearing dirty Carhartt bib overalls. He tried several times to pull me across the table towards him as our hands were locked up. I thought to myself should I let this man win so that I can get out of here alive? My ego would not allow that to happen. I looked him directly in the eyes and said, "Hope you're ready, this is going to hurt!" One of his buddies got our hands held together firmly and made sure we were equally centered.

His buddy stated, "When I take my hand off your hands that means go! I slowly reached over with my left hand and grabbed the bottom of my chair. I leaned forward as close to my right hand as possible without touching my chest. This is where most of your power comes from. The man's hand left our hands indicating "GO" and I beat him to the punch and got the jump. I slammed his right hand down so fast that he didn't even know what happened. I also waited for the left hook that he had promised me and nothing happened. It just got really quiet. The man looked at me and said, "Wait a minute, I wasn't ready, let's do that again!"

I told the man if we were going for money that I wouldn't give him a second chance, but since we were not betting any money, I would let him try again. We hooked back up and he really seemed eager to beat me now. The man said, "go," and I again got the jump and slammed his arm down to the table. His arm hit the table so hard that a couple of beer bottles fell off the table and broke as they hit the cement floor. The man jumped up and yelled, "YOU'RE ONE TOUGH SON OF A BITCH, BARTENDER BUY THAT MAN A BEER!!" The bartender brought me another Jack on the rocks and I sat at their table as if I was now one of them. We told hunting stories, fishing stories, and fighting stories. I told the men that I was scouting the area because I had an antelope tag for the area and wanted to learn the country. The man that I had just beat in arm wrestling agreed to show me the country and gave me his name and phone number. He said, "Call me anytime that you want to go look around, I will help you get a big buck!"

By the end of the night, I had made friends with all of them, even though I had probably drunk too much. I needed to get up early and look for elk on the Split Rock Ranch. I was hoping that none of them had seen my game and fish truck down by the fire hall and figured out that I was a Wyoming game warden. I had introduced myself to them as Steve.

4:00 AM came too damn early! I couldn't tell if it was my alarm clock ringing or just my head ringing from the hangover that I had. I quickly drank several large glasses of water and ate some antelope jerky and cheese sticks. I couldn't find anything good for breakfast and I didn't have time to cook bacon and eggs. I wanted to be in a location near the Split Rock Ranch before sunrise to hide my patrol truck and get in a position to locate the large herd of elk that were supposed to be in the area. I fired up my patrol truck and sped by the Ore House Bar in the dark of the night. I smiled and thought to myself, Seems, like I was just here a couple of hours ago, oh yea, I was!! I thought more about Bonnie, I had never met a girl like her before. I thought to myself, she probably needs to put on a nose twitch and tie a leg up just to brush her teeth each morning, or should I say her tooth! I laughed out loud to that thought as I sped by the bar in the night. Then I thought of the arm-wrestling match and how that could have gone very badly for me if a fight had broken out. I wasn't afraid of a good ole' fashioned bar fight, but I was out numbered and I could have been stabbed or even shot hanging with that caliber of rednecks.

As I approached the turn-off to the Split Rock Ranch, I observed a turn-off to my right that would take me to the top of a hill with a view of the ranch. I quickly turned off on this road and traveled to the top of a steep hill. Once at the top of the hill, I shut my headlights off facing my truck north so that I would be in position to glass the ranch for elk once daylight came. My head was starting to pound less and feel better. An old-time game warden once told me that he kind of enjoyed a hangover, because he knew he was always going to feel better as the day went on instead of worse. There was actually some truth to that statement.

I soon observed a vehicle drive by me on the highway below where I was parked. The vehicle was traveling slowly as it headed east with one taillight out. I watched the vehicle travel in my binoculars until it was about two miles away. I was just about to quit watching the vehicle when I observed a brake light come on from the one taillight that actually worked. I quickly grabbed my department spotting scope and mounted it to my driver's side window. As I focused the spotting scope, I could observe a large herd of elk crossing the highway in the headlights in front of the truck. I thought to myself, Holy shit, if someone wanted to poach an easy elk in their headlights this would be the time to do it! I quickly shut my patrol truck off and rolled down both windows so that I could possibly hear a gunshot if anyone were to shoot at an elk.

After watching the truck stopped in the highway with elk crossing the road in their headlights, I decided I was too far from the vehicle to actually observe any illegal activity if it were to happen. Heck, I may not even be able to hear a gunshot from that distance, I thought to myself. I made note to myself that the driver's side taillight was out on the vehicle. I quickly decided that I needed to get closer to this vehicle and I needed to do it quickly! I started up my patrol vehicle and took off down the steep gravel road at a high rate of speed with my headlights turned off. It was just getting daylight and I could barely see the gravel road. I didn't want to turn my headlights on and alert the vehicle down the road that I was in the area. I wanted to catch them doing something illegal in the dark and in a very remote area. As I approached the "T" intersection with a stop sign going down the steep gravel road, I mashed on my brakes to make a quick stop and turn left. I heard a loud "POP" and my brake pedal went straight to the floor again! SHIT, I have no brakes and need to make a sharp left-hand turn!

I was traveling way to fast to make the left-hand turn without rolling my truck. I quickly decided to blow through the T intersection and hope for the best. I hit a deep ditch on the other side of the road. My patrol truck became airborne for a short distance as I sailed over the top of a steep hill. I was now headed down towards the main highway at a high rate of speed with no headlights. I hit the top of my head on the ceiling of my patrol truck. This is also where I stored my M-14 rifle and 12-gauge pump shotgun in an overhead gun rack. I re-focused my eyes and observed a barbed wire fence coming up. I thought "OH SHIT." I held onto the steering wheel tight and hit the fence between the wooden posts! I heard a God-awful sound as the truck blew through the five strands of barbed wire and headed for the highway below. I was traveling too fast to make the right-hand turn back onto the highway, so I decided to keep it straight as I traveled through the steep barrow pit and jumped the highway in my patrol truck with headlights turned off. I don't know how much air I caught, but I sure did land hard. My head hit the ceiling again as I came to a rest up against a wooden fence post on the north side of the highway. I thought to myself I should have fixed those damn brakes by now and I'm out of brake fluid! I put the truck in reverse and backed away from the wooden post. I shoved the truck in drive and gave it the onion as I came out of the barrow pit and back onto the black top.

As I approached the highway my tires made a squealing sound when they hit the asphalt. I needed to get caught up to this guy if I was ever going to catch him shooting elk from his vehicle and in his headlights. I would assess the damages to my truck and fix the fence later once I checked on the elk crossing the highway. It was now light enough to see, and I drove very fast down the highway to catch up with the vehicle with one taillight. I drove over two miles and did not see the vehicle or the elk. I could tell where the elk had crossed the highway, because they left muddy elk tracks about thirty feet wide on the asphalt where they had crossed in front of me. I finally came to a stop in my patrol vehicle with no brakes. I did not see any dead elk in the barrow pit or the immediate area. I exited my patrol vehicle and followed the elk tracks to where they had jumped the highway right of way fence on the north side of the highway. The elk had hit the fence hard and fast. I noticed two broken wood posts and several broken strands of barbed wire. I thought to myself, between me and the elk, this fence has sustained some pretty significant damage in the past five minutes! It looked like the elk had traveled into some heavy willows next to the Sweetwater River on private property. As I followed the elk tracks towards the willows, I noticed a very distinct blood trail in the green pasture grass below. I thought, Shit, did this elk cut itself on the barbed wire fence or did someone shoot it when it crossed the highway in their headlights? Different questions raced through my mind. Was it a cow or a bull? How bad was it hurt? Was it shot or injured from something else? I followed the blood trail into the willows. The elk was bleeding pretty hard and I soon found a piece of rib bone with blood on it. This told me that the elk was probably shot and not wounded from jumping the fence. But who knows, elk can get injured from fighting other bull elk, highway accidents with vehicles or even running into and breaking off a wooded fence post? I walked back to the highway to look for any evidence in the area where the elk had crossed the highway. I searched the area very thoroughly and could not find an empty shell casing, people tracks or any evidence for that matter.

I returned to my patrol truck to assess the damage from running through the barbed wire fence. The truck only had minor scratches on each side of the front quarter panels and a small dent in the front bumper where I had hit the fence post. I thought to myself, it will buff out, I don't need to report this one! I headed back down the highway to repair the fence that I had driven through and noticed a blue and white cooler lying in the barrow pit. I thought, looks like someone lost their cooler, oh shit, that's my cooler! The cooler had flown out of the back of my truck when I jumped over the highway and came to an abrupt stop against the wooden fence post. The lid to the cooler had come open and there were cheese sticks, antelope jerky, cans of Copenhagen, flour tortillas, cheese and other various snacks lying everywhere in the barrow pit. I was happy that nobody had come along and stolen my week's-worth of camp groceries. I gathered up my belongings and repaired the fence the best that I could. I was glad that it was dark out when this happened and nobody had seen the game warden truck fly across the highway in the night with no headlights on. I was upset that I had left my location to get closer to the vehicle with one taillight and ended up missing everything and wrecking my truck. I would now need to travel to Muddy Gap store and hopefully purchase some more brake fluid.

Luckily, I found some more brake fluid at Muddy Gap. After driving several miles and pumping my brakes they were working again. I now needed to go find the herd of elk that crossed the highway and were headed for the Split Rock Ranch. I drove through the front yard of the ranch, but didn't see anyone around. Nobody came out of the house yelling or shooting at me, so I kept driving and headed north out into the badlands. As I traveled through the badlands, I thought this was some of the most beautiful looking landscape that I had ever seen before. Beautiful sandstone rock formations with mixed cedar and juniper bushes. The colors of the sandstone rocks were all different shades of white, gray, black, and even yellow. This looked like great Indian Territory to me. I worked my way through the sandstone breaks on a rough two track road. I was trying to get just north of where the large herd of elk were last headed to see if I could locate them.

I was headed south dropping off a steep hill and down into a small basin filled with beautiful sandstone outcroppings, junipers, and cedar trees. I looked up and could see a lone cow elk coming over a ridge headed right towards me. I quickly stopped the truck, shut it off and tried to blend in with the landscape. What happened next was a sight that I have never forgotten. Approximately 250 elk came over the ridge single file and headed straight towards me. There were a number of trophy bulls in the bunch and they were all bugling, grunting and occasionally fighting with one another. The whole herd of elk ended up bedding down within fifty yards of my patrol truck. I thought to myself, if Mr Schmidlin wanted me to come babysit these elk, I'm damn sure doing it right now. But how could someone poach one of these elk with a game warden parked right in the middle of them? The time was about 9:00 AM and the day was absolutely beautiful with blue sky and all the fall colors of the trees in the surrounding area. The bulls would get up and bugle for a while and then spar with other bulls. I could hear the crashing of horns as they locked up and pushed each other back and forth. The dust would roll off their feet and fill the blue sky as they pushed each other back and forth fighting for their next mate.

I had been watching the herd of elk for nearly two hours when I noticed another single bull elk come over the horizon in the same direction the herd had come from earlier. This bull was absolutely huge. It looked like he had at least six points on each antler as I zoomed in my spotting scope to get a better look at him. I soon noticed the bull was limping and I could see that he was bleeding out of the left side behind his shoulder. I thought to myself, DAMMIT, that bull has been shot and was probably shot in the headlights of the vehicle with one taillight. The blood trail that I looked at earlier is probably coming from this bull. I was furious with myself that I had decided to move to get closer and had missed everything because the brakes went out of my patrol truck. If I would have just sat on the hill with my truck turned off, I may have heard the gunshot and seen the person who pulled the trigger. But NO, I screwed it all up by getting impatient and wanting to get closer!

Now, I have a unique situation to deal with. Do I wait for the bull to die and try and recover a bullet? Do I put the bull down myself, try to recover a bullet and donate the meat to people in need of meat? Even if I recover a bullet, do I have a good suspect? I had decided to stay with the herd of elk until dark and keep my eye on the injured bull. The injured bull lay down underneath a cedar tree about fifty yards from the large herd of elk. He looked and acted very sick as he laid his head on the ground. It was a tough decision but I had decided to give the bull the benefit of doubt and leave the area and come back in the morning at first light to check and see if the bull was still alive. I drove back to Jeffrey City with a heavy heart of what to do with this situation. Did I make the right decision? Would the bull be gone in the morning and I would risk not recovering a bullet from him? Would I even find a bullet in him? Maybe it had passed all the way through his body cavity and exited on the opposite side? Mr. Schmidlin had asked me to watch over and protect these elk and I had failed my job!

I went to bed early that night with a couple knots on my head from bouncing my head off the roof of my patrol truck. My neck was stiff and I had a headache; I didn't feel up to checking my email again. I spent a great deal of time thinking about the whole elk situation and who may have shot that bull elk in their headlights. My alarm went off at 4:00 AM and I was eager to get back out to the Split Rock Ranch and see if the elk were still there. I soon arrived at the ranch just as the sun was coming up. The large group of elk had moved about one-half mile to the north but they were still in the area. I quickly drove down to the area where I had last seen the injured bull elk. As I was looking through my binoculars to find the correct cedar tree to look under, I observed three coyotes run up the hill a short distance from where I had last observed the bull lying the night before. I was hoping that the coyotes had not been feeding on the bull elk while he was still alive. I scanned more to my right and observed the bull elk lying dead out in an open grassy meadow. He had died sometime in the night and his body was bloated up with all four legs sticking straight out in one direction.

Poached bull elk.

I parked my patrol truck and grabbed my hunting knife and camera out of my backpack. I would need to sharpen my knife quick as it had become very dull from using it on other animals. This would be my first official necropsy of an elk to look for a bullet. I did not have a metal detector or any blue rubber gloves. As I approached the dead bull elk, I was hoping that the meat hadn't spoiled from him lying there all night and not being cleaned out properly. I took several pictures of the bull elk before I did any cutting or moving the carcass around. I then carefully skinned back the hide on his left side where the bullet had possibly entered. I observed a very small hole in the hide with a large amount of hemorrhaging around the hole and on the body cavity where the bullet hole had entered the rib cage area behind the bull's front shoulder. The bullet had hit a rib bone and it looked like a small chunk of rib bone was missing. I was pretty sure that the small piece of rib bone that I had collected on the blood trail the day before would match.

I then rolled the elk over to its other side and carefully skinned the hide back in the area that the bullet should have exited. I ended up skinning the entire right side of the bull and never found where a bullet had exited. I then rolled the bull on his back and split him open to look at his insides to try and determine the direction of the bullet as it passed through the body cavity. I quickly noticed the heart and lungs had not been touched by the bullet. The path of the bullet showed that the bullet had entered behind the bull's left front shoulder and traveled towards the bull's chest cavity towards its right front shoulder. I turned the bull back on its left side and removed the right front leg. It appeared that there was some hemorrhaging on the inside of the elk hide right in front of the shoulder bone. I carefully peeled back the thin layers of muscle in the chest area of the bull and located a bullet just beneath the hide on the right side of the bull. Before removing the bullet, I took a picture of the bullet still in the tissue of the meat. I then found a straight willow stick and stripped all the branches off of it to make it as straight and smooth as possible. I placed the willow branch through the bullet entry hole all the way to the exit hole with the elk lying on its back. This would show the direction of travel that the bullet made as it passed through the body cavity of the large bull. I then took several more pictures showing the travel of the bullet.

I went back to my truck and collected the small piece of rib bone that I had collected earlier. The rib bone was an exact match to the missing piece of rib bone. This evidence told me that this bull was shot while crossing the highway early yesterday morning. The direction of travel that the bullet made indicated to me that the bull was traveling slightly away from the person that shot it. Meaning the elk had crossed the highway headed to the drivers left. If the driver of the vehicle shot the bull, they would not have had a clear shot at the bull from inside the vehicle until it cleared the front of the vehicle and driver's side mirror. This bull was probably shot just after jumping the right-of-way fence as it traveled away from the vehicle that only had one taillight.

I carefully collected the bullet and examined it closely. It looked like it was a full metal jacketed bullet and about a .23 caliber bullet. I would need to show this bullet to a more experienced game warden that could measure it with calipers. I didn't have a fancy little envelope to put the bullet in for evidence collection so I rolled it up in a piece of toilet paper with the piece of rib bone and stuck it in my front shirt pocket. I labeled the toilet paper Exhibit A and Exhibit B. I now had another dilemma. I would need to load this elk whole in my pick-up as evidence by myself. I would also need to get it somewhere with a freezer or cooler to preserve the carcass. It appeared to me that the meat on the elk had spoiled during the night due to the strong smell as I performed the necropsy. It seemed like a huge waste to me that someone had shot this elk and now all the meat had wasted. Glad the pack of coyotes got a few bites! The rack on this elk was very nice, it saddened me that a legal hunter was not able to harvest this elk legally and have it mounted on their wall of their house or hunting lodge and be able to brag about how they harvested it to their buddies. I was also going to have to leave the area the rest of the day and who would watch over the 250 plus elk still in the area with numerous large bulls bugling in the background?

Loading that bull elk was great deal of work. I ended up hooking a come-along to my headache rack and around the antlers of the large bull and winched him into the bed of my patrol truck one click, at a time. I headed for Lander to find a cooler to hang him in. I would also need to find a more experienced warden and have him look at the bullet that I collected to see what caliber it was for sure. I arrived at the Lander region office at about noon time. Nobody was around the office including Mr. Schmidlin. The office managers told me that Mr. Schmidlin was out in the field, as he was tired of being in the office. They also told me that they didn't know where any of the other wardens were at but none of them were around the office. I tried to call a few of them on the radio, but nobody answered. I was able to find a temporary fish biologist to help me unload the bull elk into the cooler. He had lots of questions as we unloaded the elk. I was pretty short with him, as I was upset that someone had poached this animal. I needed to get back out to the Split Rock Ranch and look over the herd of elk before someone else found them and poached some more of them.

I watched over that herd of elk for three straight days and nobody ever showed up to hunt them. I think it was because these elk were in a new area that hunters weren't aware of yet. Plus, they would need permission from the ranch to drive through and harvest one and I don't think the owners of the ranch were going to allow any hunting unless it was close family or friends.

I drove out to the ranch on the fourth morning and I did not observe any elk in the area. I decided to learn some new country so I headed south towards Green Mountain. I hadn't spent anytime patrolling in different areas, because I had been focused on babysitting the large herd of elk on private property. It was still early in the morning when I observed some hunters pulled off the side of the Green Mountain road. It looked like they were glassing something on the east side of the road.

I pulled up behind them and visited with them for a few minutes.

Scott C. Werbelow

They both handed me their hunting licenses to look at without me having to ask to see them. I always enjoyed when hunters would do that; it just showed a sign of respect to me and my job. As I was visiting with them, I heard a loud noise coming my direction. I quickly looked up to see a man on an ATV hauling ass down the road towards us with a bird dog sitting on the front rack of the ATV. He had to have been traveling over fifty miles an hour coming down that gravel road with his dog happily perched on the front rack. The man never hit his brakes until he was very close to us. He locked up both back tires on the ATV and came sliding to a stop as he approached us. His trail of dust covered all of us as it blew by in the slight Wyoming breeze. Once the dust cleared, I could see the man was wearing a green game and fish hat with the ear flaps down and a little black pom-pom on top of his hat. He was also wearing a green game and fish coat with a shiny small gold badge mounted over his left pocket. I thought to myself, holy cow this is a senior game warden whom I have not yet met before.

He looked at me and yelled over the sound of his ATV, "Who are you, and what the hell are you doing in my warden district?" I didn't know if he was talking to me or the hunters, but he was looking at me. I said, "My name is Scott Werbelow, and I have been requested by Mr. Schmidlin to patrol this area and keep a watch on some elk that are spending time on private property over on the Split Rock Ranch. He smiled and I noticed a gap between his two front teeth. He kind of looked like a young Tom Cruise if it weren't for the gap between his two front teeth. He replied, "It would sure be nice to know that I have a trainee working in my district and babysitting my elk." I apologized to him for the lack of communication. The hunters could sense some tension in our conversation. They quickly said, "Good bye," and headed down the gravel road. The game warden that I was speaking with had a shiny gold name tag above his right pocket that read Benge Brown Game Warden.

I acted like I didn't see his name tag and quickly said, "You must be Benge Brown the legendary Rawlins' game warden?" He smiled and said, "Yup, that's me," as he held out his hand to shake my hand. We visited for a few minutes and he stated that he was in a hurry because he was working on a poaching case. The case involved someone shooting a spike elk in a 'cow-only' area and it appeared that they had shot the elk before legal shooting hours and left it lay in a field on private property. I was excited to hear about the case that he was working on. I thought that perhaps maybe the same person that shot and left this elk could also be the person that I was searching for who shot the large bull elk before legal shooting hours in their headlights.

I was excited to tell him about the case that I was working on, but I could tell he was very intent on catching up with whomever was responsible for shooting the spike elk and leaving it lay in the field. I asked him what evidence he had and if he had any suspects. He told me that only six people had permission to hunt this particular private property. He had collected three 30.06 shell casings from the area where the hunters had shot from. The three empty shell casings were all old looking brass and were even green in color because they were so old and hadn't been fired for years. He had already met with a group of three hunters who had permission to hunt the area, but they were all shooting different calibers of rifles and all their brass was shiny gold in appearance. The landowner of the private property had given Benge the names of the other three hunters who had permission and Benge was in the process of trying to find where these men were camped.

He told me that he had an idea of where these hunters were camped and he was going to try and find them. I asked him if it was alright if I tagged along and followed him to their camp. He said, "That would be fine, but you better keep up!" With that he fired up his red ATV and gave it the onion as he headed down the county road with his dog still on the front rack of the ATV. It soon became apparent to me that I may roll my truck trying to keep up with him. I never saw anybody drive that fast on an ATV before, especially with a dog on the front rack. This guy was driving like an asshole, hopefully I could at least keep up with his dust to be able to find him again. I was a little hesitant to drive too fast as I still hadn't gotten my brakes repaired.

After several miles of chasing dust, I could see Benge's ATV parked off the main road in a camp of local hunters. As I pulled up in my truck, Benge was already interviewing the hunters. They must have thought they were in deep trouble when I pulled up in my patrol truck. Now they had two game wardens in their camp. I wanted to watch a Senior Game Warden at work to see what I could learn from him. As I approached the three men, I just stood back a short distance and listened. The men looked to me like they were all in their early 80's. As Benge questioned them, all three men denied hunting in the area and knew nothing about a dead spike elk. Benge then asked if he could see their ammunition. They all reached into their pockets and pulled out green colored 30.06 caliber ammunition. Benge then asked them if they minded if he fired each of their rifles. They all looked at him kind of cross-eyed and hesitantly said, "Yea, I guess that would be alright."

Benge leaned over his ATV and aimed at a large pine tree about fifty yards away. He slowly and meticulously fired each of their rifles one at a time and collected the empty shell casing from each rifle. He pulled out a little notebook from his front shirt pocket and tore out three pieces of paper. The first piece of paper he labeled "Bob" and placed the empty shell casing on the small piece of paper that belonged to Bob's rifle. The second piece of paper he wrote the name "Larry" and placed an empty shell casing on that piece of paper. And finally, he pulled out the third piece of paper and labeled it "Roger" and placed an empty shell casing on that piece of paper indicating that bullet was fired from Roger's rifle.

He then pulled out three empty 30.06 shell casings that he had gathered at the scene of the poached elk. Then he grabbed his binoculars and turned them upside down and looked at each empty shell casing through the large end of the binoculars. I didn't know this at the time, but this works very well as a magnifying glass. Benge explained to the men that each rifle leaves a unique mark when the firing pin of the rifle strikes the primer of the bullet. He also explained that each rifle leaves a unique mark on the empty shell casing when the shell casing is extracted from the chamber of the rifle. After observing the empty shell casings very thoroughly through his upside-down binoculars, Benge grabbed Bob's rifle and brought it over to my patrol truck away from the other hunters. He looked at me and said, "This is the rifle that killed that elk."

He then pulled out a small plastic egg that he had in the front pocket of his game and fish coat. The small plastic blue egg contained "Silly Putty" My heart raced as I seen the small blue egg filled with silly putty! This reminded me of the Silly Putty that I had stolen out of Dunning's Department store when I was five years old and nearly went to jail for. I still had not forgotten the ass beating that my ole' man gave me when he returned home from work that day to find out from mother that I had stolen from a store. Benge grabbed the "Silly Putty" and shoved it down the end of the barrel of Bob's hunting rifle for approximately one inch. He carefully pulled the putty out of the barrel and laid it on the white piece of paper that was labeled "Bob". He then pulled a small brown envelope out of his front shirt pocket and emptied the envelope onto the tailgate of my truck. Benge had collected a bullet out of the poached spike elk earlier that morning.

Benge asked me if I knew anything about bullets. I told him that I thought I did, but now I wasn't sure I really knew anything about anything. Benge carefully showed me the lands and grooves that are left on the base of a fired bullet when it leaves the barrel of a gun. Benge tipped his binoculars over and looked closely at the bullet that he had collected from the spike elk. He said, "Looks like the bullet has a right-hand twist with six lands and grooves. He showed me how to look through the binoculars backwards and what to look for on the base of the bullet. He then grabbed the Silly Putty and looked at it through his binoculars. As he looked, he said in a low tone of voice, "This looks like the gun that fired the bullet; it has the same lands and grooves as the bullet collected out of the elk."

At this point I thought this guy was God! Who strolls into someone's hunting camp, shoots all their rifles at a tree with his bird dog still sitting on the ATV? Then grabs a hunter's rifle and shoves "Silly Putty" down the barrel to determine if that rifle fired the same bullet that was collected as evidence. Benge showed me the brass that he had collected in the field and the brass that he collected from Bob's gun. The firing pin had left a distinct mark in the primer of the shell casing that was the same as the shell casings that Benge had collected in the field. Based on the evidence, Bob's rifle is the one that killed that spike elk. The spike elk was also unique as one of the spike horns had been previously broken and stuck straight out of the skull to the side instead of straight in the air.

Benge went back to the three men's camp and asked if he could speak with Bob. Bob was about eighty-two years old, heavy set and wore bib overalls. Benge explained the evidence to Bob and told him that his rifle had killed the spike bull elk. Bob looked at the ground and started to weep. He looked up and said, "I'm sorry Benge, I did kill that elk before legal shooting hours this morning. I thought I was shooting at a cow, but

Poached spike elk.

it was too dark to tell for sure. When I walked up to the elk and seen that I had shot a spike elk on a cow license I got scared and left it lay." He then started crying even harder and said, "I lied to my friends. They don't even know that I killed that elk this morning." Benge thanked the man for his honesty and issued him a citation for shooting before legal shooting hours, taking the wrong sex of elk, and failing to properly tag the elk.

I was really impressed with Warden Brown. It seemed to me like he was only in their camp for about twenty minutes and completely solved the case, even though all three of them lied to him initially. The only evidence that he had was three empty green shell casings and he made the case. This told me that I had a lot to learn about becoming a good game warden. What game warden carries Silly Putty in their front pocket for Christ Sakes? What game warden shoots three different hunter's rifles off his ATV in their hunting camp nearly using his dog as a rest? I would later learn in my career, that game warden was Benge Brown! God threw away the mold when he made Benge Brown!

I thanked Benge for teaching me all this neat game warden stuff and said, "Oh, by the way, I have been working on a case." I pulled the bullet out of my front shirt pocket that I had recovered out of the large bull that was shot in the headlights. I said to Benge, "Can you tell me the caliber of this bullet that I recovered out of a bull elk the other day?" Benge looked the bullet over carefully. He said, "I can tell you in a minute as he unzipped his backpack that was strapped to the back of his ATV. He pulled out a set of bullet calipers and measured the bullet. He handed the bullet back to me and said, "It's a .223 caliber bullet. You have a good day. I need to get going on another case that I'm working on!" He jumped on his ATV, took off like it was stolen and I wasn't sure I would ever see him again. I thought to myself, how in the hell did he ever train his dog to stay on that ATV? I spent the rest of the day patrolling the Green Mountain area. I never did run into Benge again that day. Every camp that I stopped and checked said Benge had just checked them, minutes prior to me showing up. Several hunters said, "How in the hell does that dog ever stay on that ATV?" Benge officially retired from the Wyoming Game and Fish Department on April 12, 2022 after protecting Wyoming's treasured wildlife for 30 years. We will miss you Benge, happy sailing!

I ended up back in Jeffrey City that evening. I was hungry and needed a drink, so I headed back down to the Ore House bar. I hadn't been in there for several days. I parked my patrol truck south of the bar down by the fire station again, so that nobody would recognize my truck and figure out that I was a game warden. I walked through the front door and noticed Bonnie was again bellied up to the bar smoking hand rolled cigarettes and drinking shots of tequila. She seemed excited to see me again, and gave me a big smile as I entered the bar. I had forgotten about her missing front tooth until that moment. Yup, it was still missing! She smiled and said, "Get this handsome man a Jack on the rocks, bartender." She asked me what I had been up to the past several days. I told her that I was just passing through town again and had been out scouting for a nice buck antelope.

I really wanted to tell her about my day with game warden Benge Brown and everything that I had learned from him. I also wanted to tell her about the bull elk that someone had shot from the highway in their headlights but I didn't dare tell her that I was a game warden. I didn't really feel like I had much to talk about and I felt uneasy that she was friendly and had bought me a drink. Would she try to take me home? Was she still dating the crazy redneck that challenged me to an arm-wrestling match last week? I was happily married and would never cheat on my wife Lana. Even if I were single, I would have a hard time bringing home a gal to ma and pa who could drink and chew more than I and was missing her front tooth. But something about Bonnie intrigued me, I wanted to get to know her more, and try and learn why she lived such an unusual and possibly very rough life.

We visited about a lot of things and she kept buying me more drinks. I'm glad she was paying for my drinks because I was paying for her drinks. It greatly out-numbered what I was drinking and the shots

Rawlins game warden Benge Brown.

were much more expensive! She told me that she had broken up with her narcissist boyfriend because he was controlling and had a drinking problem. She told me that he had tried to kill her twice, once with a gun but missed and the other by strangulation. This guy sounded like a real peach to me and I was hoping that he would not show up at the bar and see us sitting next to one another having a big and rich time. It was now midnight, the bartender yelled "LAST CALL FOR ALCOHOL!" Bonnie ordered us both a double shot of tequila, I had never seen any women drink this much in my life.

I was tired and felt like I should have left the bar hours ago, but I was having a good time listening to all of Bonnie's crazy stories. There were only a few other people in the bar that night. I was just getting up to leave when Bonnie's ex-boyfriend came crashing through the front door of the bar. He was intoxicated and very loud as he came towards us. He grabbed Bonnie by the arm and yelled, "GET YOUR ASS OUT HERE RIGHT NOW!" Bonnie screamed as the large man drug her out the front door of the bar. She screamed at the bartender, "CALL THE POLICE!" I thought to myself, the only thing wrong with this picture, IS THAT I'M IN IT!!

I sat there on my bar stool for several minutes trying to figure out if I should intervene or not. I'm not sure how far away the police were, but my guess is they probably wouldn't show up anytime soon in Jeffrey City. I had only met one other law enforcement officer in the area. He was a deputy sheriff. His name was JD Darnell. I finally decided I better go out and check on her and make sure he wasn't beating her half to death. I really didn't want to get in the middle of their affairs, and I certainly didn't want him to think that I was flirting with his ex-girlfriend.

As I exited the bar, I noticed about a 1972 brown Ford pick-up parked right in front of the bar. The truck was covered in mud and looked like it was pretty beat up. I could hear voices yelling across the street, but it was too dark to see anybody. He would yell at her and Bonnie would yell back at him. I thought it might be best to just hang out in the shadows of the bar and watch them for a while from a distance to make sure that he wasn't going to beat up on her. I was leaning over the bed of the old brown Ford pick. Of course, being a game warden, I had to look in the bed of the truck to make sure there weren't any dead animals in the back of the truck that may have been poached. I did not find any dead animals in the back of the truck, and I wasn't even sure who the truck belonged to. After standing there in the night listening to the argument going on across the street, I decided to peek into the cab of the truck.

It was difficult to see into the cab of the truck as the only light I had was from the flashing neon bar light that was attached to the outside wall of the bar. The flashing neon light was red and white and very bright and read "COORS LIGHT" I noticed the driver's side window was rolled down on the old truck. The passenger side window was covered in mud and I could not see anything through it. As I peeked through the driver's side window, I observed a scoped rifle propped up on the bench seat with the barrel resting on the floor board of the truck. It was difficult to tell what caliber the rifle was, as I could only see it for a second every time the neon bar sign would flash the bright white light. The closer I looked at it, it looked like an AR style rifle. I could see a long magazine sticking out of the rifle below the hand grip. I then looked up on the dash of the truck and observed two boxes of ammunition. When the bar light flashed a bright white, I quickly read the caliber of bullet printed on the box of ammunition. It read .223 Remington. HOLY SHIT, I thought to myself. This is an AR-15 rifle that shoots a .223 caliber bullet!!

I thought about stealing a round out of one of the boxes of ammunition to see if it matched the bullet that I had collected out of the poached bull elk. About that time, I heard a loud voice screaming and it was coming towards me in the dark. I quickly ducked below the bed of the Ford truck and moved around the corner of the bar to hide in the dark alleyway behind a garbage dumpster. I heard voices screaming and the sound of a truck door slamming. The old truck fired up and the rear tires squealed as it left the parking spot and sped out onto the main highway. As I peeked over the dumpster to watch the truck speed down the highway, I noticed the driver's side taillight was out on the truck. I thought HOLY SHIT, this may be the guy that poached the large bull elk in their headlights the other night. And this guy was Bonnie's ex-boyfriend, the guy that I beat arm wrestling a while back in the bar. I stayed hidden behind the dumpster and I could hear the sound of someone crying close by. I looked up to see Bonnie walking back into the bar. I jumped up and quickly greeted her at the front door of the bar before she entered. I said, "Is everything alright?" She sobbed and replied, "Yes, thank god we are finally done!!" I told her to have a good evening that I was tired and needed some sleep. She asked me where I was staying the night and if I was alright to drive. I told her that I was fine and that I would probably head on down the road. She looked around and said, "Where is your truck parked?" This made my heart skip a few beats because I did not want her to know that I was a game warden and that my patrol truck was parked one block south of the bar behind the fire station. I responded "It's parked just down the street a bit, I'm doing fine you have a good evening!" I didn't want to leave her standing there in the street but it was time for me to get out of the situation and get home and get some needed sleep. Bonnie wiped the tears from her eyes and said, "Have a good night." I turned and walked away from her.

I walked down the street about a block and noticed a sheriff's deputy coming down the street towards me. The deputy saw me walking down the sidewalk and stopped to talk to me. As he rolled down his driver's side window, I could barely make out his face. This was Jeffrey City's finest deputy JD Darnell. JD asked me my name and I replied "Scott Werbelow" JD said, "Oh, Scott Werbelow the game warden? The game warden that I rescued last year on a cold and rainy night out in the Buffalo Basin who didn't have a lug wrench to change a flat tire? The guy who was antelope hunting with Bob Trebelcock and the Director of the Game and Fish? HOLY CRAP, this was the same deputy that rescued me that cold and rainy night while we were parked up on the tall hill flashing

Flashing neon bar sign.

our headlights. I was embarrassed and said, "Yup that would be me!" He reached out, shook my hand and said, "JD Darnell, a pleasure to meet you again!" I said, "Likewise, what are you doing out this hour of the night?" He replied, "Oh, I got a call of a couple having a domestic over at the Ore House, just responding to the call." I explained to JD what had happened between Bonnie and her boyfriend. He said, "Oh, you know Bonnie?" I said, "not very well but I have met her and her ex-boyfriend." JD responded, "Ex-boyfriend?" I said, "yea they broke up tonight!' JD said, "GOOD, he is a piece of shit and a poacher!"

After hearing that response from JD, I perked up and said, "So, what do you know about her ex-boyfriend?" JD said, "His name is Roy, works in the oil field and drinks a lot. I have also caught him out late at night spotlighting a couple of times. I haven't caught him with any dead animals, but I suspect he is up to no good!" I told JD about the vehicle missing a taillight and the poached bull elk that I had recovered the .223 bullet out of. I also told him about the rifle and ammunition that I observed on the dash of the old Ford truck. JD said, "That wouldn't surprise me a bit if he was the one that poached that elk." JD also told me that he had been watching Roy and that old Ford truck for quite some time and that he would eventually catch him leaving the bar drunk one night and arrest him for driving under the influence. JD shook my hand again and said, "Hell, I might just catch up with him later tonight if you just saw him leave the bar." I thanked JD again for rescuing me out in the hills and told him that we needed to have a cup of coffee and get caught up sometime. I also gave him the phone number of the Jeffrey City warden station and told him to call me anytime. He said, "Will do!!" as he rolled up his window and sped off. I was happy that JD didn't ask me where my vehicle was parked and what I was doing out so late at night! Dammit, I had forgot to ask him what he knew about Bonnie.

I made my way to the warden station and crashed. I had a headache and it had been a very long day. I lay in bed wondering how I could make a case against Roy. I had circumstantial evidence that pointed to him, but

I would need to prove the case. Without a confession or an eye witness this would be difficult to do. Questions went through my head. Was this the same truck missing the taillight? Was this truck registered to Roy? I hadn't even thought about getting a license plate number, how could I be so stupid? My last question to myself was, if this was the same truck and it was registered to Roy, could I prove that he was actually driving the truck and shot the elk in his headlights off the highway? I was beginning to realize that sometimes cases can be difficult to solve even when you think you know what happened. My last thought before I went to sleep was, Bonnie and Roy just broke up, would she rat him out if I met her at the bar and bought her a shot of tequila? Sometimes ex-girlfriends can be a game warden's best friend.

I finally fell asleep. It must have been about 3:00 AM. I was suddenly awakened by the sound of a phone ringing on the kitchen wall. I thought to myself, are you shitting me right now! Who could be calling me at this hour of the night? I hadn't even heard this phone ring before, nor had I given this number out to anyone except JD? I answered the phone, "Hello." I heard a voice on the other end. "Hey Scott this is JD, I got some headlights out here on Beaver Rim!" I replied, "Ok, are they doing anything illegal?" He said, "Nothing that I know of, just wanted to let you know that I'm watching some headlights out here in the hills." I wasn't sure how to respond to JD, I was very tired and needed some sleep. I responded, "Thanks for the heads-up JD, call me if you see them doing anything illegal!" JD responded, "Will do, thanks Scott!" I laid back in bed and thought to myself, really, he called me because he saw headlights out in the hills? Does he really need any help? Could this be Roy?

My stay in Jeffrey City was coming to an end as the elk were no longer coming down out of the mountains and hanging out on private property. The elk simply did not need babysat by the game warden anymore, as they were back on Green Mountain where they had adequate cover in the timber. The whole deal with Bonnie and Roy was really bothering me. I felt strongly that Roy was my suspect in the elk poaching case. I would need to go back down to the Ore House and try and gather some more information.

It was a Monday evening. I was craving a cheeseburger and a Monday night football game. I headed down to the Ore House and again parked my game and fish patrol truck a block south of the bar so that nobody would recognize me as a game warden. I walked through the front doors of the bar and couldn't believe what I was seeing. Roy and Bonnie were sitting together at the bar. I started to turn and walk right back out the front door when Bonnie made eye contact with me and said, "Well, hello handsome." I smiled and nodded my head as to say hello back and kept walking to a small table in the back of the bar. I felt very awkward. They had just broken up a few days earlier. How was I going to get any information out of Bonnie about her ex-boyfriend if they were dating again? I ordered a crown and coke, cheeseburger and fries, and started to watch the football game. About that time a short chubby bald-headed man came through the front door of the bar and yelled, "WHO OWNS THE GREEN TRUCK IN FRONT OF THE FIREHALL, YOU'RE PARKED IN MY SPOT AND WE HAVE A FIRE MEETING TONIGHT!" I didn't make eye contact or respond to the man, I figured I could finish my cheeseburger, drink and just get the hell out of there for the night.

About that time the bartender went racing out the front door of the bar. I figured I better follow him and explain the situation to him. I walked outside to see the bartender looking down the street to the south. He looked at me and said, 'Do you have a semi-truck that you need parking space for somewhere? If you do, you can park it right over there in that large parking lot to the north." I said, "No, I don't have a semi-truck just a regular pick-up truck." He said, "Where is your truck parked?" I replied, "It's that green one down the street." The bartender looked down the street for a moment and turned and looked back at me. His eyes were the size of a silver dollar! He looked at me and said, "You're A F---ING GAME WARDEN!!" I said, "Yes, Sir." The man crinkled up his face and ran back into the bar without saying a word to me. I followed him back into the bar to watch him run around the bar and yell. He was pointing his finger at me and yelling, "THAT GUY IS A F---ING GAME WARDEN, THAT GUY IS A F---ING GAME WARDEN!!"

I was embarrassed, but I smiled and waved at everyone in the bar and went back to my table to finish my meal. I was watching Roy and Bonnie out of the corner of my eye. It looked like they were having a "quiet" argument and they both kept looking back at me while they argued with one another. Everyone in the bar became quiet and most of the other patrons just sat there and starred at me as if to say they wanted to kick my ass. I just wanted to finish my meal, pay my tab and get out of there. About that time, Bonnie stood up and came walking towards me with a drink in her hand. Her lips were quenched tight as she smoked her rolled cigarette. She pulled her cigarette out of her mouth and smiled at me with her missing front tooth. She yelled, "I BOUGHT YOU A JACK ON THE ROCKS ASSHOLE!" and threw the drink in my face!

She marched back to the bar, put both her arms around Roy's neck and gave him a huge French kiss right in front of me. She looked at me and said, "Roy and I got back together asshole!!"

I never had a crush on Bonnie. Apparently, she thought I did. It was at this very moment in time that I had realized that I had worn out my welcome in Jeffrey City and needed to make a mile. I wiped the drink off my face, paid my tab without a tip and got the hell out of there. The elk in the headlights case was never solved and I have never been back to that bar since.

Chapter 4

LYSITE

It was October 9th, 1996, I had returned back to the Ocean Lake house in the Lander region. I needed to take a few days off and get my truck brakes repaired. I felt like I had been working harder than an ugly Wyoming pole dancer for the past month with no days off. The busy part of hunting season hadn't even begun yet. October 15th would be one of the busiest days of the year for all game wardens in the state. This is the date that most deer and elk seasons officially open up. This is also the date that the majority of the non-resident deer/elk hunters will be showing up. I hadn't spent any time with my wife and kids all fall and it was only going to get busier for me in a few more days.

The fall weather was beautiful and I had heard that the trout on Boysen Reservoir were really biting. I called my wife Lana and told her that I would really like to take her and the kids fishing on Boysen for a day. Lana thought that sounded like fun and agreed to hook onto my boat in Shell and meet me at Boysen Reservoir at daylight the next day. Back then there were no cell phones with weather Apps that would tell you exactly what the weather was going to be like every hour for the next month. This would have been a handy tool to have, because we never knew what the weather was going to do unless you stayed up late at night to watch the local news channel. And most of the time they were wrong with their weather predictions! I never understood how people could get paid to be wrong so often? Besides, only old people watched the news! If I wanted to know the weather, I would just ask the next old person that I ran into and they will tell me the weather predictions for the next year, and according to the Farmer's Almanac.

Well, it would have been great to know that the wind was going to blow over 50 mph the next morning. I met Lana at the boat dock on Boysen Reservoir. I was so excited to see my family and know that I had the entire day off to take them fishing. My kids were so cute, they were excited to go fishing with their father. The wind was blowing so hard that I could observe, three to four foot-deep, swales on the lake, with, one to two-foot white caps. It would be very dangerous for us to be out on the water in my small 16' Crest-liner fishing boat. But, I'm now a "trained professional," and I can safely maneuver a boat in any kind of weather in Wyoming. I just spent four months doing watercraft enforcement out of the Casper region, which required operating a boat in some of the roughest water that you have ever seen.

The lake was so rough that I told my wife Lana that I would unload the boat at the boat ramp and take it by myself over to the area of the dam on the north side of the lake out of the wind. She was to drive the vehicle with the kids over to a cove out of the wind where I would pick them up later. She agreed, that would be the safest thing to do with the young kids involved. But also made the comment, "Honey I don't think you should do this, let's just go fishing another day!" I told Lana, "Don't be ridiculous, I'm a "Trained Professional." Lana unloaded me and the boat in the water and drove north out of sight towards the dam. I turned the key on the boat, and to my surprise, it actually started. I hadn't run this boat all year and from my experience it's always a miracle when a boat actually starts, especially when you only have one day to fish and the wind is blowing. I throttled up the boat and headed south to go around a point that would then head me north towards the dam. I would only have to face rough treacherous water for a short distance, until I got around the point and out of the wind. Just as soon as I hit the rough water, I turned the boat into the north wind and gave it full throttle to get around the point. I heard something "POP" behind me and my boat instantly quit running. I could literally see my wife and kids waiting in the cove out of the wind a short distance away.

I quickly tried to start the boat, nothing happened!! The motor would not even turn over, it was completely dead! I was now drifting out to sea in the rough water with no paddle, slowly getting further and further away from land and my family. I walked to the back of the boat and removed the fiberglass cover that protects the engine. Smoke was rolling out of the engine and the engine felt VERY hot! I quickly yelled at my wife Lana, "PICK ME UP ON THE OTHER END OF THE LAKE!!" I wasn't sure where I was going to end up, but I knew it wasn't going to take me very long to get there. It was very scary drifting out to sea with no paddle and engine. I guess I was once again in God's hands. I said a short prayer and went with the flow. As I was drifting off to sea, I looked around to see if there was anybody else on the lake who could help me. NOPE, I was officially the only dumbass on the whole lake that day! I quickly grabbed my life jacket and secured it tight on my body. I thought, if the boat ends up sinking, I can still drift to shore as long as I have my life jacket and don't end up dying of hypothermia.

All I can say is God was again with me that day. The boat ended up drifting into a nice sandy beach area where Lana could drive the truck and trailer and pick me up. The boat was difficult to load in the wind and I got really wet and cold in the process. Once I was finally in the truck soaking wet and shaking, I reached over and turned the heater on high. The kids were both bawling because they were hungry, tired, and didn't get to go fishing. I looked over at my wife Lana with a disgusted look on my face. She just smiled and said, "You big Dumbass, trained professional huh!" I responded, "That's MR. Dumbass to you!" I would later learn that the water pump went out, the engine overheated and completely seized up the motor. So much for my new/used boat that I only got to use a few times.

The day was pretty much shot. Lana ended up taking the boat and Wesley home to Shell. Wendy wanted to stay with her dad and go antelope hunting the next day. I was so excited to do something with my daughter because we hadn't gotten to spend much time together. She was now four years old and full of energy, I mean Piss & Vinegar. Wendy and I went back to the Ocean Lake house and I grilled her a cheeseburger on the barbeque grill. She was so excited to have a new place to play. She ran circles around the house in the yard and played in the sand down by the lake.

We woke up early the next morning and headed to the Red Desert to try and find a trophy antelope. I had worked that area earlier in the season and had seen some really nice bucks. But, today would be different, I had my four-year-old daughter and we were going to have to find something pretty close to the road. Besides, the weather was cold and windy. I kept telling Wendy that we needed to shoot an antelope so that we had something to eat for dinner.

I finally spotted a pretty nice buck antelope that was bedded down about three hundred yards off the main county road. I pulled out my spotting scope and got it focused on the antelope. I told Wendy to stay in the truck and watch the antelope through the spotting scope, and to be very, very quiet. I quietly got out of the truck and started crawling on my belly through the sage brush and cactus towards the antelope. I ended up about 150 yards from the still bedded-down antelope. I set up my by-pod and got the antelope in my scope. The buck antelope stood up and started walking towards me, I thought to myself, this is perfect! Once the antelope was about 100 yards away, I slowly pulled the trigger and held my cross hairs right behind his front shoulder. "CLICK" the rifle didn't fire and the antelope heard the sound of the firing pin and started running away from me. I ejected the shell casing and chambered another round. The antelope stopped a short distance later and stood broadside for a moment. Long enough for me to get my cross hairs back on him and behind his front shoulder. "BANG" the rifle went off and the antelope hit the ground. I heard the door slam on my truck and I looked up to see my daughter Wendy running full blast towards the dead antelope through the sagebrush. Wendy and I actually arrived at the dead antelope at about the same time. She screamed, "DADDY, DADDY, CAN WE EAT HIM NOW!" I just laughed and said, "Just as soon as we get him dressed out and back home in the freezer, pumpkin."

I drove Wendy back to Shell and dropped her off with her mom. It was really good to get to spend some quality time with my daughter, even if it was only a day. I headed back to the Lander office. I was really getting behind on case reports, monthly reports and email. Actually, I still had not been able to log into my laptop computer to check my email in over three weeks. After one full day in the office, I was caught up on everything and finally able to log into my computer, with the help of some gal in Cheyenne headquarters. Once I got logged on, I clicked on the mail icon and a message popped up. You have 324 unread messages! I thought to myself, Oh, dear Lord, how much trouble am I in for not responding to important emails! It took me several hours to wade through all the emails, most of them were junk and needed no response. However, there were a couple from Casper supervisor Terry Cleveland that demanded a response by a deadline and I had missed those deadlines. I quickly responded to Mr. Cleveland and apologized for missing his deadline. I soon learned that the Game and Fish Department used email to communicate on a statewide basis, and with all the different divisions, it was very important to stay caught up on your email. Wardens were expected to read and respond to emails on a daily basis.

This was a new form of communication for me. I was used to picking up the phone and calling someone. But now I realized that if I had a poached animal or a suspect that I was looking for, I could simply send a quick email to every game warden in the state requesting any assistance with one click of a button. Heck, I could even take pictures of evidence with my new .35 mm camera. I would wait a couple weeks for the pictures to be developed, scan those pictures with a copy machine and save them on my computer. Or, I could use my old Polaroid camera and have instant photos available to scan. Except the film for this camera was extremely expensive and the camera had no zoom capabilities to capture detail. This way, if I had a headless deer on the winter range and tire tracks for evidence, I could send pictures to every game warden in the state requesting assistance on any poaching case that I may come across. This new technology was pretty cool, I just needed to learn more about it and keep up with it.

The date was October 14th 1996. I would be back at the Ocean Lake house in the evening preparing myself for the biggest day of the year, October 15th, opening day of hunting season. I would need a good meal and a good night sleep. The next several weeks were going to be very long days and nights. I would need to make sure that I had all my law enforcement equipment available and that all my firearms were clean and functioning properly. I quickly went through my mental list. Ticket book, pen, game tags, donation coupons, seizure tags, evidence kit, metal detector, camera, warm clothes, food, portable radio, knife, saw, binoculars, spotting scope, oh yea Copenhagen, and sunflower seeds, how could I forget? The older I become, I realized that my mental list got much longer. My mental list now includes two pair of reading glasses, hearing aid batteries, vitamins, prescription drugs, Aleve, Pepto, and a roll of Copenhagen. I found you need two pair of reading glasses for that moment when that little screw comes partially out and you need another pair of reading glasses to see the screw to put it back in. I was pretty excited about opening morning. My truck brakes had been repaired, and I had even washed my truck.

My alarm went off at 4:00 AM. I had decided to check deer hunters in the Lysite area. There were a couple big ranches up in that area owned by Spratt and Hendry's. I hadn't been in that area before and wanted to see some new country. I found as a Trainee that I was lost most of the time and was never very sure of the hunt area boundaries. Sometimes I would have to check two or three hunters in row and look at their license just to see what hunt area I was in. I always figured that if I checked three hunters in a row and they all had the same license with the same hunt area listed on it, I was pretty sure what hunt area I was at least in. The public expects the game warden to know everything about the area and the regulations. This is difficult when you travel all over the state and you don't have your own warden district to learn inside and out. I found over time that I knew a little bit about a lot, but I didn't know a lot about anything.

The sun had just peaked over the mountain top to the east. I was traveling down a maintained county road. There were bright green alfalfa fields on my right. Every other fence post had a brand-new fluorescent orange sign hanging off of it that read, NO TRESPASSING. It was very evident to me that this particular ranch did not allow any hunting to the general public. Someone had spent a great deal of time posting all those new signs. I thought maybe this property was owned by Spratt's, but I wasn't really sure. Back then we didn't have ON-X or GPS units. All we had was a handful of crusty old topo maps if we were lucky, none of the maps showed landownership.

As I drove down the road, I noticed a really nice four-point buck mule deer standing in the alfalfa field next to the main county road. I hit my brakes (and they actually worked) and thought to myself, this buck deer would make a really nice "REAL LIVE DECOY." If I can find a place to hide my truck and watch this deer, someone will come along and shoot it from the road and hunt on private property without permission. I looked up and there was a two-track road to my left that crossed a canal. The bank of the canal would allow me to hide my truck and watch the buck deer. I had just got into place and hadn't even got my truck shut off yet. I looked below me to see a blue Ford truck come sliding to a stop right across from the deer. I call this the "modified stop." Anytime you hear the sound of tires coming to a sudden stop in gravel, they are going to shoot the animal! I can't imitate what this sounds like with words, but you know what I mean. SCREEEEECH!! An older man and a young child jumped out of the truck. They both leaned over the hood of the truck and shot at the

No Hunting sign.

large buck deer from the middle of the road, using their vehicle as a rest. Neither person had any fluorescent orange on, and neither one of them hit the large buck deer. The deer bounded off towards the river bottom that was near-by and had heavy cover with willows and cottonwood trees. There was a sign made out of a tire that hung on the fence post right in front of them as they shot. The sign read "No Hunting."

As the deer ran away from the hunters, they both continued to shoot. To my amazement, the buck deer made it to the cover in the river bottom without being hit! I was getting ready to jump out of my patrol truck and run down and visit with them, but they had both jumped the fence and headed after the deer through the alfalfa field. This blew my mind. They left their truck parked right in the middle of a county road with both doors open. They jumped the barbed wire fence right where a bright fluorescent orange sign hung that read "NO TRESPASSING" I just assumed that maybe they both had permission to hunt this private property. They certainly were not trying to be sneaky about it. I sat in my patrol truck with the windows down and truck shut off, so that I could hear if they took anymore shots at the deer. The hunters soon went into the willow bottom out of sight. I could no longer see the hunters or the buck deer. I sat and listened for about ten minutes. BANG, BANG, BANG, I counted nine more shots. SURELY, THEY HIT THE DEER BY NOW! I thought to myself.

I drove my patrol truck down to the county road and parked right behind the blue Ford that was still parked in the middle of the road. After a short wait, I observed the two hunters walking back across the alfalfa field towards their vehicle. Once the hunters crossed back over the barbed wire fence, I stepped out of my patrol vehicle. I played stupid, which I'm really good at! I said, "Good morning, did you guys have any luck?" The older man was still breathing hard and responded, "Shit, we just missed the biggest buck that I have ever seen in my life!" I then asked them for their licenses. Neither one of them had their license on them. They had to get them out of a backpack that was in the back of their truck. After looking at the licenses I discovered this was a father and his 14-year-old son. I played stupid and asked them how many shots they had fired, and where did they first shoot at the deer. The man told me that he couldn't remember how many times that he or his son had shot. He also stated that both of them jumped the fence before shooting, because he knew it was illegal to shoot from a public road. I walked over to the driver's side door of his truck and picked up five empty shell casings that were lying in the road. I said, "If you guys shot from the other side of the fence, how come all these shell casings are lying in the road next to your truck?" The man didn't respond to me, he just hung his head.

I then asked the man if they had permission to hunt the private property. He replied, "PRIVATE PROPERTY, I thought this was BLM land!" I replied, "Have you ever seen the BLM plant alfalfa and post no trespassing signs on their public property. I ended up writing the father a citation for trespassing, shooting from the road, and failure to wear fluorescent orange. I did not issue any citations to his 14-year-old boy. After issuing the citations, I pulled out my BLM Topo map and showed the father some areas that he could legally hunt in the area. He wadded up the map on the hood of my patrol truck and threw it on the ground. He put his face really close to mine and looked me right in the eye and said, "YOU PRETTY MUCH F---CKED UP OUR HUNTING TRIP, I THINK WE ARE GOING TO HEAD BACK HOME NOW!"

I couldn't believe this guy, I just wanted to head-butt him. I asked him to please pick up my map and hand it back to me. He bent over and picked up the map and threw it at me. I said, "You have a great day sir!" As I left that situation, I hoped that they had not hit and killed the buck deer. It showed me just how excited some people can get at seeing a trophy deer. Some people get tunnel vision and just lose all common sense. I began to question myself as a game warden after this incident. Should a game warden allow someone to shoot something illegally just to document a violation and issue a citation? Should I have protected that buck deer and sat down on the county road and not let anyone shoot at it? Should I have scared it off? I essentially used a live deer to document a violation and the deer could have been killed illegally right in front of me, so that I could catch someone shooting from the road and hunting on private property without permission. This is something that I would need to think more about.

It was still early morning hours. I continued to head up the county road that I had never been on before. I drove around a sharp corner and observed a man wearing camouflage standing on the edge of another hayfield about 200 yards away. I stopped and mounted my spotting scope on my driver's side window to get a better look at the man. He was carrying a scoped rifle and was not wearing any orange clothing. I noticed that he was also looking back at me through his binoculars. He only looked at me for a second and he quickly disappeared down into the creek bottom with heavy cover. I quickly found a two-track road that would take me down to that location. That was weird, was this man trespassing as well? Was he trying to blend in with his full camouflage outfit? I didn't get a very good look at the man, but he looked Hispanic to me. I parked my patrol truck, put on my jacket and headed down into the creek bottom. I was trespassing on someone's ranch whose owner I didn't know. I was up on a small hill looking down into the creek bottom, now about a half mile from my patrol truck. I sat down in some cover where I could see the creek bottom.

After glassing for several minutes, I noticed something dark lying behind a rotten log on the ground. The closer I looked, it looked like a person lying next to an old cottonwood tree that had fallen over years ago. I watched the dark-colored object for what seemed like forever. It never moved. I wasn't sure what I was looking at, but my curiosity finally got the best of me and I snuck down the hill into the creek bottom. I walked very slowly and quietly to the old cottonwood log. As I peeked over it, I could see a Hispanic man lying face down in the grass with arms tucked at his side. I was hoping he wasn't dead, but this was weird! I stood there looking at him for a few minutes. He never moved. Finally, I said,

"Excuse me, sir!" The man rolled over very quickly and jumped straight up. He seemed very nervous. I asked him if he was hunting. He said, "Yes he was." I asked him for his hunting license and he showed it to me. His name was Jose from Sacramento, California, he had a non-resident doe/fawn license. I asked him if he had permission to hunt the private land, he stated he did. I asked him what the landowners name was. He couldn't remember the name, and I didn't know it either.

His license was not signed on the back by the landowner, indicating to me that he didn't have permission to hunt that private property. I asked him why he was not wearing any fluorescent orange. He stated he had forgot his orange hat in his truck earlier that morning. Then I asked him why he was hiding down in the creek bottom. He stated that he had seen a huge buck in the area earlier that morning, and was hiding from the deer hoping that it would come back out of the thick trees. I smelled a RAT. This guy did not have permission to hunt private property. He was hiding from the game warden, not the deer! He saw me in my patrol truck and raced down to the creek bottom and hid. I asked if I could look into his backpack, he said "Sure." I unzipped the backpack and pulled out a fluorescent orange hat. I said, "Is this the hat you left in your truck this morning? Why don't you wear it?" I asked the man for his driver's license and had him follow me back to my patrol truck.

The man was Hispanic and spoke very good English. I could not yet prove the trespass case until I talked to the landowner. I asked Jose' where he was camped. He tried to tell me, but I didn't know the area and I had no idea what he was talking about. I ended up issuing him a citation for failure to wear fluorescent orange clothing while hunting. The bond amount was $50.00. I told Jose he would need to pay that amount or go to jail. Jose' smiled and pulled out his wallet. He dug through about $5,000 dollars in one hundred dollars bills to finally find a $50.00 bill. He handed me the $50.00 dollar bill with a smile on his face and apologized for not wearing any orange. I left the area knowing that I was only scratching the surface to what was really going on with Jose'. I leaned as a warden, sometimes you have to play stupid and dig deeper. I would need to find his hunting camp and learn who else was in camp, and who owns the land that we both just trespassed on. Wardens have the right to enter private property without permission, if they have probable cause that a violation has occurred. I always respected the rights of landowners and rarely entered private property without the landowner's permission.

I jumped into my patrol truck and headed back up the road. I didn't make it very far up the road because I kept running into hunters violating the law. I came across a pick-up that was pulled off the edge of the road. It looked like there might be a deep canyon right off the edge of the road to the right of the truck. I pulled in behind the truck and looked in the back of it for dead animals. No dead animals. I peeked over the edge of the hill to look down in the canyon below and spotted an elderly man dragging a two-point buck deer up the steep hill towards his truck. He was about one hundred yards away, but it was straight up the hill and very steep. I decided to hike down the hill and help the elderly man drag his deer the rest of the way. He was very glad to see me, and acted like he may have been very close to a heart attack just prior to my arriving. I told him to take a rest. I grabbed the small antlers on the deer and dragged the deer up the steep hill. I even loaded the deer by myself into the back of his truck before he made it back up the hill.

Once he reached the truck, I asked him for his license. He pulled his license out of the glove box. The license was still in the envelope from Cheyenne; he hadn't even opened it yet. I explained to the elderly gentleman that technically he needed to have his license filled out before he left the site of kill. This seemed confusing to him, as if he didn't understand the regulation. I explained it to him and told him it was not a big deal at all, but that I would document the violation with a warning citation. The man was not happy! I wrote out the warning citation and asked him to sign it. He ripped it out of my ticket book, wadded it up and threw it on the ground. I thought to myself, WOW, it's just a warning citation! He yelled, "I WON'T SIGN ANYTHING, YOU CHICKEN-

SHITTED SON OF A BITCH. YOU MUST BE ONE OF THOSE NEW BABY WATER WARDENS!!" I didn't need his signature on the ticket, so I reached down, picked up the citation and put it in my pocket. I did not want the situation to escalate anymore, so I jumped into my patrol truck and drove off. He never even thanked me for dragging his deer the rest of the way up the hill and loading it in his truck. I drove off thinking, I hope this wasn't the landowner that I just trespassed on!

I looked up and here was another truck pulled off the left side of the road. There was a man loading a deer into the back of his truck by himself. I stopped, helped the man load his deer, and checked his license. Everything looked all right with this situation. I was standing on the side of the road visiting (Bullshitting) with the hunter when I heard a vehicle coming down the road. I looked up and it was the guy whom I had just written a warning citation to. He romped on the throttle (gave it the onion) and swerved to try and run over me while I was visiting alongside the road with the hunter. He nearly hit me. I had to jump backwards as his driver's side mirror nearly hit me in the face. He held his middle finger out the window as he went by and yelled, "F---K YOU!!" The hunter whom I was talking to also had to jump back to prevent being run over. He looked at me with wide eyes and asked, "WHAT THE HELL WAS THAT ALL ABOUT?" I said, "Oh, just some crazy ole man, I just wrote a warning to for failure to properly tag his deer."

I would end up checking a bunch of hunters and deer that day. It seemed like I couldn't ever get anywhere and learn some new country because it was so busy on the main county road. Finally, I found myself on an old two-track road that headed out into the hills on some BLM (Public) ground. This land was located near the private property where I had written Jose' a citation earlier that morning. The day was overcast and cold and snowing lightly with a slight breeze. I looked at the ridge ahead of me and it looked like there was smoke coming out from behind the hill in front of me. I could also see some fresh vehicle tracks on the road ahead. I eased forward and noticed the road had ended, but vehicle tracks were evident in the sagebrush going over the ridge in front of me. I followed the tracks and popped over the hill. To my amazement there was a large hunting camp set up in the bottom of an old dried out reservoir. Were they trying to get out of the wind or were they trying to hide from the game warden?

I popped over the hill. The smoke was coming from a stovepipe that was sticking out of a wall tent. There were no other vehicles around. I would have never found this hunting camp if it weren't for the smoke coming out of the wall tent. I parked my truck down in the bottom of the reservoir and got out to look around. There were several pup tents set up around the wall tent. There was also an enclosed trailer parked nearby. I walked around the backside of the enclosed trailer and could not believe my eyes. There was at least a half dozen doe deer strung up by their heads hanging against the wall of the enclosed trailer. There was one small 2x3 buck hanging by its neck with its tongue stuck out. What really got my attention was the amounts of lungs, heart, liver and windpipes that were hanging on the backside of the trailer. I thought to myself, do people really eat the lungs and windpipe of a deer? This seemed a little eerie to me. Why was their camp hidden out of sight? Where was everybody? This was opening day of deer season and they had already killed six deer?

I walked over to the wall tent to make sure no one was around. I banged on the tent flap and yelled, "ANYBODY HOME?" No answer. I then went over and checked the licenses that were attached to the deer. The licenses were valid in a different hunt area that was probably at least two hours from this location. All the names on the licenses were Hispanic and they were all from California. Except the license that was on the small buck deer. It was a resident youth general license. If everybody was from California, where did the resident general deer license come from? The other thing that I found interesting was that three of the deer's hides were soaking wet. The only water in the area was down on the creek on private property. It was possible that these deer were killed over two hours away, but not likely. I was starting to feel a little nervous about the whole situation. Not knowing who these people were or how many of them may be in camp when they all showed back up. I decided to leave the area. I didn't like not being able to see out due to the fact that I was sitting in a hole. I also did not have any service on my mobile radio to call SALECS if I were to get in trouble and need help. Just as I was about to jump into my truck, a vehicle came racing over the hill right in front of me and parked next to the wall tent.

Two Hispanic men got out of the truck. They were both wearing heavy army green colored coats with hoods on. The hoods had white/grey colored fur wrapped around them. They had the strings sucked up tight on their hoods to the point that I could not see much of their faces. They saw me and did not want to talk to me. They both headed for the wall tent as if I didn't exist. I jumped out of my truck and stopped them before they entered the wall tent. I didn't know what was in the tent for firearms so I was concerned about that. I approached both men and asked them how they were doing. They both said, "No Comprende." They couldn't speak a word of English. At least that is what they wanted me to believe. They wouldn't look me in the eye and both of them had their hands in their pockets. One of them kept circling around to my backside. I caught myself walking in circles to keep an eye on both of them. This was making me very nervous. I was in a location where nobody would ever find me if I were in trouble.

I tried to talk to them but they were trying to tell me that they were cold and wanted to enter the small pup tent. This seemed weird to me because the large wall tent had a stove in it and it was already warm in there. Why would they want to go into a small cold pup tent? The one guy was still trying to get behind me when we talked and I couldn't see his face because his hood was sucked up tight. I finally decided it was time to take control of the situation to protect myself. I ordered both of them to take their hands out of their pockets and place them on the hood of my patrol truck. They slowly complied as if they understood what I was saying too them. I placed my hand on my pistol. They knew I meant business. As soon as both of them had their hands on the hood of my truck, I got behind them and frisked them. When I say "frisked" them I only reached into their coat pockets to check for weapons. The guy who had been circling me had a .45 caliber handgun in his right coat pocket. I grabbed the pistol and quickly unloaded it and placed it in my patrol truck. The men were scared, at least they acted like it. I told them to "STAY" like a dog.

I was very nervous as I tried to keep an eye on both of them. I walked over to the small pup tent and unzipped the zipper to the front door. I opened up the tent flap trying to keep an eye on both men at the same time. Inside the tent I found several assault rifles and two semi-automatic .40 caliber Glock pistols. I didn't know what to do. Were these guys trying to get into that tent to grab a firearm to kill me? Or were they just cold? I hadn't had any time to do an investigation with the deer that they had harvested, so I didn't know if I even had any violations. What was my authority at this point? Heck, everyone has loaded firearms in their camp, what do I do? I zipped the tent flap back up, returned to my patrol truck and gave them their un-loaded pistol back. I jumped in my truck and said, "Adios Amigo," because that was all the Spanish that I knew. It was time for me to do some investigative work and possibly get some back-up.

I was most concerned about the resident general youth tag since everyone in camp was from California. I decided to drive to Shoshoni and visit with the high school principal to see if he had anybody in school with the name that I was looking for. I figured a resident youth would be under 18 years old and going to school. The only school in the area was Shoshoni. I hauled ass to Shoshoni and met with the principal. The principal was very helpful and told me that the person who I was looking for did indeed attend school there. He also told me that if I wanted to interview the kid, I would need his parent's consent since he was under the age of 18. Long story short, the parents were contacted and met me at the school and gave me consent to visit with their son. I told the boy that he was not under arrest and free to go at any time. I also told him that he could be represented by an attorney and did not need to answer any of my questions. I was kind of new to all this and didn't want to screw anything up.

The young boy was very nervous as I interviewed him in front of his parents. I asked him if he had bought a general deer license this year. He responded, "Yes." I then asked him if he had harvested a deer. He responded, "No," I knew he hadn't harvested a deer because he got on the school bus at daylight and was in school all day. I then asked him if I could see his license. He responded, "I don't have it with me." I said, "Where is it at?" he replied, "At my house on my dresser." I said, "No, it's not, it's on a buck deer hanging in a California camp north of your house. Can you tell me about that?" The young boy told me that one of the hunters had offered him $500.00 dollars for the license, so he sold it to them. You should have seen the look on his parent's face. I asked him who bought the license and he stated, "Jose'." I thanked the boy for his honesty and told him that I would be in touch with him later.

I then met with the boy's parents out in the parking lot of the school. They were both Hispanic as well and managed the ranch that I caught Jose' hunting on with no orange. My guess is they gave the California hunters permission to hunt on the ranch, but really didn't have permission from the actual landowner to allow hunting. That's why Jose' couldn't remember the name of the person who gave him permission. I thanked them and jumped back into my patrol truck. It was getting late in the day and I had a lot of work to do before nightfall. The more I thought about it, it became clear to me that all those deer were shot on private property at night in the wrong area. I knew this because they were wet from being dragged across a creek. There were no other creeks in the area. Plus, they had six dead deer by noon? I suspected the reason that Jose' was down there in camouflage at first light is because he was still dragging deer out of the creek bottom and back to camp.

Daylight was burning and it was time for me to get some back up. As I sat there in the school parking lot in Shoshoni, Wyoming, I grabbed my radio mic, "GF-38, GF-97." I heard a response, "GF-38 go ahead" GF-38 was the legendary longtime Riverton game warden. Chris Daubin. Chris knew the area and the hunters well in his district and nobody messed with Chris Daubin. "GF-38, GF-97, could you give me some assistance with a California camp near Lysite?" "10-4 GF-97, I'll be 10-76 (enroute.) I know exactly what camp you are dealing with!" I told Chris that I would meet him in Shoshoni and fill him in on the details. Once I met with Chris, he knew the camp well. He said they pull this crap every year and they just bring lots of cash in case they get caught. I told him about all the cash in Jose's wallet and he said, "Yep, that's exactly what I'm talking about." Chris said, "We will want to get to their camp ASAP, because they start drinking tequila at sundown and will be dangerous to deal with after they get lit up."

Chris and I headed back towards Lysite. By the time we got back to their camp it was dark out. We took separate vehicles for safety reasons. We both headed over the dike of the reservoir at the same time and lit up their camp like a Christmas tree with our headlights and overhead spotlights. They had a bonfire going in the middle of their camp. There must have been at least 8-10 Hispanics standing around the campfire. They were all yelling, playing loud music and drinking copious amounts of tequila. We shined both of our spotlights right on their bonfire. I was nervous but I stepped out of my patrol truck and yelled, "I WANT TO SPEAK TO SOMEONE WHO SPEAKS ENGLISH!" One guy walked over towards me away from the fire. He spoke broken English. I did my best to interview him, but he didn't know anything. I told him that I wanted Jose' as an interpreter. He called Jose' over and I started asking questions to another hunter. I looked at Jose' and he said, "No Comprende." I knew that was bullshit because I had written Jose' a ticket earlier that morning and he spoke perfect English. I told them if they didn't start cooperating, they were all going to jail. Jose' seemed to understand this concept.

Chris and I would end up interviewing everyone in camp over the next two hours and we finally got confessions that they had shot the deer on private property without permission from the landowner. They had killed deer in the wrong hunt area and used a spotlight to kill them in the night. They also purchased a resident general deer license from a 17-year-old boy for $500.00 and killed a small 2x3 buck. When you look at the totality of circumstances, they really had not done anything right. I ended up writing over $5,000 dollars in tickets and ordered them to pay their fines in cash. Jose' said, "That's Mucho Dinero." I replied, "Mucho Dinero or go to jail!" He certainly understood the word "Jail." Jose walked back to the campfire and I saw everyone get their wallets out and contribute to the fines.

Chris and I got out of there alive that night, and did our jobs, I was thankful for that. I was also very thankful for having Chris as my backup. He kept them all gathered around the campfire and in his spotlight while I interviewed and issued citations. I would end up getting back to the Ocean Lake house after midnight. I went to sleep with a smile on my face. It always felt good when you catch the bad guys and come home safe. I believe these hunters are still hunting in this area today and are still pulling the same old crap over 25 years later!

I would show up at the court house in Riverton on Monday morning to turn in citations and cash. I laid all the copies of tickets out on the counter and put the cash amount with each ticket. The entire counter top was covered with tickets and cash. The other Riverton game warden Brad Gibb walked through the door to turn in a citation and saw me standing there with all the tickets laid out. He said, "Damn. Look at you go buddy, all I have is a failure to purchase a conservation stamp citation, good job!!" That made me feel good as a "Trainee." Brad was well-respected in the community and a great game warden. I would later work with Brad on a great winter range deer poaching case in the Pinedale area.

I traveled on to Lander to meet with my supervisor Kent Schmidlin. I was excited to tell him about my busy weekend. After telling Kent the story about the Hispanic poaching camp, he gave me a big smile and said, "Congratulations," as he shook my hand. He said he knew that camp well and that it was about time they had gotten "shook" down. Mr. Schmidlin then asked me if I would be interested in assisting him with a case just south of town near the Red Canyon road. He went on to say that he had received reports of some spotlighting going on in this area. He suspected that maybe some Native Americans may be responsible for shooting deer in their headlights on private property off the Red Canyon road. I was appalled that Mr. Schmidlin would ask for my assistance as a Trainee. I replied, "You bet, when do, you want to do this?" He replied, "Let's plan on getting set up sometime after dark." We agreed to meet at the Lander office at 6:00 PM. I was so excited to get the opportunity to work with my supervisor on a poaching case. I thought to myself, heck maybe I can catch these guys and really impress my supervisor.

We took separate vehicles. Mr. Schmidlin showed me the area that the reports had come from and recommended that I back my patrol truck up a draw and shut my lights off. The draw would allow me to see the fields where the poaching reports had come from. Mr. Schmidlin said he would go on down the road several miles and set up on a hill where he could glass the whole river bottom. He said he would call me on the radio if he observed any suspicious activity. I was excited, I shut my truck off and turned the key back a click so that my mobile radio would be turned on. I even took some electrical tape and placed it over the glow of the light on my radio so that I could be completely "Blacked Out." I sat in position for over an hour. No vehicles had passed by and no radio traffic had come from Mr. Schmidlin. I felt that if anyone was going to do something wrong, they would do it late at night when everyone else had gone to bed.

I sat there for what seemed forever. Only a few vehicles had passed by, none of them stopping or looking at deer in the nearby hayfields. Finally, my radio blurted "GF-97 I have a vehicle located very close to your location. They are traveling very slow and occasionally stopping to look at deer in their headlights." I grabbed my radio and replied, "10-4, I will watch for them." My heart rate sped up, I thought are we going to actually catch these guys shooting deer in their headlights? I looked up. The vehicle had stopped in the highway right in front of my patrol truck. They couldn't have been more than fifty yards away from me! Mr. Schmidlin got on the radio and said, "GF-97, go to Roy's channel." ROY'S CHANNEL, WHAT THE HELL DID THAT MEAN? The only Roy that I knew was a Federal Agent. Did this mean they had their own covert radio channel that nobody else could scan? Now that I thought about it for a second, I had heard other wardens talk about Roy's channel before. I think Roy's channel was channel 180? I reached down to quickly change channels and accidently hit the button that turned on my sirens and my red and blue lights. WHOOP, WHOOP, WHOOP, with red and blue lights going everywhere. SHIT, I panicked, I couldn't find the damn button in the dark to shut everything off!

I looked up and the suspect vehicle quickly sped off into the night. I finally hit the right button and shut off my sirens and lights. "GF-97, GO TO ROY'S CHANNEL" the radio blurted out. I finally got on the correct channel. I responded, "Yea, go ahead!" Mr. Schmidlin responded, "I think they were getting ready to shoot a deer but something spooked them off." I can still see their taillights, but they are already clear out to the main highway, hauling ass!" I didn't know how to respond, that someone that spooked them was me! I responded back, "10-4, they may have seen me parked up the draw as they were within 50 yards of me." I was too embarrassed to tell him that I had screwed the whole thing up by lighting them up with my lights and sirens. I will never accidently hit that button again!

My time in Lander was coming to an end. It was early November I would wash my patrol truck and turn in all my equipment to Mr. Schmidlin. This was a sad day for me. I would now be without a job until April or May. I wasn't even sure if they were going to hire me back for the Reservoir Crew in Casper. If they did, I would have to retake the competitive warden's exam again and go through all the background and psychological testing again. I drove back home to Shell with a heavy heart. I missed my family, but really enjoyed my time as a game warden trainee in Lander.

While back at home I read an ad in the local Buyer's Guide paper advertising a regional arm-wrestling tournament in Cody. This sounded interesting to me as I was always good at arm wrestling but had never competed at any professional level. My wife Lana was also very strong. Maybe I could talk her into arm wrestling in the tournament as well. The tournament was that coming Saturday at 1:00 PM at the Sportsman Bar in Cody, Wyoming. After some sweet talking, Lana agreed to have a date with me and attend the tournament.

We showed up on Saturday for weigh-ins. I weighed 204 lbs. which put me in the heavyweight division. If I would have been four pounds lighter, I would have been placed in the middleweight division. As it stood, I would be competing with men that weighed over 300 lbs. Lana came in at 128 lbs. and would be placed in the lightweight division. I soon learned that these guys take their arm-wrestling very seriously. They were not only strong, but they also knew certain techniques that would give them the advantage over those who didn't have any technique. I didn't know any technique I was just very strong. I went through my competition that day and never lost a match. I even signed up left-handed and won all those matches as well. Lana would wade through her competition and also win first place.

At the end of the day a man named Trenton from Big Sky, Montana offered to buy me a beer. He had won the middleweight division that day at 180 lbs. After visiting with Trenton, I learned that he had won the world championship the previous year in the middleweight division. He asked me if I would arm-wrestle him in an exhibition match just for fun. I agreed. I had never been beat at this point in my life, so why not. This guy was tall and slender with a black cowboy hat. He didn't look tough at all. He had told me earlier that he rode bulls and bucking broncs for a living. I hooked up with him. After several minutes of wrestling for the proper hand and arm position, a certified referee started us. The referee would put his hand on top of our hands and when his hand left contact with our hands, that meant go.

I felt like I got the jump on Trenton and gave it my all. Trenton beat me so fast and effortlessly that I couldn't believe someone smaller than me had actually beat me that easily. I felt helpless. We would arm wrestle a couple more times, he easily beat me each time. I joined Trenton for a beer after the match. He said, "Man, you are the toughest person I have ever arm wrestled." I said, "How do you figure? You just whooped my butt effortlessly!" He replied, "You are very strong, but you just don't have any technique. I can feel your strength," Trenton said, "I would like to teach you some technique that will help you very much." I was excited and worked with Trenton over the next hour learning several different arm-wrestling techniques. At the end of the day, Trenton told Lana and me if we were to win the state tournament next week in the pro-division, that we would qualify for the national tournament. Lana wasn't nearly as excited about this as I was. This would be a chance for both of us to compete at a professional level.

Lana and I practiced our technique every night at home for the next week. She was very strong and fast for her weight. We would end up competing in the state championship the next weekend. Both of us won first place again in the pro division, both left and right-handed, which qualified us for Nationals to be held in Deadwood, South Dakota. Lana told me her arm was sore and she was done with the nonsense. I told her my elbow hurt as well, and I didn't think that I wanted to take it to the next level. My good friend, Lander game warden Bob Trebelcock watched both of us win the competition. He said, "If you guys will take it to the National level, I will sponsor you and help pay for your trip," We thanked Bob, and told him that we would let him know depending on how our arms healed up over the next several weeks.

I had taken nearly two weeks off from work and was getting restless at home. It was nice to spend time with my family and do some fishing in Shell Creek. I would need to find a job for the winter to pay the bills. I had contacted Elk Feed Ground Supervisor Ron Dean who lived in Etna, Wyoming several times over the past years trying to get a job feeding elk over the winter months. There were a number of permanent game wardens who had started their career feeding elk on elk feed grounds in western Wyoming. This was a good job to get you through the winters and then go back to work on the Reservoir Crew in the spring. However, Ron had never returned my calls. He probably thought that I lived too far away and had a family with young kids. Many of the feed grounds involved a small one room cabin that you or the family would have to live in for the winter months. Feeding elk was a seven-day-a-week job for several months. Probably not the best situation for a wife and two kids to spend the winter. Bob Trebelcock had showed us pictures of him feeding elk on a feed ground. Lana and I both thought that would be an awesome job. As we both grew up on a ranch feeding livestock every morning, feeding elk would be much more appealing than feeding cattle or sheep.

It was November 9th, 1996 at about 10:00 AM. The faded yellow wall-mounted phone above the kitchen counter rang. I almost didn't answer it because I was headed out the door to do some fishing. It was probably someone looking for Lana anyways. I laid my fishing rod down and hesitantly answered the phone. "Hello," "Hello, is this Scott Werbelow?" "Yes, it is." "This is Bernard Holz, regional wildlife supervisor for the Pinedale region, how are you today?" I replied, "I'm doing fine, sir, how are you today?" Bernard replied, "I'm well, thanks for asking. The reason for the call is that I would like to offer you a position as Feed Ground Manager for the Pinedale region on a contract basis." I could not believe what I was hearing. Heck, I had applied to feed elk for years and nobody would ever return my calls. Now, they were offering me a Feed Ground Manager position. I quickly responded, "Yes sir, I would be very interested." Bernard responded, "Great, can you meet me at the Pinedale regional office on November 12, at 8:00 AM?" I replied, "Yes, sir!" Bernard replied, "Great, you will eventually need to find a place to rent or buy, but you're more than welcome to stay in the department's small camper trailer in the compound until you have found something else." I said, "Yes, sir, I will see you Monday morning at 8:00 AM."

What, did I just agree to? I thought to myself! I hadn't even asked my wife Lana what she thought about living in Pinedale. I was just so excited to have a job with the Game and Fish Department over the winter months that I didn't even care where or what the job was. Hell, I didn't even know where Pinedale was located for sure. I would have to pull a Wyoming map out of the closet to see where Pinedale was located. For some reason I thought it was southwest Wyoming. It took me awhile to find it. It is located just south of Jackson Hole. I thought to myself, this might be a really beautiful spot to live. I couldn't wait to tell Lana the great news. She was gone riding her horse somewhere, again! I decided I would just go fishing and tell her the great news over dinner. Heck, maybe I should take her out for dinner and break the news over a candlelit meal. That would be a great idea!

I picked up the phone and made a dinner reservation at Wagon Wheel Restaurant in Shell Canyon. This place had the best prime rib that I had ever eaten before. I was in the mood to celebrate; this was awesome news for me today. Lana returned home later that evening. She walked in the front door tired and asked, "What do you want for dinner?" I said, "Honey I'm taking you out to dinner tonight." She responded, "Why, it's not my birthday or anything special." I said, "It's a surprise, I will tell you over dinner later tonight."

We had an awesome candlelit diner. Lana finally asked, "So what's the special occasion?" I said, "Honey, I accepted a job in Pinedale today as a Feed Ground Manager for all the elk feed grounds in western Wyoming." She said, "That's great, when do you start?" I said, "I have to leave Sunday morning and meet Bernard Holz the regional wildlife supervisor on Monday morning at 8:00 AM." "MONDAY MORNING! Where are you going to live?" I replied, "I don't know, maybe a small camper trailer in the compound for now." "Is this a permanent job?" Lana asked. I said, "No, It's just on a contract basis for now." "What does that mean?" Lana asked. "I don't know," I replied. "I thought you wanted to be a game warden, how are you going to be a game warden and a feed ground manager?" I said, "That's a good question, I don't know?" "Sounds like you have a lot to figure out. Congratulations on the new job. You go down and figure things out, once you get a permanent job, I will move me and the kids to Pinedale."

I packed my personal belongings in my truck and headed for Pinedale Sunday morning. I was really excited, but I had many questions about what I had just got myself into. I wanted to be a game warden, but this may be a better opportunity at a permanent job. I didn't even know what the job was all about. Heck, I haven't even been to Pinedale before. I stopped in Lander and visited with Bob Trebelcock to tell him the exiting news. He was very excited for me and congratulated me. He thought that I would love the job and that Lana and I would love Pinedale. He asked me if Lana and I were going to compete in the National arm-wrestling tournament in January. I told him that we were still undecided with everything that was going on in our lives.

I left Bob's and headed south towards Farson. The closer I got to Farson, the uglier the topography got. It was flat sagebrush ground for miles with a few hayfields along the highway. I thought to myself, what did I get myself into, this place is ugly!" I finally arrived in Farson and turned to my right to head to Pinedale. I noticed the Farson Mercantile on my right. I had always heard that they had awesome ice cream cones there. I wheeled my truck into the parking lot and ordered me a double cheesecake/cookie dough ice cream cone. I headed north towards Pinedale with ice cream clear to my ears on both sides of my face and a partial load in my lap. Seems like when you order a "double" that's just the way things work out. As I continued north, all I could see was miles and miles of flat sagebrush ground. The wind was blowing out of the west about 30-40 mile per hour with an occasional tumble weed traveling across the highway in front of me. The landscape was depressing. What had I got myself into? About twenty miles south of Pinedale I crested a hill and could now see the whole Pinedale valley. A smile came across my face, ice cream and all. I thought to myself, what a beautiful valley nestled between the Wyoming mountain range and the Wind River mountain range, I think I'm going to like this place!!

I pulled into Pinedale at about 4:30 PM. It was cold and gloomy out. Just as I entered town, I noticed a sign that read Wyoming Game & Fish Department with an arrow pointing to my left. I turned down the street to my left and headed one block south of Main Street. Located on my left was a green building with a sign that read Wyoming Game and Fish Department. Right in front of the sign on the building stood three cow moose. I had never seen moose in town before. This was going to be a really cool place, I thought to myself. I parked my truck right in front of the main entrance of the building. The moose had no fear of me.

Cow moose in front of Pinedale office.

It was Sunday and no other employees were working. The main office was locked up. I walked around the building and noticed a green and white 16' wilderness camp trailer parked on the north side of the building. This was going to be my home. As I approached the trailer, I noticed that it had a flat tire on one side. I also noticed the front door was locked. I walked around the front of the trailer and noticed there were no propane bottles in the rack on the front of the trailer. I also noticed there was no extension cord plugged into the trailer to provide electricity. I had forgotten to get Bernard's phone number in case I needed to call him. Large fluffy snowflakes started to hit the ground, illuminated by the street light in the compound. I decided it may be best to get a motel room for the night.

I walked across the street and checked into the Sundance Motel. Not a bad place and pretty inexpensive for Pinedale on a November night. I was hungry and looked forward to a Sunday night football game. The motel didn't get the game so I hiked down to the Stockman's bar just down the street. They had the football game on and a nice juicy cheeseburger and fries. While sitting at the bar, I met several new people that night. After visiting with them for a while they told me they worked as elk feeders for the Wyoming Game & Fish Department. They asked me what I did for a living and I stated, "I think I might be your new boss!"

Chapter 5

PINEDALE - FEED GROUND MANAGER

Morning came early. I jumped out of bed, took a warm shower and dressed up nice for my meeting with Pinedale regional supervisor Bernard Holz. I was nervous. I had never met the man before. I walked a short distance to the office and entered the front door of the green-colored office building. I was greeted by a cute gal who sat behind the front desk. She had a slender build, long hair and a pretty smile. She smiled and said, "Good morning, can I help you with something?" I replied, "My name is Scott Werbelow, I have a meeting with Mr. Holz at 8:00 AM." She said, "I think he is in his office on the phone right now. My name is Des Brunette. I'm the Office Manager for the Pinedale region." I smiled, shook her hand and said, "It's a pleasure to meet you, ma'am."

Des knocked lightly on the door to Mr. Holz's office. I heard a voice from the other side of the door say, "I'll be with you shortly." The door was oak and had a glass window with a shade that had been pulled down to prevent anyone from seeing inside his office. I visited briefly with Des and told her that I had been offered a job as the Pinedale region Feed Ground Manager. She looked surprised when I told her the news. She responded, "REALLY"? About that time Mr. Holz opened his door, shook my hand and said, "You must be Scott. Pleasure to meet you." I gave him a firm handshake and told him that it was a pleasure to meet him as well. He invited me into his office and shut the door behind us. His office was very orderly. Mr. Holz sat down in his oak chair with rusty metal wheels attached to the legs and rolled his chair next to his vintage style oak roll top desk. The desk had an old kerosene lantern sitting on top of it next to a small glass jar filled with ink. I noticed an old-style ink pen dipped in the jar of ink.

Mr. Holz was a short slender man, probably only weighed about a buck fifty. He wore a neatly pressed red shirt and brand-new wrangler jeans. The cuffs of his jeans were turned upwards which showed off his cowboy boots and spurs. His neatly trimmed beard was black and he wore a cowboy hat with a round brim. I noticed he had a large Cuban cigar sticking slightly above his left shirt pocket. I said, "Pleasure to meet you, Bernard." He replied, "Please call me Bernie." Bernie asked me how my summer and fall had gone and a little about my background. We had a nice visit for some time. Bernie then told me that he was looking for a feed ground manager on a contract basis. The previous feed ground manager had suddenly left the department. Bernie stated that he had contacted Casper supervisor Terry Cleveland and Terry had told him to give me a call. Mr. Cleveland had told Bernie that he thought I would be a perfect fit for the job. Bernie asked me questions like, have you ever harnessed and driven a team of draft horses? Do you have experience riding snow machines? Can you weld and do you do carpentry work?

Heck, I felt like I was a perfect match for the job. I had actually harnessed and driven a team of draft horses several times back on the ranch. I also had a degree in Industrial Technology and was a certified woods and welding instructor when I left college. I also owned my own construction business at one time and had spent my whole life on a snow machine. I answered yes to all of his questions when Bernie said, "Great, welcome aboard, we are excited to have you in the region." Bernie then went on to explain the job to me. He told me that I would be in charge of 13 of the 22 state-operated feed grounds in western Wyoming. Most of them were primarily in Sublette County. He told me that Ron Dean from Etna, Wyoming, was the Feed Ground Supervisor and would be my immediate supervisor. He gave me Ron's contact information and told me to call him very soon.

Bernie then provided me a list of what my responsibilities would be. The list looked something like this:

* Make hiring and firing decisions for contract elk feeders

* Maintain an annual budget of 1.5 million dollars

* Care for 30-40 draft horses located on the Soda Lake unit north of Pinedale

* Work closely with Ron Dean to purchase 6000-9000 tons of hay annually for all feed grounds

* Perform needed maintenance work on all feed grounds on an annual basis

* Weigh hay, test hay, complete all hay purchasing and hauling contracts with hay producers and hay haulers

* Maintain all feed ground equipment including hay sheds, horse corrals, feed-sleds/wagons

* Maintain/purchase draft horses and equipment to include double trees, single trees, bobsleds, tongues, and harnesses

* Attend all public season setting meetings and regional wildlife personnel meetings.

* Assist region game wardens with damage situations, including moving elk off private property to elk feed grounds

The list went on and on, but those were the high points. After reading the list, I felt over-whelmed. None of this list included being a game warden. Was I making the right decision? Would this change my path to becoming a game warden someday? I looked at Bernie and said, "I'm very excited about this opportunity. Do I need turn in all of my law enforcement equipment? Bernie looked up at the ceiling in his office as if he was in deep thought. He then looked at me and said, "I don't know, let me make a few calls on that and get back to you."

I was looking over Bernie's shoulder out of his office window and I observed a mule standing in the horse corral next to the office. I asked Bernie if that was his mule. Bernie responded with a smile "Yes, that's Woodrow, I ride him to work as often as I can. I live about seven miles out on Pole Creek road. I had him at a high trot this morning and made it to work in less than 15 minutes."

Bernie then took me around the office and introduced me to everyone. We went up-stairs in the small building. The offices upstairs were broken up into four small cubicles with five-foot high walls around each work space. Each work space was about 10'x10' in size. He showed me my office space which was located in the back corner of the building. With the slope of the roof, I only had room for a desk and a chair. If you slid your chair back to get away from your desk, you would hit your head on the ceiling. Bernie said, "This will be your work station right here, I will have Des find you a computer somewhere in the next few days. I thanked Bernie. He then said, "Oh, let me show you where your truck and horse trailer are located. We went outside into the compound on the south side of the building. Bernie pointed across the parking lot and said, "There is your truck and trailer parked over there," as he pointed across the parking lot. Your truck will be GF-226 and the horse trailer parked next to it is assigned to the feed ground program. Get with Des for the keys, and I believe your snow machine is parked in the Quonset hut out at Soda Lake. Get with Des to see which snow machine is assigned to you. If you have any questions about anything, get with Des. She will order you a planner, get you a gas card, and get you a set of keys for all the feed ground locks, equipment, and buildings."

Bernie said he had a meeting that he was late for and needed to "make a mile" I thanked him for everything and he yelled as he was walking away, "If you need anything don't hesitate to ask someone. They will steer you in the right direction." He seemed in a hurry! A few minutes later I looked up to see Bernie and Woodrow trotting down the street headed for Main Street. Bernie, must have had a lunch date with someone, I thought.

I walked over to look at my new truck (GF-226). It looked like about a 1992 regular cab Ford pickup. It was game warden green with the game and fish shield in the center of each door. The closer I looked, the truck was beat to shit and looked like an old ranch truck. The front window was cracked in several different places. Hell, it didn't even have a rear window! The front bumper was hanging down and bent slightly forward on the driver's side. The tailgate was missing and the entire bed of the truck was filled with frozen loose hay and a mangled mess of red and blue hay-bale twines. The hay had gotten wet and then frozen. The whole bed of the truck felt like it had been poured full of concrete and dried. It was a waste of time to lock the truck because the rear window was missing. The doors were unlocked and the keys were in the ignition. I tried to start the truck and the battery was dead. CLICK, CLICK, CLICK went the ignition. I went to pop the hood and noticed about 6-8 inches of manure stuck to the driver's side floorboard. It was also frozen and harder than a rock!

I walked over to the heated shop to get a battery charger, extension cord, hammer and a chisel. There was a warden's truck parked in the heated shop with water and mud dripping off of it onto the concrete floor.

I noticed a large man lying underneath the truck. It looked like he was putting tire chains on the front tires of the truck. The man was wearing a snow machine suit and Sorrell snow boots. I startled the man when I said, "How are you doing today?" He raised up quickly and hit his head on the under frame of the truck. The man slowly crawled out from underneath the truck. He was wearing a green Elmer Fudd looking hat with the ear flaps down. A chunk of snow and mud had dripped down on his cheek and was now running down his chin. He stood up and said, "OH, I didn't know anybody was around today. I don't believe we have met. My name is Duke Early I'm the north Pinedale game warden." I said, "Pleasure to meet you sir, I'm Scott Werbelow, the new feed ground manager." We shook hands. Duke smiled and said, "Oh, I'm just putting some chains on. It's a little warmer in here than it is outside. I got some elk in a hay stack north of town that I need to go try and get out in the morning. I just didn't want to get out there somewhere and get stuck in the snow and then have to put my chains on, if you know what I mean!" Duke giggled and smiled. I replied, "Oh, I know exactly what you mean, I'm just trying to get this old feed ground truck up and running." Duke said, "Well, pleasure to meet you and good luck getting that truck going." Giggle, Giggle. I told Duke that I would catch up with him later when we both had more time to visit.

I charged the battery on the truck and spent over three hours with the hammer and chisel chipping frozen manure off the floorboard of the truck. I needed to park the truck in the heated shop to thaw out all of the frozen hay in the back. But I couldn't do this because Duke had his truck parked in there. I didn't dare ask Duke, a Senior Game Warden to pull his truck out of a heated shop. Those were things you just didn't dare try as a Trainee/feed ground manager. As I was cleaning the truck, I noticed an empty whiskey bottle under the driver's side seat. I also noticed a handful of empty beer cans as well. The more I looked, I found broken glass, Dentine gum, and cinnamon fire balls under the seat. I looked at the bench seat on the driver's side and there was a dark colored stain in the area that would be between your legs when you were driving. I recognized this stain as one made from when you were driving with an open beer between your legs. My old man's truck had the same stain in the same spot! I thought to myself, was the previous feed ground manager fired for drinking on the job? If I had done this job for twenty years, would I be drinking on the job as well?

I got the truck started and vacuumed and cleaned out the interior of the truck, at least the best that I could. I took the truck across the street to Belveal's Repair Shop to ask them if they could order me a rear window. They actually already had the window in place, someone had ordered it several weeks prior. They said they weren't that busy and could install the window right now, if I had a few hours to wait. I said, "You bet, I have some things to do right across the street." I headed across the street to my 16' Wilderness camp trailer. I would need to find a key to open the trailer. After asking Des and searching for over an hour, I finally broke into the trailer with a heavy-duty screwdriver. The place was a mess. Mouse shit everywhere! It even smelled like Hantavirus. There was no bedding on the bed. It was cold enough in there to hang a beef for the winter. I cleaned up the trailer and found some propane bottles in the Quonset hut that had been hooked up to some Zon Guns (propane cannon used to scare wildlife.) I grabbed a crescent wrench out of the shop, hooked up the propane bottles and lit the heater in the trailer. Things were starting to look up.

By now my truck was done. I would look at a map in the front office to figure out where Soda Lake habitat unit was located, and go check on the draft horses and figure out if my snow machine was out there in a storage shed somewhere. Des looked at her inventory sheet and told me what snow machine I was supposed to have. Her inventory sheet read 1994 Artic Cat ZR-440. ZR-440? What a piece of crap! I thought to myself. I had been riding snowmobiles my whole life and was an Arctic Cat fan. But they make much better snow machines than this one! I had just purchased a 1994 Arctic Cat ZR-700 Mountain Cat. This snow machine had been customized with a 163" long track and had paddles that were two inches long. Nobody had even heard of the new 2" Camoplast track yet. This machine was sitting in my garage back in Shell. I hadn't even had time to ride it yet since I had bought it from a guy in Billings back in October.

I soon arrived at the Soda Lake unit. I stopped and read the informational sign as you enter the unit. The unit encompassed over 5000 acres of wildlife habitat and was owned by the Wyoming Game and Fish Department. The unit was beautiful and full of migrating deer and waterfowl. There was also an elk feed ground that sat right next to Soda lake. I could see the horse corrals and stack yard off in the distance. I didn't have my binoculars, but it looked like about 30 draft horses up on the side of what they called Fremont Ridge. The gate was locked into the unit. I checked all my keys on the key ring and none of them fit. I looked in the tool box of Gf-226 to see if there was a hide-a-key located somewhere. I didn't find a hidden key but I did find a coffee can completely full of keys. There must have been over 200 keys in that can. I think I tried nearly every one of them and "WALLA" the lock opened. I entered the unit and found the Quonset hut that had snow machines stored in it. It was also locked and a different key than the front gate. I would need to get all of these keys figured out over time.

The snow machine was in good shape with surprisingly low miles. The two-place trailer that hauled the snow machine was a complete mess. No trailer lights, two flat tires, and the wooden bed was nearly rotted out. The trailer was probably about a 1960's model. I would need to do some work on it. This Quonset hut was huge and full of lots of equipment. I noticed two flatbed semi-trucks, one four-wheel drive tractor with a ten-pack (used to load and unload small hay bales) mounted on the front. They must have used the trucks to haul hay to the feed grounds, I thought. There were also at least six other trailers with snow machines sitting on them. Most of the trailers were single wide and would only hold one snow machine. I also noticed an old snow plane back in the corner. It had a huge fan on the rear of the plane with pontoons to travel on ice or snow. The plane didn't fly in the air, but was probably used by wardens to check ice fishermen on the many frozen lakes in the area. There were also some old army snow-cats with snow plows mounted to the front of them. I thought to myself, this must be some deep snow country over here! Oh Shit, I just remembered I was supposed to call my boss Ron Dean ASAP. I would need to drive back to the office and call him, bag phones were not yet invented.

I had a good phone conversation with Ron. He was excited to meet me and wanted to drive down to Pinedale in the morning to show me where some of the feed grounds were located. He informed me that he had scheduled an elk feeder meeting tomorrow night at 7:00 PM at the fire hall in Pinedale. He asked me to make sure that all my elk feeder contracts were completed, so that they could all sign them at the meeting. He also asked me if I could make contact with all of the elk feeders to remind them of the meeting. He had sent them a letter several weeks earlier informing them of the meeting, and hoped that they had not forgotten about the meeting. I agreed to do all of it, and agreed to meet him at the office at 10:00 AM in the morning. After I hung up the phone, I thought to myself, I don't even know who my elk feeders are or how to get ahold of them. Many of the elk feeders didn't even have a home phone. I would need help from Des.

It was almost 5:00 PM. I was in a panic! I asked Des if she could help me complete all the elk feeder contracts for tomorrow's meeting. She smiled, reached down on her desk and handed me a pile of contracts. She said, "I have already done them for you." What a sweetheart she was, I couldn't believe it. I didn't know how to even find a contract, let alone fill one out with all the proper budget codes and dollar amounts. I also told her that I needed to contact all my feeders to let them know of the meeting tomorrow night. She again smiled and said, "I have already contacted all of the ones who have home phones and they plan on coming. She gave me a list of the ones who didn't have phones and told me that I could probably find most of them at the Stockman's bar during happy hour. I smiled and said, "I think I met some of them last night. That's where I went for dinner."

I stepped into my Wilderness camp trailer to change clothes for dinner. I thought I might head down to the Stockman's bar again and see if I couldn't meet some of my elk feeders. The trailer house was warm, the heater was working properly. That put a smile on my face! I quickly changed my clothes and walked down to the Stockman's bar. I bellied up to the bar and ordered a Crown and Coke, I was ready for a drink after such a long day. I felt like I had accomplished a great deal for only my first day on the job. About that time, one of the largest human beings whom I had ever encountered in my life walked through the front door of the bar and sat next to me. He must have been about 6'-5" and weighed about 340 lbs. He had long brown hair that hung straight down to the middle of his back. He was wearing a black leather Harley Davidson jacket. His head looked like it could have easily weighed 30-40 lbs. minimum. He had a mustache and a long, pointed goatee.

He ordered a double Crown and Coke and drank the first one like it was a glass of ice water. He ordered another double and turned around and looked at me and said very slowly with a deep voice, "Where are you from? I don't think we have ever met." I responded, "My name is Scott Werbelow, I'm from Shell Wyoming, I don't think we have met." I reached over to shake his hand. He said, "Nice to meet you, my name is Cash Rich." His hand was so big that it just swallowed up mine when we shook hands. He said, "Shell, I don't think I have ever been there before, what brings you to Pinedale?" I explained to Cash that I had just been hired as the new feed ground manager for the Wyoming Game and Fish Department. Cash said, "Oh really, my dad Dean Rich worked for the Game and Fish forever. He was a hay hauler." We sat there and visited for quite some time. Cash asked me when I had started working as the feed ground manager. I responded, "Today."

Cash looked around the bar and said, "Well, if you haven't met some of your elk feeders yet, there are several of them in the bar right now." I said, "Oh really, where are they at?" He looked around and said, "That little short guy standing down at the end of the bar that is Greg Grassell. He feeds at Franz feed ground." I looked over at Greg and he had just taken a shot of something, slammed the shot glass down on the bar and was laughing uncontrollably. Every time that Greg would take a breath, he would snort like a pig because he was laughing so hard. It looked like he was having a great time. Cash said, "And that lady over there with the ponytail sticking out of her cap and the safety glasses on, that is Kathy Rebescher. I think she is the new feeder for Fall Creek feed ground? The guy that she is talking to, I think his name is Tim Baxley or something like that. He is new in the area and told me that he was feeding elk for the Game and Fish last time I visited with him." Tim was wearing a dirty confederate cowboy hat. He had a full dark scraggly beard and was wearing leather chaps with tall lace up "White" snow boots. He was wearing pink colored sun glasses in the bar. It looked like he was having a big and rich time visiting with Kathy. Both he and Kathy were drinking bottled beer and chewing Copenhagen.

Cash looked over on the other side of the bar and said, "OH, and that guy with the dark beard who is playing dice, that's Frosty Hittle. He has fed at Muddy Creek feed ground for years." Cash then stood up and said, "Come on, I will introduce you to these guys." Cash was a great guy, and I damn sure wanted to be on his side if there was ever a bar fight. Cash introduced me to all of the elk feeders. They were all great people and they knew how to have fun. As the night went on the elk feeders were buying me drinks and I was buying them drinks back. We were getting to know one another better every minute. Greg Grassell had me laughing so hard that I blew whiskey through my nose several times and my stomach ached from laughing so hard. He was a little short guy that didn't look tough at all. The bar crowd was starting to thin down a bit. Greg held up his drink and faced everybody at the bar and yelled, "ANY OF YOU PUSSIES WANT TO LEG WRESTLE? I'LL KICK ALL

YOUR ASSES!" I had forgotten about leg wresting I was surprised that anyone else had ever heard of it before let alone had actually ever done it. About that time, one of the biggest red-haired women whom I had ever saw in my life came lumbering down the aisle walking towards us. She had a determined look on her face, like she might kill anyone that got in her way. She was wearing pink sweat pants with black combat boots and a very tight white tee-shirt.

Greg was busy telling a story and snorting like a pig when she tapped him on the shoulder and said, "Hey, honey, lets leg wrestle." Greg's eyes were as big as silver dollars as he looked up to see her face. A drunken cowboy standing nearby blurted out, "I WOULD RATHER SCREW A TACKLE BOX!!" She gave Greg a shove and nearly knocked him over. I again blew whiskey out of my nose. She yelled, "COME ON, YOU LITTLE BASTARD PUT YOUR MONEY WHERE YOUR MOUTH IS. LET'S GO!" Everybody started clearing chairs and tables out to give them room to lie on the floor. One guy even tried to start up a Calcutta on the side. Once a small area was cleared the two lay down on their backs and put their right legs straight in the air. One, Two, Three, they counted out as their legs went back and forth. On three, the heavy-set lady quickly reached over and hooked Greg's right leg and threw him completely over the top of her. His limp drunk body sailed about ten feet and knocked over a near-by table and chairs.

The whole crowd was on their feet yelling and cheering for the lady. Greg slowly got up, started laughing and snorting and said, "DAMN, I'm sure glad I'm not married to you. Somebody needs to buy that big ole redheaded sumbitch a drink while I sit down and catch my breath!" It was getting to be about 2:00 AM. I decided I had better make a mile and get back to my trailer house and get some sleep. I would need to meet with my boss Ron Dean in the morning at 10:00 AM. I said my good byes to all the elk feeders and told them I would see them tomorrow night at 7:00 PM for the elk feeder meeting. Most of them thanked me for the reminder, they had already forgotten about the meeting. I walked back to my trailer and entered through the front door. Shit, I had forgot to run a power cord to the trailer and I had no lights. To top it all off, the heater had quit working and it was freezing cold in the trailer. I was too tired to mess with it, I crawled in my sleeping bag and went to sleep. I woke up the next morning and I'm not sure I had ever been that cold in my entire life. My toothpaste, shampoo, and shaving cream were frozen solid. I would end up going upstairs in the office to take a hot shower.

I met with my new boss Ron Dean at 10:00 AM. Ron spent the morning with me and showed me where Black Butte, Franz, Jewett, and Bench Corral feed grounds were located. I really enjoyed visiting with Ron. He was a wealth of knowledge and had been the Feed Ground Supervisor for over 20 years. I gave him a hard time for never hiring me as an elk feeder to get through the winter months. He laughed and told me that he didn't remember ever seeing my application. He explained a great deal of feed ground history to me. He explained that the National Elk Refuge in Jackson Hole started feeding elk around the early 1900's, primarily to keep elk from starving to death. Ron told me that many of the state-operated feed grounds started in the forties, fifties, and sixties. He told me that there were 22 state-operated feed grounds that fed an average of about 17,000 elk per year in addition to the National Elk Refuge that fed between 5000-10000 elk per year. Some feed grounds like Green River Lakes, Gros Ventre, and Forest Park feed grounds were started to prevent elk from starvation. The other feed grounds were strategically placed at lower elevations to short stop elk and prevent elk from entering onto private property and causing damage to cattle feedlines and hay stacks. Brucellosis was also a huge concern. Some of the elk had brucellosis. It was very important for the Game and Fish to keep elk and cattle from co-mingling and spreading the disease to cattle. There was, and still is a great deal of controversy surrounding elk feed grounds as it pertains to disease issues and over-crowding of elk.

Ron also held a PHD in animal nutrition. He gave me the name and phone number of a previous feed ground manager who would be a

Scott C. Werbelow

great resource for me if I had questions or problems. Ron attended the elk feeder meeting with me and introduced me to all of the elk feeders. He explained to me how we paid the elk feeders and how to properly complete a monthly elk feeder report. This report tracked the number of bales and tons of hay fed each month by the feeders. Most of the feeders had been feeding for years and some of them had their own team of draft horse that they got paid to use. All I had to do is call them when it was time to start feeding and make sure they had their draft horses in the corral with all the necessary equipment they needed to feed the elk.

The elk feeders were only paid about twenty-five dollars a day. They also received pay based on the number of tons of hay fed each month and about sixty dollars per month if they provided their own team of draft horses. If they owned their own draft horses this was actually a pretty good deal for them. As they didn't need to pay for any hay to feed their horses all winter and the horses got worked daily. The job didn't pay that much but it generally paid better than most ranch jobs feeding cattle and only took about 4-5 hours a day to feed elk. Most feeders had at least two different jobs. They also got paid a small amount to vaccinate their elk for brucellosis each winter.

Tim Baxley was the only new elk feeder. Tim was from the South. It was his dream to come out west and feed elk. Tim was hired to feed two different feed grounds that winter. He would be feeding at North Piney and Finnegan feed grounds. He told me that he was going to live in a small camper trailer at each feed ground and run a trap line between the two feed grounds each day. I really liked Tim. He had a great attitude and was just happy to be alive. You would never see Tim quit smiling or laughing, even when he didn't have anything to smile or laugh about. Kathy Rebescher had come from New York. She really enjoyed life out west and could work harder than most men. Kathy had fed Finnegan feed ground the previous year and would now be living in a small camp trailer and feeding elk at Fall Creek feed ground just northeast of Pinedale.

We also had long time elk feeder John Fandek who had been

feeding elk previously at Black Butte feed ground for years. John had been fired the previous winter. Apparently, John had put in for a bighorn sheep license for over 30 years and was unable to draw a license. He became upset with the draw system and wrote a letter to the Chief Game Warden in Cheyenne. In his letter he stated that he was going sheep hunting without a license. Apparently, the letter didn't go over very well, as John was not hired back to feed elk the next year. I don't think that John ever had any intentions of shooting a sheep without a license, but he sure wanted to get someone's attention to try and make the draw odds a little better. John was now hired back and he was excited to be back in action. John still feeds elk at Black Butte feed ground with 43 years of service feeding elk for the Wyoming Game and Fish Department. John was kicked in the leg by a draft horse back in about 1986. The horse broke his leg and he missed some days feeding. Aside from that incident John has only missed two days of feeding in his 43 year career.

John Fandek with his team of horses.

Scott C. Werbelow

The winter of 1996-1997 was horrible. It seemed like it snowed nearly every day and temperatures were well below zero almost daily. I hit the ground running. It soon became apparent to me that all feed grounds needed started up, and none of them had draft horses hauled to each feed ground. I didn't even know where many of the feed grounds were located yet. The snow was piling up and many of the feed grounds were difficult to drive into, especially in the deep snow pulling a large horse trailer full of heavy draft horses. I drove out to Soda Lake to figure out just how I was going to catch the horses on the departments 5000-acre pasture.

I finally located the herd of draft horses. They were in an aspen stand just north of the wetlands. There were no roads even close to where the horses were hanging out. I walked about one mile through the deep snow to get a better look at the horses. As soon as I approached the horses, they grabbed their asses, and ran away from me up the hill through the heavy timber. It was like they knew I was coming to catch them and they weren't ready to go to work. I walked back to my truck. I would need to figure out a better system to catch horses. I drove over to the old Soda Lake feed ground and located a smaller area that had been fenced off. Inside this five-acre pasture there was an old stack yard with an eight-foot-high elk fence around it. If I could get the horses into this pasture, I could maybe bait them into the old stack yard and catch the ones that I needed.

I grabbed a load of some really pretty green native grass hay out of the stack yard. I had to stack it on top of all the frozen hay still in my truck. I would need to thaw my truck out so that I could get down to the fifth wheel ball in order to hook up my horse trailer to haul horses. I soon found the draft horses clear at the south end of the unit. They had traveled about four miles since I last saw them. I yelled at the horses, "COME ON BOYS, HERE BOYS!" as I banged on the hood of my truck to get their attention. I fed out a partial bale of hay on the ground behind the truck. Pretty quick, here they came a-running to get some fresh hay. They gathered around my truck and started kicking, biting and fighting

Draft horses standing on hill at Soda Lake.

with one another to establish a pecking order of who got to eat first. I had never seen such beautiful and majestic horses in my life. These horses all weighed between 1400-2000 lbs. Their manes were long and their feet were huge. It was dangerous to stand near the horses while they were eating, because they were doing so much fighting and kicking. I jumped into my truck, cranked up the heater and drove a short distance away to watch them feed. It took some time, but I was finally able to get them to eat out of the back of my truck. I drove very slowly for about three miles, and they followed me into the five-acre pasture. Once they were all through the gate, I quickly jumped out of my truck and ran behind the herd of 30+ draft horses and closed the gate behind them. I thought, "WHEW" I did it, I got them all corralled.

I then fed out four bales of hay inside the old stack yard and opened a large gate on the south end of the stack yard fence. The horses knew what I was up to; they had been through this procedure before. They all stood right in front of the gate and would not enter the stack yard area. No matter how good the hay tasted, they were not going to walk through that gate and be trapped. I would need to get them all caught soon, because they all needed their manes roached, and their feet trimmed. Their feet looked horrible. I don't think they had been trimmed for a very long time. I wasn't even sure how I was going to trim them. I couldn't imagine trying to hold the legs up on these horses and trim their feet. Maybe that is why they hadn't been trimmed before? The horses would also need to be wormed. I wasn't sure I was even tall enough to put a syringe in their mouth to give them the wormer paste.

I tried to walk up to the horses. None of them would let me touch them. I even tried to herd them through the gate. This idea went south in about ten seconds. All the horses turned and nearly ran me over as they bucked and farted across the pasture. I knew one thing for sure, I would need to spend more time around these horses if I was ever going to catch one of them. I would need to start feeding them horse cubes and grain and spoil them a bit. I would also need to figure out if there was someone in town who could trim, roach, and worm the horses. I left the gate open so that they could go in and out of the old stack yard and eat their hay. Maybe they would get used to this over time. I would need to start feeding them every morning and get them used to my presence.

I drove back to the office to clean out my truck and see if I had any tire chains. Duke was now out of the heated shop, so I quickly slipped my truck into the warm shop to thaw it out. I walked into the front office to say hi to Des and give her all the elk feeder contracts from last night. She was smiling as usual and asked how the meeting went. I told her that some of the elk feeders were absolute characters. She said, "Did you get to meet Greg Grassell?" "Oh, boy did I ever!" I said with a smile and a laugh. I was telling Des the bar story about Greg and another senior game warden walked into the front office to check his mail. Des looked at me and said, "Have you met Dennis yet?" I said, "No, I haven't."

Dennis looked at me and held out his hand to shake my hand. "Dennis Almquist, pleasure to meet you, I'm the south Pinedale game warden." I shook his hand firmly and replied, "Dennis, I'm Scott Werbelow the new feed ground manager, pleasure to meet you." Dennis was probably in his fifties. He was considered an "Old Time" game warden. I couldn't imagine the things that Dennis must have been through and the stories that he could tell during his long career with the department. I was looking forward to spending more time with Dennis and picking his brain about being a Wyoming game warden for so many years. After visiting with Dennis for a short period of time, he invited me to ride along with him in the morning. He agreed to show me the feed grounds that were in his warden district. This would be Fall Creek, Scab Creek, and Muddy Creek feed grounds.

Dennis Almquist and his wife Mary Ann at Elbow Lake.

I was finally able to thaw my truck out and dig all the frozen hay out of the back of it. I ran an extension cord over to my trailer and re-lit the heater. The trailer now had lights and a working refrigerator. When I re-lit the heater, I turned the thermostat to high. I lay in bed that night wondering how my family was doing in Shell. I was missing them. I found a book in the trailer titled "Elk Management in Wyoming" I started to read the book under the dim light above my bed.

The next morning, I again awoke frozen solid. The damn heater went out again! The only thing that wasn't frozen was in the refrigerator. I looked out the trailer window and could see Bernie unsaddling his mule, Woodrow. There was a horse corral right next to my trailer that Bernie would put his mule in on the days that he rode him to work. I wasn't sure why Bernie liked to ride his mule to work. It had to have been a damn cold trip from his house that morning. I jumped out of my trailer to head for the office to take another warm shower. Duke pulled up next to me and rolled down his window. He smiled and said, "Are you staying warm in that trailer?" I replied, "Hell no, can't keep the damn heater working." I told Duke that if I couldn't get the heater working, I was going to start sleeping on the floor in my office. Duke laughed and told me that he and his wife were going to be gone for the weekend and that I was welcome to stay in his warden station which was located right across the street from the regional office. That was very kind of Duke to make me that offer and I was ready to take it. I told Duke that I would take him up on his offer. He took me over and showed me the house and where he hid the key to the front door. He asked me if I would mind taking care of his old German shepherd dog named Champ while they were gone. I told Duke that I would be happy to do that. Duke said, "Just make sure you let him out to go poop at night."

I walked across the street and met up with Dennis Almquist. Dennis was kind of grumbly that morning and said, "Well, are you ready to run up and see some new country?" I replied, "Yes, I'm excited to learn some new country." Dennis said, "Well, let me put this damn dog in the back and you can jump in the passenger seat. Dennis opened the passenger door and said, "Come on Brady, get in the back of the truck." Dennis dropped the tailgate and Brady jumped in the back of the truck. "Brady, get in your damn kennel, thank you." Dennis replied. Apparently, Dennis had named the dog after a trainee game warden that was stationed in Jackson. We headed south of Pinedale and then east to travel up to Fall Creek feed ground. The road into Fall Creek was rough and steep in places. We crawled along bouncing from one rock to another. "DAMN, this road hasn't gotten any smoother!" Dennis blurted out. I asked Dennis if we actually were able to get a semi load full of hay up to the Fall Creek feed ground. Dennis replied, "Yes, they do, I don't know how, but they do."

I spent the whole morning with Dennis. He was extremely knowledgeable about his warden district. He had been the south Pinedale game warden for over 20 years. The landowners, sportsmen, and outfitters had a great deal of respect for Dennis. I heard a lot of comments from hunters over the years, "You never know when or where you are going to run into Dennis. It could be at 13,000 feet elevation on his mule or in your backyard in town." Dennis dropped me back off at the office later that afternoon. I grabbed an air tank and headed out to Soda Lake to check on the draft horses and air up the tires on my snow machine trailer, so that I could pull it back to the office and put a new floor on it and repair the taillights.

The horses had cleaned up all the hay in the stack yard. I would need to let them back out into the 5000-acre pasture as there was no water source in the fenced area that I had them penned up in. I opened the gate and they took off a farting and bucking as they ran through the gate. I grabbed my snow machine trailer and pulled it back to the heated shop.

As I was leaving the shop Des said, "You need to call Kathy Rebescher. She has about 600 elk that just showed up on the feed ground and she needs to start feeding before the elk drop off onto the Fayette Ranch. She would like you to catch her draft horses and haul them up

Scott C. Werbelow

ASAP, before you can't drive up there anymore." I grabbed the phone and called Kathy at a house that she was renting in Bargerville. She asked me if I could catch her horses named Bonnie and Clyde. She said they were both sorrels with white socks on their front legs. I said, "Shit, I just let all the horses out of the small pasture thirty minutes ago." I told her that I would go out first thing in the morning and try and catch her horses. She offered to help and I said, "Naw, I can get it Kathy." She also told me to grab the harnesses for Bonnie and Clyde out of the Quonset hut in Pinedale and bring them up as well. "Oh, and grab me about four sacks of grain for my horses, please." I agreed and told Kathy I would be at the feed ground before noon.

I hooked up my horse trailer and had everything ready by nightfall. It was snowing hard again. I walked over to the Quonset hut and loaded up the harness and collars for Kathy's team. Hopefully I had the right harness and collars as there were about ten pair of them hanging on the wall. But hers had little tags on them that read Bonnie and Clyde. I even found four tire chains hanging on the wall. I threw them in my tool box along with some bungy cords.

I was pretty excited that I got to stay at Duke's warden station that night and not freeze to death in the trailer again. I grabbed some stuff out of the trailer and walked over to Duke's house. The house was warm. I turned on the TV and watched a western movie. This was a real treat. I hadn't watched a movie forever. That movie was so good that I watched another one. I woke up at about 6:00 AM, with my clothes still on, sitting in Duke's recliner. Shit, I thought to myself. I had fallen asleep at some point and forgot to let Duke's dog Champ out to go poop! I jumped out of my chair and could smell something nasty. I looked in the dining room, Champ had had an accident on the carpet. This was the biggest accident that I had ever seen in my life. There was nasty diarrhea strung the entire length of the dining room, and man did it stink!! I looked at Champ and said, "Sorry buddy, my fault." I don't deal well at all with dog poop or baby poop. I started gagging and went outside and puked in Duke's front yard. Champ followed me and tried to clean it up the best that he could. I think he felt bad for pooping on the floor and just wanted to make it right with me. I went back into the house. I honestly could not stomach to clean up the dog mess. This would require like a professional shampooer and a ventilator mask. I did not know what to do, so I just left it. I would play dumb with Duke and tell him I didn't know anything about it!

I warmed up my truck and headed out to Soda Lake to catch Kathy's horses. I entered the unit. The horses saw the horse trailer and ran to the top of Fremont Ridge with their tails in the air. I don't know how many miles I hiked that day or how many new curse words I came up with, but it was a lot. It was now noon. I had finally coaxed the horses into the new stack yard and shut the gate. There were now about thirty-five draft horses running up and down the aisles in the stack yard. They were kicking, fighting, squealing and running back and forth. Out of all the horses there were only four sorrel-colored horses. And all four sorrel-colored horses had white socks on their front feet. It was a crap shoot for which horses were actually Kathy's. After about 75 laps around the hay shed it became apparent to me that I was not going to catch any horses. I finally got them all in a corner and ran a long rope across the alley way so that they couldn't escape. I grabbed an old rubber feed bucket out of the horse shed and put some rocks in it. I still hadn't had time to stop by the feed store and purchase any grain.

I grabbed a couple of halters and hung them around my neck as I entered the stack yard. I shook my bucket and talked calmly to the horses. (Even though I was pissed.) It took several attempts, but I finally got two sorrel horses caught and put in the horse trailer. I was actually pretty proud of myself. I opened the stack yard gate and turned the horses loose. It was about 2:00 PM, I jumped into my truck and started to head down the road. I looked up and there was a two-tone brown Chevy pickup with a topper coming down the road towards me. As the truck pulled up next to me, I noticed it was Kathy. She jumped out of the truck and said, "Did you get them caught?" I said, "Yes ma'am!" She walked over to the horse trailer and said, "NOPE, wrong ones. Those aren't Bonnie and Clyde!" I was so mad I couldn't even say SHIT! Kathy said, "I have some grain in my truck, I will help you catch the right ones." We drove back to the feed ground and found the draft horses again. Kathy jumped out of her truck, grabbed a bucket of grain and a couple halters and started walking out to the horses. She yelled, "COME BONNIE, COME CLYDE!" Both horses left the herd of horses and trotted down to her. She caught both of them in less than five minutes. I couldn't believe what I had just witnessed. Those horses both knew Kathy and they hadn't seen her since last spring.

I headed for Fall Creek feed ground. It was snowing hard and the snow was getting deep. I pulled over and chained up my truck all the way around. There were a couple of spots where I didn't think that I was going to make it. I gave it the onion and just kept chewing my way up the steep hills. When I arrived at the feed ground there were about 600 elk standing there wanting fed. This was one of the coolest things that I had ever seen in my life. I don't think I had ever seen this many elk in one bunch before, and some of the bulls were huge. I couldn't wait to actually get out and feed elk with the feeders. This was going to be the best job in the whole world, I thought to myself. As I got out of my truck, the snow was level with my floorboard. I couldn't believe that I actually made it up there with a horse trailer loaded with draft horses.

I returned home to my trailer house. The heater was out again. I walked over to Duke's house to let Champ out. The smell in the house from Champ's accident was absolutely horrible. There would be no way that I could stay in the house a second night with the rancid smell. I felt horrible about the situation, but I could not bring myself to clean it up. Just walking in the house made me gag! I would sleep on the floor in my little cubicle upstairs in the office. At least it would be warm and I could make a few phone calls from my office phone.

I called my boss, Ron Dean, that night and told him that the draft horses were in dire need of having their feet trimmed, manes roached, and they all needed wormed. He told me there was a guy in Star Valley named Dale Clark that had a trimming table. The table picks the draft horses up off the ground and lays them on their side. Once on their side in a squeeze chute you can roach their mane, trim their feet and worm them. I also told Ron that the snow was piling up and that I would really need to focus on getting draft horses delivered to feed grounds while I could still drive into them. It was only mid-November. I felt like it was time to start feeding on all feed grounds. I got a hold of Dale Clark later that night. I explained my situation to him with snow getting deep and my need to get horses delivered to the feed grounds. Dale said he was plenty busy but understood my situation and agreed to meet me at the Soda Lake feed ground on Monday morning at 7:00 AM. I was pretty pleased with that level of service. I also learned that Dale and his family had a long history of feeding elk for the department over on the Star Valley side. I would need to spend all day Sunday and repair an old horse corral that I had located near Soda Lake. I would also have to figure out how to get the horses in the corral and provide them with food and water so that they would be ready for Dale when he arrived.

I didn't sleep very well that night on the floor in my office. My mind was racing all night on how I was going to get 35 draft horses in a small corral and ready for trimming by Monday morning. I was also stressing about how I was going to get all the horses delivered to the feed grounds with the snow piling up so quickly. If elk showed up on feed grounds and there was no hay for them to eat, they would quickly move down country and cause damage to cattle feed lines and rancher's hay stacks. We would then spend all winter moving the elk back to feed grounds with snow machines. Once elk reach lower elevations, it becomes more difficult to move elk back up country in the deep snow. Elk don't migrate up country when the snow continues to get deeper as they go.

I looked at the thermometer in my truck. It read -24 degrees when I tried to start my truck, it turned over very slowly about three times and went click, click, click. Shit, the battery was dead. And it was Sunday and the feed store would be closed. I had meant to pick up some four-way grain that might help me catch horses. It was about this time, I wondered if any of the game wardens were working in the -24-degree temperatures on a Sunday morning. All the hunting seasons were closed by now. They were probably in their warm beds sleeping in.

I hooked up a battery charger to my truck and plugged in the block heater for about an hour. The truck finally started, although It took forever to warm up. The bench seat was frozen solid and the power steering pump made a loud whining noise. If I would have been thinking I could have parked my truck in the heated shop. While my truck was warming up, I walked over to the Quonset hut and entered a small room that stored feed ground supplies and equipment. I found a hammer and a can full of large nails, some barbed wire and a chain saw. I would need to mix oil and gas for the chainsaw and hope that it would start. I picked up an old green army tarp full of mouse shit. Low and behold, there sat a half bag of four-way grain that I could use to help catch the draft horses. This put a smile on my face. I loaded up all the supplies and equipment that I could find to repair the old horse corral and headed for Soda Lake.

On my way to Soda Lake, I noticed Duke's patrol truck parked at the Wrangler Café. I figured I would stop and have a quick cup of coffee with him and maybe even a big breakfast. The Wrangler Café had just been moved by a large truck and trailer and placed in its current location. They served awesome food. All the wardens loved to eat there and have coffee with the local ranchers and sportsmen. I walked through the front door and Duke greeted me with a big smile and a wave. He said, "Swerb, come over and join me for a cup of coffee." I loved Duke. He was always happy and had a great attitude. The people in Pinedale also loved Duke. He had such a great personality and always made people laugh. Duke just had one of those personalities that made it difficult for anyone to ever be mad at him. If a rancher would complain to Duke about having elk eating and destroying all their hay in a hay stack, Duke would respond something like, "You don't know just how blessed you are to look out your window every morning and see a herd of elk eating your hay. Some people never get to experience that." And then he would laugh, pat them on the back and keep walking.

I bellied up to the table with Duke. He had been telling stories with an old timer named Tommy. Tommy was in his mid-eighties and drove a yellow Camaro. Tommy had just told Duke a funny story. Duke was laughing out of control. Duke said, "Tommy, this is Swerb. You need to tell him the story that you just told me," Tommy went on to tell me a story about the time that he was making some toast for breakfast. Somehow a .270 bullet had rolled out of a cupboard above the toaster. Unbeknownst to Tommy, the bullet had landed in his toaster, and after several minutes of toasting the live round went off. It blew the toaster plumb to pieces and shattered the front window in his kitchen. Tommy said that it scared the crap out of him and was the loudest damn noise that he had ever heard in his life. Duke finally finished laughing and looked over at me and said, "Champ must have had a bellyache while you were dog-sitting." I replied, "Why, he seemed fine to me." Duke replied, "I got home late last night, took my shoes off at the front door and could smell something absolutely horrible. I walked across the dining room to turn on the light and stepped in dog poop. Champ had crapped all the way across the dining room floor." Duke went on to say that he couldn't stomach it anymore and had to leave the house. I couldn't think of a good response, I just said, "Oh the hell, ya say!"

Duke loved to visit (Bullshit) with the locals. Sometimes I would show up for breakfast at the Wrangler and talk so long with locals that I would end up ordering lunch as well before I got out of there. I had a big day ahead of me and needed to get going. I soon arrived at Soda Lake and found the herd of draft horses near the corral. I spent several hours repairing the old corral and fence. The chainsaw actually started and was fairly sharp. I put five bales of hay in the corral and spread it out. I poured some oats in a bucket and walked towards the herd of horses shaking the bucket. A couple of horses turned and started walking towards me. Once they figured out that I had a bucket of goodies, it became a dangerous situation. All the horses wanted a bite of grain at the same time and began fighting, kicking, and biting one another. I ended up almost running towards the corral to keep out of their way. I dumped the bucket full of grain in several different places in the corral and jumped over the fence. I couldn't believe it all the horses had entered the corral for a bite to eat. I quickly shut the gate with a big smile on my face. The corral system that I had built actually allowed the horses to drink water out of Soda Lake while they were in the corral.

As I left the horses that day, I felt much less stressed. The horses were all caught and would be ready for the horse trimmer in the morning. Once I had the horses caught and trimmed, I would leave them all in the corral and spend several days hauling horses to various feed grounds. I would haul all of the horses and not worry about that anymore. I drove back into Pinedale and stopped by the local veterinarian's office. It was Sunday afternoon and I couldn't believe the doctor was actually there. He was walking a horse sick with colic. He handed off the horse to his vet technician and introduced himself to me. His name was Dr. Dean. We visited shortly and I asked him if he had any wormer for draft horses. He soon fixed me up with a large bottle of liquid Ivermectin with a stainless-steel attachment that screwed onto the top of the bottle to administer the wormer. It was simple, set the amount of CC's that you wanted to administer to the horse and pull the trigger back. Dr. Dean was very knowledgeable and helpful, and I was thankful that he was at the office that day.

I drove back to the office and rifled through the small room in the Quonset hut that contained feed ground equipment and supplies. I found an old box that contained electric horse hair clippers. I also found an old generator and was able to get it running. Before I knew it, I was ready to worm and roach draft horses in the morning. I wasn't sure how this trimming table was going to work, or how the large draft horses were going to react to it. Anything that can pick a 2000 lb. draft horse off the ground and lay them on their side has potential for things to go really wrong.

The next morning was only -15 below zero. I had parked my truck in the heated shop. It started much better this time and the bench seat wasn't frozen. I arrived at Soda Lake feed ground at about 6:30 AM. To my amazement, the horse trimmer was already set up next to the horse corral and already had three horses caught and tied outside of the corral. I could hear the sound of a generator running in the background. I walked over and introduced myself to Dale. Dale gave me a firm handshake and said, "Pleasure to meet you, sir." I thanked him for changing his schedule and coming over to Pinedale at a minute's notice. I asked him to show me how everything worked. Basically, you lead the horse into a large squeeze chute. Place a heavy-duty belt under the horse's chest behind its front legs and another heavy-duty belt around the horse's mid-section. The machine lifts the horse off the ground. Once the horse was off the ground Dale would pull another lever and the chute would slowly turn the horse onto its side. Once the horse was off the ground, they really couldn't fight it much. I asked Dale if it would be alright for me to roach the horse's mane and worm them while they were strapped on the table. Dale said, "That will be fine, but we will have each horse trimmed in less than five minutes, so be quick." As the horse lay on its side, there was another heavy strap that went across the horse's neck so that they couldn't flail around and hurt themselves. Dale had a couple young boys assisting him, they both seemed pretty horse savvy.

I quickly got set up and plugged my clippers into Dale's generator. Dale led the first horse into the squeeze chute, hooked all the straps up and pulled a hydraulic lever. The sound of the generator bogged way down as it lifted the heavy horse off the ground. The horse was not impressed, but only fought back for a short bit. Once the horse was on its side, Dale and the two boys would strap Velcro hobbles around the horse's lower legs. This prevented the horse from being able to kick them. They each quickly pulled out a large pair of diamond horse nippers and went to work trimming. They essentially did three feet at one time. Once they were done with that, Dale pulled out a large Makita grinder and cleaned up each foot while another guy finished trimming the last foot. They were done trimming the horse quicker than I could roach the mane and worm the horse. I would need to speed things up on my end. My first couple haircuts looked pretty pathetic but I got better as I went. It was fast and furious for about three hours. Dale shut the generator off and all 35 horses were standing in the corral trimmed, wormed, and had a beautiful haircut. I couldn't believe we were done that quickly and that it went so easily. I thanked Dale and shook his hand. Dale gave me an invoice for his work. I think he charged $30.00/horse. I wasn't sure how I would get him paid, but I would figure it out. I don't believe those horses had ever been trimmed on a table before or for that matter ever trimmed at all. I was pretty proud of my accomplishment that day and would make this an annual event each fall.

I would meet with Bernie Holz on Tuesday morning and give him an update on my progress with the draft horses and deep snow conditions on several feed grounds. I told Bernie that I had all the draft horses trimmed, roached and wormed in three hours yesterday. Bernie replied, "WOWZER, that's a good lick!" Bernie then handed me a fat red three-ring binder book that read "Feed Ground Operational Plans" he said, "You'll want to read this when you get a minute. There are certain employees in the region who have developed a "Cook Book" plan to feeding elk." Bernie then advised me that it would be a good lick to get the draft horses hauled into Finnegan and North Piney feed grounds before the snow got any deeper. Bernie offered to show me where those two feed grounds were located, as he used to be the Big Piney game warden and those feed grounds were located in his old game warden district. He offered to help me catch and load the horses for both of those feed grounds first thing in the morning.

Bernie jumped in with me the next morning and we headed out to Soda Lake. I was always nervous when I was around Bernie. He was just kind of hard to talk to and communicate with. Maybe I would get to

Draft horse being trimmed.

know him better on this trip and feel more at ease when I was around him. Bernie was a very intelligent man. His thinking was very analytical, which was probably why he became a supervisor. We arrived at the horse corral. Bernie was impressed with how well the horses looked. He also liked my new corral system. He jumped out of the truck and asked, "You want me to catch Kent and Doug for Finnegan feed ground? I said, "Sure, I don't even know which horses go up there." He said, "Yea, Kent and Doug have been at Finnegan for years. Kent is named after Kent Schmidlin, Lander supervisor, and Doug is named after long time Jackson game warden, Doug Crawford." Both Kent and Doug were huge draft horses. Doug Crawford stood over 6'-5." Maybe that's why someone named the horse

Draft horse on trimming table.

after him?

Bernie loaded Kent and Doug up and asked, "What horses do you want for Tim Baxley up at North Piney feed ground? I told Bernie to catch the matching pair of sorrel Belgians with the white socks. Apparently, this team was very young and had just been broke by one of Ron's feeders on the Jackson end the previous winter. My guess was this team was 3-4 years old. They were a beautifully matched team and very big and stout. Bernie recommended that if we were going to put a young team in North Piney, we should also grab a spare older horse in case something went wrong. It was difficult for me to pick a spare horse because I didn't know any of the horses and I didn't want to mess up another feeder's team of horses. I learned over time that when the draft horses are settled in a herd, their mate will usually be right next to them or very close by. They spend so much time together cooped up in a corral all winter and working together as a team that they become really close to one another. Bernie looked up and said, "I'll grab Joy, I know she is a spare horse because I have fed with her before on North Piney. Joy was another large draft horse mare that was bay-colored. As Bernie loaded Joy, he said, "I think they named this one after a previous Office Manager in Jackson." I replied, "Hopefully she's not a little Bucky!"

We got loaded up and headed for Big Piney. I was really happy to have Bernie's help. Once we got just north of Big Piney, Bernie asked me if I had ever met the new Big Piney game warden Brad Hovinga. I told Bernie that I thought I had met him when I took the Wyoming game warden's exam in Cheyenne awhile back. I could remember Brad was there to help proctor the exam. He was a young guy, probably close to my age. Bernie said, "I really like Brad, he's a great game warden," I had never heard Bernie compliment anyone before, so those words stuck with me. Bernie told me to pull into the warden station in Big Piney and he would introduce me to Brad. The Big Piney warden station also had a large metal Quonset hut for storing equipment. There was also a horse corral located next to the Quonset hut that had running water running through the corral. Bernie recommended that I leave the three North Piney horses in the corral and haul them tomorrow. He felt that it would be too long of a day to fight our way into both feed grounds with the deep snow. Bernie told me that getting into North Piney and back would be a full day in itself. Brad was not home. I would have to meet him another day. We dropped the three horses and headed for Finnegan.

We had to drive right through a rancher's front yard as we headed up the hill towards Finnegan. Bernie told me that the department had a long history of fighting with this landowner because he didn't like the department having an easement right through his front yard. Bernie said, "Don't piss this guy off, because he can close 13 gates between here and the feed ground if he wants to. Apparently, this guy would close all the gates with a fence stretcher every fall when we were trying to haul hay with a semi through his place. The hay hauler would have to stop on every hill with a loaded truck of hay to open each gate. The loads of hay were heavy. It was difficult to get the semi-trucks moving forward again because of the steep terrain. Hay haulers had gone through several clutches and transmissions while hauling hay into Finnegan over the past few years. Evidently, last year, the landowner parked a ranch truck in the way, so that the hay hauler couldn't get through the complicated corral system while pulling a pup. The hay hauler barely made it through without running over the ranch truck. So, the landowner backed it up a few more feet so that the hay hauler couldn't get back out later that night. The hay hauler realized what he had done, got mad, and just ran over the ranch truck with his semi-truck. This situation was still in some sort of a lawsuit when I arrived.

I would do my best to get along with this landowner. We headed through the front yard of the ranch house. Nobody came running out shooting at us, so that was good. It had been snowing all day and the snow was piling up. Bernie recommended that we put tire chains on before we get to the last steep hill before the feed ground. We chained up all the way around. The snow was drifted and deep and the hill was steep. I parked at the bottom of the hill. It didn't look like there was any way I could pull a horse trailer up that hill with the deep drifting snow conditions. Bernie looked at me and said, "We may want to unload the horses here and walk them in." The word "Can't" was not in my vocabulary. I looked at Bernie and said, "Hold on, this is going to be a tank slapper!" I put the truck in four-low and gave it the onion!! We almost made it to the top and I finally spun out. The hill was so steep and slick that once I spun out, I immediately headed back down the hill backwards with a horse trailer full of draft horses. Bernie's eyes were big as silver dollars, and I think he thought about jumping out of the truck for just a second. The thought even crossed my mind! I held the steering wheel tight and away we went for about 100 yards backwards. We finally came to a sudden stop. The horses fell down in the trailer. I looked at Bernie and said, "I think we should probably go ahead and walk the horses in from here!" Bernie giggled and said, "Damn, that was scary!" and I'm pretty sure Bernie wasn't afraid of anything.

We ended up walking the horse's uphill in knee-deep snow for the next two miles. The wind was starting to pick up and visibility from blowing snow made it difficult to see anything. As we approached the feed ground, there were about 300 elk standing by the stack yard waiting to be fed. We put the horses in the corral, made sure their water system was working properly and dragged a bale of hay from the stack yard over to the horse corral to feed the horses. The elk were not afraid of us at all. We walked right through the herd dragging the bale for the horses. Several elk acted like they wanted to eat the bale while we were dragging it. Bernie looked up and said, "Shit, we better drag about 10 bales of hay out and feed these elk before they leave and end up on the ranchers place below us. This was why that feed ground was created years ago, to keep elk off private property. We couldn't harness up the team and use them because the harnesses were still in the front of the horse trailer at the bottom of the hill. Crap, we should have harnessed the team before we walked them in. I would need to bring the harnesses up tomorrow with a snow machine. I could probably fit my snow machine in the horse trailer with the three North Piney horses and run them in tomorrow.

I formulated that plan while Bernie and I dragged 10 bales of hay out of the stack yard and spread them on the feed ground. The elk were trying to eat the hay as we spread the bales around. It was a beautiful sight with the large wet snowflakes blowing around and the elk standing so close in the background. Bernie took me over and showed me what they called the "Brown Turd." It was an old beat-up brown camp trailer that sat on the feed ground for the feeder to stay in. This would be Tim Baxley's home for the next 5-6 months. I opened the door and observed a packrat's nest on the bed that was made out of loose hay and bailing twines. The

Scott C. Werbelow

trailer was completely full of mouse turds and stunk like rat piss. I thought, OH DEAR LORD, THIS TRAILER IS GOING TO REQUIRE SOME SERIOUS CLEANING.

Bernie and I barely made it out of there that night, even with an empty horse trailer and down-hill travel. The road had drifted in and would no longer be passable with a truck. I thought to myself that was perfect timing to get the horses in. I felt like Bernie and I bonded that day. We had to accomplish some important work together and we did it. On the way back to Pinedale I asked Bernie if he had a chance to visit with Wildlife Administration about me being able to keep my law enforcement equipment and doing some game warden work. He told me that that decision had not yet been made. He also told me the reason that the previous feed ground manager had left and why. Apparently, he had a drinking problem and had been fired. The previous employee that had been fired had 90 days to appeal the decision. We wouldn't know anything until that ninety days was up. I appreciated Bernie's honesty and was told to keep that to myself.

Chapter 6

ONE HELL OF A WINTER

I was getting really tired of sleeping on the floor in my office. I would have to get up very early every morning and get showered before any other employees showed up to work. It was embarrassing to me to sleep on the floor in my cubicle in my sleeping bag. I had been so busy with work that I had not had any time to look for a rental. I couldn't even think about buying a place at this moment in time, because I didn't even know if I would have a job in three more months. I had visited with a few other employees and they told me that it was nearly impossible to find a place to rent, and if you were lucky to find a place it would be very expensive. What if the guy that got fired, appealed the decision and was allowed to come back to work? I thought to myself.

All feed grounds needed started and all horses needed to be hauled immediately. There was only one of me and not enough time in the day to get my work completed. I would need to run up to North Piney and Finnegan and get Tim Baxley started immediately. There was also a trailer at North Piney feed ground that Tim would be staying in. He would need to ride his snow machine between North Piney and Finnegan feed grounds daily to get both feed grounds fed. Tim was supposed to work on purchasing a snow machine and get moved into the trailer houses.

I had waited too long to get the draft horses into North Piney. I drove my truck up to the Forest boundary on the Middle Piney road and that was as far as I could make it. I ended up loading the harnesses for Kent and Doug on my snow machine and hauled them into Finnegan feed ground. Tim was not there. I was hoping he had snow machined into North Piney. His old brown Ford (named the Brown Turd) was parked at the forest boundary with a solar panel hooked to his battery to keep it charged. The old brown Ford was on its last leg and had seen many tough miles. Tim had a little sleeper mounted in the back of his truck, just in case he needed a place to stay away from home. I also noticed that there was a grey cat running around the inside of the small sleeper. It was meowing at me with its little face pressed up against the window. I didn't know how to get into North Piney yet, as I had never been there. The snow was extremely deep and the wind was blowing. I went back to meet with Big Piney game warden, Brad Hovinga, to see if he could help me snow machine into North Piney. I soon arrived at Brad's warden station and banged on his front door. Brad opened the door and said, "Good to see you, Swerbe, welcome to the Pinedale region. Come in for a cup of coffee." I was impressed that Brad had remembered who I was and even knew my nickname, Swerbe. We had a cup of coffee and I explained my situation to him. Brad said, "You bet I can help. Give me a few minutes to hook onto my snow machine trailer."

We went out to the Quonset hut and Brad showed me around the building. He showed me a spare Game and Fish truck that was parked in the Quonset hut. He said, "This truck belongs to the feed ground program and is used to feed elk at Bench Corral feed ground, along with that flatbed trailer." I asked, "Where is Bench Corral feed ground?" Brad replied, "Just north of here, I will take you out and show you that one when you have time." I looked the truck over. Heck it was in much better condition than the truck that I was currently using. I may have to consider trading the two trucks out down the road. I unloaded the three draft horses and left them in Brad's corral. Brad told me that we could probably walk the horses in from the bottom through the Gutherie and Rathburn place if need be. Brad only had a single-wide snow machine trailer so I ended up loading my snow machine in the back of the horse trailer and followed Brad to the forest boundary. Once we arrived in the parking lot, we ran into Tim. Tim had tried to snow machine in from the parking lot up the draw headed northwest, but couldn't make it up the steep hill. Tim was covered in ice and snow and said he had been stuck most of the morning. Brad said he would show us the way up through the forest boundary, as he had never been on the trail over Johnson ridge before. Brad told us that we may need to get a hold of the previous North Piney feeder to have him show us the trail over the top and down through the trees. He said, "I think it can get a little hairy when you drop over the ridge down through the thick timber. You'll want to know where the trail is or you may get stuck and never get out of there."

Tim was riding an old beat-up snow machine. Brad gave Tim a hard time about his beat-up snow machine, four bald tires on his Ford truck and his solar-powered battery charger. Tim just laughed and took the sarcasm in stride and said, "Sometimes you gotta do what you gotta do to survive in today's world. I only got $500 invested in that truck and $200 invested in this here snow-eating son of a bitch of a snow machine. We both laughed and Tim said, "We better get going. I have lots of elk to feed." Brad said, "You don't even have any draft horses to feed with yet." Tim said, "That's alright man, I can pull one bale at a time with this here snow machine. And, I even have a homemade snow machine sled that I built sitting at the feed ground."

We all three headed into North Piney. Brad started out in the lead and soon became stuck in the deep snow. I went around him and cut trail as far as I could go and became stuck as well. Tim was nowhere to be found. We both got unstuck and turned around to look for Tim. I soon noticed a set of snow machine tracks that went off a steep embankment to my right. I stopped and observed Tim clear down in the creek bottom below us. He was so stuck that all we could see was his windshield sticking

171

out of the snow. Brad and I laughed. I yelled, "TIM WHAT THE HELL ARE YOU DOING DOWN THERE?" Tim yelled back, "I'M ALRIGHT BOSS MAN, JUST GOT SUCKED OFF THE TRAIL A BIT, I'LL BE UP IN A MINUTE!" Brad and I cut a trail down to him and we both ended up stuck a couple of times trying to get him out. We finally made it back up to the main road again. The wind was blowing and the visibility was very poor. We agreed that we would leap frog into the feed ground. When one person became stuck the other was not to let up, just go around whoever was stuck and keep the momentum up breaking trail until we reached the feed ground. It took us several hours to reach the feed ground. We were tired and wet. The elk were standing on the feed ground wanting fed when we arrived.

We had to dig the gates out to the stack yard with a scoop shovel to get them open. We used all three snow machines and dragged one bale at a time until we had fed the elk about 20 bales. We then took the snow machines down country and broke a trail in the snow to walk the draft horses in from the bottom up. I looked at my odometer on my snow machine, I would have to walk the three draft horses nine miles to get them to the feed ground. We turned around and went back through the Forest boundary. It was much easier this time as we had already broken a trail. Once we got back to Tim's truck, Brad agreed to help Tim break trail into Finnegan and help him feed with the team. I would run back down to Big Piney and grab the horses and walk them into North Piney. I was hoping that I could remember all the roads that I needed to take to get my truck and trailer to the location where we had turned our snow machines around. Brad had given me keys to all the locked gates that I would need to travel through on private property.

I filled my snow machine up with gas, and loaded the horses and snow machine in the horse trailer. If you haven't ever tried to load a running snow machine with a headlight into a horse trailer with three draft horses you truly haven't lived life to its fullest. I finally arrived at the locked green gate on the Gutherie place. I dragged my snow machine out of the back of the trailer and unloaded the horses. I put the harness on each horse, pig-tailed them together and led the horses into the feed ground behind my snow machine. If you have never tried leading three draft horses behind a snow machine in belly-deep snow for nine miles, you should also check that off your bucket list of stupid things to do. The problem was, I couldn't go slowly on the snow machine or I would get stuck. If I got stuck, I couldn't get going again, because the lead horse was tied to my rear bumper and would spook and pull back. This exercise had already shot me over the handle bars once. I couldn't hold onto the lead rope with one hand and run the throttle with the other, because the lead horse would pull back once in a while and jerk the lead rope out of my left hand. I finally found that once I got the horses lined out, and in a trot, that worked the best. I had to lead Joy the mare because the two matched Belgian's were young and full of piss and vinegar and didn't want to play nice.

I finally made it to the feed ground just before nightfall. Man, what a day!! I had to shovel the snow away from the gate so that I could get the horses in the corral. I dragged the horses over two nice green looking hay bales and made sure their water system was working properly. I would arrive back at Brad's house at about 8:00 PM. Brad was home and invited me in for a drink. Brad and I sat down at his kitchen table and he poured me a Jack Daniels on the rocks. This may have been one of the best drinks that I had had in a long time. Brad told me that they got the elk fed at Finnegan with no problems. I was really happy to have Brad's help. We couldn't have done it without his help. I was tired, but I visited with Brad for a couple of hours. We talked about a lot of different things. I really liked Brad. We were similar in age and had a lot in common. I told Brad that I really wanted to be a game warden, but wasn't sure what path I was currently on. He told me to hang in there and stay positive and it would happen someday. I really looked up to Brad and his advice. If Bernie liked him, that meant something to me as well. Brad had told me that becoming a Wyoming game warden was a dream come true for him. He also told me that he had recently divorced and was going through some tough times.

The next morning, I stopped into the office to check my mail. I had a large box shoved in my mail box. I hadn't ordered anything so I was curious what was in the box. I quickly opened it and found a telephone in a small black carry bag. I guess they called this thing a "Bag Phone," something that you could plug into your cigarette lighter and carry with you in your truck. I couldn't wait to try mine out. Man would it be handy to be able to make calls while you were on the road. I had heard of them before, but never had enough money to afford one. Now, the department has purchased me one for my work.

Dennis came walking into the office with his snow machine suit on. He asked me if I had time to help him move some problem elk over on Richie's place. I was plenty busy, but I knew Dennis rarely asked for assistance unless he really needed it. Besides, I had never officially went on an elk drive yet. I told Dennis that I would be glad to help him. He said, "Thank you, I'm just waiting on Duke to show up and we can get out of here." Duke finally showed up, I think he was having breakfast at the Wrangler Café and got held up. I followed Duke and Dennis south of Pinedale out to the Richie place. Apparently, there was a group of about fifty elk that had been getting into a hay stack and causing damage. There were cattle nearby and Dennis did not want them to end up on a cattle feedline co-mingling with cattle due to brucellosis concerns.

Dennis had a brand-new purple panther arctic cat snow machine. The machine was 500 CC'S, liquid cooled and came with reverse. Dennis pulled his reverse lever and backed it off his trailer while Duke and I broke our backs dragging our machines off the trailer backwards. I think the only reason Dennis wanted to move elk that day was to try out his new machine with reverse. No one else in the region had a snow machine with reverse and he was pretty proud of it. Dennis's warden district was an absolute rock pile. It was not fun moving elk in his district due to all the large boulders that were hidden just beneath the snow. Dennis explained to Duke and me where the elk were located and where he wanted to try and move them over the sound of his running snow machine. I was excited. This would be my first official elk drive on a snow machine. I wished that I had my personal sled as it had way more horse power and track to get through the deep snow. Dennis explained that he wanted to try and take the elk up Muddy Ridge and on over to Muddy Creek feed ground.

Dennis on his brand new purple Panther.

I followed in behind Duke and Dennis as we sped wide open across an open hay field. We finally got the elk moving north up a steep hill covered in boulders. We all carried portable radios and could communicate with one another when need be. Dennis told us that we couldn't make it up the hill due to all the large boulders. So, we would have to go a long distance to get around the steep hill and get caught back up with the elk. We would all get separated and nobody knew where the elk were located. I finally located the elk and they were headed back down towards the hay field. I hauled ass towards the herd of elk to try and turn them back to the north. I came across a small river that had open water and many huge boulders. If I didn't hurry and get across the river, the elk would be right back where we started with them. I wasn't sure just what to do, because I didn't want to lose the elk and I didn't want to tear up my snow machine on the rocks in the open water. I started across the river very slowly and ended up getting stuck in the middle of the river between two large boulders. I wasn't sure what to do because the water was about waist deep if I were to get off my machine. I really didn't want to get that wet. About that time, I heard the sound of two snow machines. I looked up to see Dennis and Duke hauling ass right towards me. I thought they were coming to rescue me. NOPE, they hauled ass right by me, one on my left and one on my right. Both of them threw a wall of ice-cold water on me from both sides as they hovered across the top of the water in the creek. Neither one of them got stuck, they just kept going after the elk and got them turned and headed back to the north.

I was soaking wet, and a little miffed that they didn't have the common courtesy to stop and help me get unstuck. I soon learned that these guys were "trained professionals" at moving elk and didn't let anything get in their way. I jumped off my machine into waist deep ice-cold water and jerked my machine off the large boulder and got it turned around. I went back the same way that I had come and turned around. This time I gave it the onion and sailed across the river. I followed their snow machine tracks for miles before I caught back up with them. They just looked over at me and gave me the thumbs up as if to say, "Glad you finally made it." I soon learned that if you got stuck on an elk drive, you are probably going to be on your own. We would end up getting this group of elk successfully back to the Muddy Creek feed ground.

Dennis asked me if Frosty had started feeding yet. I told him that I wasn't sure, but that I would call him from my new bag phone once we got back to the truck, and tell him to throw some hay out. Dennis said, "You better make sure you have this cleared first with the BFH crew first." (Brucellosis, Feed ground, Habitat) Apparently, we have BFH biologists that have a say when we actually started feeding at each feed ground.

Maybe this was the large red three-ring binder that Bernie had given to me and I hadn't had time to look at yet. Dennis said, "Oh yea, don't throw any hay out too early or you will get your ass chewed!" I would need to look into this. I was a ranch kid, it seemed pretty simple to me, if you had elk standing on a feed ground wanting fed, feed them before you lose them! Once you lose them, you spend all winter chasing them off private property back to the feed ground that you could have held them at in the first place. But apparently the department had gone through a process called TQM (Teaching Quality Management) and had decided to try and save some money by holding off and feeding the elk later. The department hired BFH biologists to improve habitat conditions with an effort to reduce time elk spent on feed grounds. Basically, start feeding them later and quit feeding them earlier. This would save the department money and reduce the prevalence of brucellosis by not congregating elk as long on feed grounds. I would need to visit more with Ron and Bernie about this.

We returned back to our trucks and loaded up our snow machines. Dennis and Duke came walking over to my truck and said, "Bag phone, what the hell is a bag phone?" I showed them my new bag phone and made a call to Frosty Hittle the elk feeder at Muddy feed ground. I told Frosty to throw out some "Monitoring Bales" I was now getting the proper terminology down for initiating feeding on a feed ground. Dennis and Duke wanted to know where their bag phones were. I said, "I don't know, didn't you get yours yet?" Dennis had a sled with reverse, but he didn't have a bag phone yet.

I would call my wife Lana that night from my new bag phone. I was so happy to have this new technology. I begged her to come see me and bring my new snow machine up with her. She asked, "Where are me and the kids going to stay? In your meat locker of a trailer house or on your office floor?" I asked her to see if she could get a babysitter for a couple of days and come see me. I told her I would pay for a motel room, as Duke had not offered me his house again.

I spent the next day hauling horses into Scab Creek feed ground. Bob Klaren was the feeder at this feed ground. He had been feeding for many years and didn't need much help getting started. All he needed was his team of horses and some grain and he was good to go. Bob didn't have any water source to water his horses at Scab Creek. He would pull a small sled behind his snow machine daily with thirty gallons of water for two draft horses and his black and white collie dog. I was really excited to actually get to hitch up a team of horses and feed elk. Bob said we could go ahead and hook up his team and feed out some hay. Bob's feed ground was a rock pile, and he didn't have much area to spread the elk out due to rough terrain and huge boulders. Bob had been feeding there long enough that he knew where all the bad rocks were located to avoid running over them with the hay sled in the deep snow.

Bob and I stacked about twenty bales of hay onto the feed sled. Bob cut all of strings on the hay bales with a large knife and told his team to "Get Up". The draft horses dropped their heads and I felt a jerk as the sled started moving forward. I couldn't believe the power of the draft horses. They pulled a sled full of hay up a steep hill in the deep snow almost effortlessly as they parted through about 600 elk. The elk were talking and mewing to one another. Occasionally a couple of cow elk would stand on their hind feet, lay their ears back and strike at one another with their front feet. Bob had a line in each hand and maneuvered his team around the large rocks. I saw something that day that I had never seen before. Bob's black and white collie dog was feeding hay to the elk. The dog would use its front paws and nose to flake hay off the sled to the elk. If Bob wanted the dog to stop feeding elk, Bob would turn around and say, "That will do," and the dog would stop feeding. This was the first time that I actually got to feed the elk using a team of horses and a hay sled with bobs. I thought to myself, this is the coolest job in the world. I returned back to Pinedale with a smile on my face.

The horse-catching was getting easier. I had learned to grab the horses that I needed each day at Soda Lake, haul them to the office and

Elk being fed on a feedground.

keep them in the corral over-night. This way I could feed and water them
and get an early start each day hauling draft horses. My next feed ground
to haul horses to would be Jewett. Donny Calhoun was the feeder at this
feed ground. Donny was an older guy, probably in his fifties, and had
been feeding elk for the department for many years. Donny met me out at
Soda Lake and showed me which draft horses went to Jewett. We picked
out an extra horse to put at Jewett just in case one of the others became
lame or sick. Jewett feed ground was located in deep snow country right
at the base of the Wyoming Range mountain. Once Jewett snowed up, you
would not be able to get another horse in there if you needed to.

Scott C. Werbelow

I followed Donny in his white Ford Bronco up to Jewett feed ground. It was a long way up there, but the county road had just been plowed. We drove through a large ranch called the Antelope Run ranch. This ranch was huge and looked like a beautiful ranch to me. Donny stopped at the ranch headquarters and introduced me to the ranch manager. Apparently, the Game and Fish had an easement through the ranch. I visited with the ranch manager briefly. He seemed like an old time Wyoming cowboy to me. I really enjoyed my visit with him. I would like to stop by when I had more time and get to know him better. I had a great deal of respect for this man just knowing the work that must be done daily on a ranch of this size. It sounded like the owners of the ranch were millionaires and only visited the ranch a couple times a summer. The owners had a nine thousand square foot home that sat on top of a large hill where they could see most of the ranch from their home. They called it the "Hill House," the ranch manager called it the "Hell House." They also each owned their own leer jet and had a runway on the ranch that was larger than the runways in both Pinedale and Jackson.

We drove another 3-4 miles from the ranch headquarters to finally arrive at Jewett feed ground. The feed ground actually sat on a state section and was completely surrounded by private property. The hay sheds at this feed ground were much longer than other feed grounds. It looked to me like they held much more hay underneath them compared to others that I had been to. I also noticed that there was a row of pine trees that had been planted on the west side of the hay sheds. The pine trees had fences built around them with some sort of irrigation system to water the trees. I asked Donny what the deal was with all the pine trees. He said, "The damn owners of the ranch didn't like looking at the hay shed from their house, so they planted all these damn trees to hide the sheds." We drove down a steep hill into a draw west of the feed ground. This hill would be difficult to come back up pulling a horse trailer. I noticed a cute little log cabin that sat right next to the horse corral. I asked Donny if the department owned the cabin and corral. He explained to me "The owners of the ranch didn't want the elk feeder traveling through their ranch every day, so they built him a cabin to stay in during the winter months". Donny also explained that they put the horse corral and cabin down in the draw because they didn't want to see any of it from their (Hill house.) "The only damn thing that the owners wanted to see was the damn elk," Donny blurted out. The cabin was small but very nice. The horse corral had a lean-to for the horses to get in out of the wind and a place to harness them each morning.

Donny would park his vehicle at the ranch house and ride his snow machine into the feed ground. He would stay at the feed ground all week and go home for one day each weekend to catch up on chores at home. Donny had two daughters and a son who would occasionally help him feed the elk. I dropped the horses and harnesses off and followed Donny back out of there. He wanted me to follow him back home to look at his snow machine. He said he couldn't get it to start. I was always pretty good with working on snow machines, so I agreed to stop and look at it. Once at his house, Donny invited me in to meet his wife and children and have a cup of coffee. They were a very simple and hard-working family. They lived in a small rustic cabin. Donny and his family did whatever they could to make ends meet. They lived off the land, so to speak. Donny and his family loved to hunt for shed antlers and trap coyotes and bobcats to help pay the bills. Both of his daughters rode for the Green River Cattleman's Association in the Upper Green River area.

After a quick cup of coffee, I took a look at Donny's snow machine. It was an old Polaris with no hood. I'm not sure how old it was but it had seen better days. It had fuel, spark, and compression. It should run but it didn't. I removed the spark plugs and they looked fouled. I cleaned them up and sprayed some starting fluid on them to dissolve the raw gas. I put the plugs back in, held the throttle wide open and pulled the rip cord. The machine started on the first crank and ran like a top. You should have seen the smile on Donny's face. He said, "Damn, I didn't know you was such a good mechanic." I really wasn't much of a mechanic, I just got lucky once in a while. I left Donny's house that night with a strong appreciation for him and his family. They stuck together through thick and thin and each family member worked hard to put food on the table.

I drove back to the office in the dark. It was a Friday night, and I was missing my wife and kids. I wasn't sure what I was going to do for the evening, as I had nothing to entertain myself. No television, no house, no nothing! All I had was my cold house trailer and my cubicle in the office. Maybe I would go down to the Stockman's and eat dinner and shoot some pool or something, I thought to myself. I pulled up in front of the office and could not believe my eyes. My wife Lana was parked in front of the office with my truck and my new snow machine sticking out of the bed of my truck. I don't know if I was more excited to see her or the snow machine! Just kidding!! I didn't think she would come over; therefore, I had not gotten a motel room. We would end up going out for a nice dinner at the Stockman's restaurant. Finally, a date with my wife! We even got a motel room. I was excited to see Lana, apparently Grandma had agreed to watch the kids. I was excited to show Lana around the next day, but didn't feel like I could officially take a day off with everything that still needed to be done.

The next morning, I took Lana out to Soda Lake feed ground to show her the draft horses that I hadn't yet hauled. We even got to see a couple hundred of elk up on Fremont Ridge. I think Lana was starting to get more excited about coming over to Pinedale once she saw the country, the elk, and the horses. Her parent's guest ranch was closed during the winter so Lana had some time off from working as a wrangler on the guest ranch. She actually had gotten a job with a company to lay a new gas pipeline out in the hills near Greybull. This was really good money, and really hard work! She told me to keep my ears open for any jobs in the Pinedale area and to start looking for a place to rent. I think she was maybe ready to move to Pinedale. With her job laying pipeline, she only had one day off a week and needed to get headed back home to Shell. I thanked her for the surprise visit and for bringing up my new snow machine. I couldn't wait to try it out in the deep snow and blow the doors off Dennis's purple panther with reverse. We unloaded the snow machine at the office. I gave Lana a hug and kiss goodbye and told her to drive careful as the roads were very slick all the way back to Shell.

The next morning Duke asked several of us if we could help him move about 150 elk from some private property on south Beaver Creek to Franz feed ground. The snow was piling up and the elk were in a cattle feed-line about eight miles from the Franz feed ground. This would be my second official elk-drive, I was very excited to try out my new ZR-700 Mountain Cat. We all met at the Wrangler Café for breakfast. The "A" Team to move the elk that day would be Brad, Dennis, Duke, and Pinedale wildlife biologist Doug McWhirter. During breakfast Duke would give us all our instructions for the elk drive. This included where the elk were located, and how we were going to get them to the feed ground. Duke explained where we would park our trucks and unload our snow machines. Once we had the elk located, we would develop a final game plan on how to get them to the feed ground. We left the Wrangler in a convoy. Everyone had a single cab truck pulling a single place snow machine trailer. The locals always knew when the Game and Fish was moving elk somewhere because of the number of trucks traveling in a convoy through the town of Pinedale.

The day was sunny but the temperature was about -10 below zero. The snow was so deep that it covered most of the fences in the area. Some places the fences were completely covered and other places you could only see the top wire sticking above the snow. It was important to be able to navigate fences when moving elk. If you couldn't find a gate or snow-machine over the top wire, the elk could sometimes get away from you and end up in a heavy willow bottom with deep snow. Once the elk beat you to the willow bottoms, you were generally done moving elk for the day. You simply couldn't find them or get to them due to the thick willows and deep snow.

We dressed warm, unloaded our machines, and followed Duke to the top of a large hill south of where the elk were supposed to be. We would need to cross the Green River and climb a steep hill to get to the top. The ice on the river was open in most areas. Sometimes you would have to just hit the open water wide-open and hydroplane across the water. However, this didn't always work. Sometimes your skis would go under the ice on the other side of the river and cause a sudden stop. This in turn would generally pitch you over the handle bars and windshield of your snow machine. Everybody in our group was very experienced at riding in adverse weather conditions and traversing difficult terrain. We all made it across the river except Brad. He hit the bank on the other side of the river and over the handle bars he went into a cartwheel. It looked to me like

Sometimes elk drives don't go as planned when crossing the Green River.

he may have hurt himself and his windshield was missing. I pulled up next to him to check on him. He was lying on the ground laughing. I think he was going to be just fine. We all helped him get his snow machine pulled out of the river and headed to the top of the hill. Once we got to the top of the hill, we spotted the elk in the heavy willow bottom below us. The willows were so thick that we could only see a few elk here and there, but we knew there was about 150 head in the herd. Duke was not optimistic about getting the elk out of the willow bottom.

It was decided that Brad would take the west flank and drop off the hill. He would set up in the willows west of the elk to prevent them from traveling further west. Dennis would do the same but take the east flank. Doug and I were to bail off the steep hill and head directly at the herd of elk while shooting bird bombs into the air. The bird bombs were shot out of a pistol and make a very loud whistling sound leaving a trail of smoke behind them for about seventy-five yards. We could also fire another device that made a huge BOOM sound. It would shoot about fifty yards and resemble an M-80 when it went off. Both devises were highly effective at getting elk to move. Except, sometimes the elk didn't go the direction that you wanted them to, and they can travel very fast.

Duke told us that he would stay on top of (Poo Hill) and be our spotter. Poo Hill was named after a biologist who couldn't get his wool pants off in time after eating one of the Wrangler Café's finest greasy bacon and eggs breakfast. He made a small mess in his pants and the hill was officially named. Duke would communicate with us on his portable radio and let us know where the elk were and if they were coming out of the willow bottom. It was always important to have a spotter because once you were in the thick willows you couldn't see anything. You could become stuck in the deep snow and be completely incapacitated so as not be able to react to where the elk were headed. Poo Hill became an official land mark for game wardens moving elk for many years to come. Nobody ever forgot that story, including the biologist.

Doug and I flew off the steep hill making as much noise as we could with our bird bomb pistols. As we got close to the willows, we needed to cross a barbed wire fence. The top wire on the fence was sticking out of the snow about ten inches. There were no gates in the area to open. If you stopped, you were stuck. You can't move elk when you are stuck. I quickly hit the "Loud Lever" (throttle) and gave it the onion. I blasted right through the top wire of the fence and sailed into the willow bottom nearly hitting a cow elk in the thick willows. Doug on the other hand got hung up in the fence and was stuck, REALLY stuck! If I didn't have my personal machine with the long aggressive track, I would have been stuck as well. I was pretty proud of my new machine as I navigated through the deep snow in the willow bottom. Duke got on the radio and announced, "The elk are breaking out of the willow bottom headed north." Perfect, I thought to myself, (our plan had worked.) I soon got on the elk trail in the willows and would be bringing up the rear. Once the elk were out of the willows, Brad stayed on their west side and Dennis stayed on the east side. I settled in about one mile behind the herd of elk and put just enough pressure on them to let them know they were being actively pursued.

We never called this "moving" elk, we called it "hazing elk." We never pushed the elk hard. We would always let the elk go at their own pace. The snow was chest deep and you certainly didn't want to move them too hard, as we had about eight miles to go with them. Once you had the elk moving you tried to keep everybody in position. There was no going back to help Doug. Hopefully Duke would drop off the hill and assist Doug with getting out of the fence. We all communicated well on our portable radios to let each other know where the elk were and how they were doing. Sometimes, no one could see the elk anywhere. Those times the elk could be making a break for it and be headed the wrong direction. In this case, you would be called on the radio to provide back-up and help turn the elk back on course. It took a great deal of team work to have a successful elk drive. It was always a good feeling to get the elk safely to a feed ground and out of a costly damage situation or an, elk/

cattle co-mingling situation with risk of spreading brucellosis to cattle.

It looked to me like the elk had made it to the feed ground. I decided to follow the main elk trail in the snow to make sure that all of the elk had made it safely. Approximately one mile from the feed ground I came across a lone cow elk lying in the elk trail facing me. I pulled up close to her on my snow machine. She stood up and walked towards me grinding her teeth with her ears laid back. She was not afraid of me at all. I stood up on my snow machine, waved my hands at her and yelled, "GO ON, GIRL!" She stood her ground and faced me. I decided to turn around and leave the area to go get Doug for help. As I went towards her to turn my snow machine around, she charged me. She stood on her hind feet and struck at me with her front feet. Both feet came down on the hood of my snow machine. She pawed at the hood until she had broken my windshield and smashed the hood of my brand-new snow machine. Not only did she smash my hood, she broke both of my spark plugs off that were located on top of the engine. My machine died with her lying on my hood. This scared the shit out of me. Now it was just me and the mad cow elk.

She eventually got off my hood and stood right next to my snow machine, grinding her teeth with her ears laid back. I spoke to her very softly and said, "Easy girl, I won't hurt you." I slowly unlatched and lifted up my broken hood. She saw the movement and struck at the hood a few more times. While she was busy striking my hood, I slowly grabbed my tool kit out of the back compartment of my snow machine. Thank God I had extra spark plugs and a spark plug wrench. I slowly changed the spark plugs while she glared at me, daring me to come another inch closer to her. I never thought I would be under duress changing spark plugs. This was a very stressful moment in my life! Finally plugs were changed. I slowly pulled my broken hood back down. Now I would need to pull my starter rope, get the machine started and get out of there without being attacked again. I pulled the cord, she fired and I hit the "Loud Lever" and got out of there as quick as possible. The cow elk struck at me as I went by. One hoof hit my helmet and made a loud "POP" as I went by her.

I later found Doug and explained the situation to him. He told me that he would run back to his truck and get a body sled. Apparently if elk stalled out and didn't make it to a feed ground, they would be placed on a body sled that was pulled behind a snow machine and be taken to the feed ground. Doug didn't even ask me what had happened to my windshield and hood. He told me to wait right there and he would soon return with the sled. Once Doug returned, he explained that I should haze the cow elk with my snow machine into the deep snow and he would bulldog her. I had never worked with Doug before and I certainly had never bull dogged an elk. I was a rookie at this stuff and he was a trained professional. I told Doug that she was very cranky and had already destroyed the hood on my machine. He just smiled and said, "C-mon Swerbe we got this!"

We soon arrived at the cow elk and I was able to move her into some chest-deep snow with my snow machine. Doug quickly pulled up along-side of her and tackled her from his snow machine. This didn't work out very well for Doug. The cow stood on her hind feet and started striking at him. Doug turned around and ran for his snow machine. The cow elk chased him on her hind feet and struck him in the back and head until she had him down in the deep snow. I didn't know what to do. I didn't want to have to shoot her, but this was getting pretty serious. Doug lay face down in the snow with his arms protecting his head. He had his helmet on for protection and a heavy leather snow machine suit. The elk finally decided that she had ended the immediate threat and got off him. Doug crawled over to his snow machine and used it to pull himself back up. He stood up and raised the visor on his helmet. His helmet was completely packed with snow. He wiped his face with his gloves to remove the snow. Once the snow was removed, I could see that Doug was laughing. He said, "DAMN, she is a little cantankerous!"

We made another game plan and decided that we would both have to tackle her in the deep snow to get her down and place some hobbles on her legs. It was a good thing that I had some wresting experience as it came in handy. We finally got her down. I held a front leg back with my knee on her neck (similar to how you hold a calf down while branding) while Doug put hobbles on her front and hind legs. We then blindfolded her with Doug's neck warmer and loaded her on the body sled. Doug hauled her the rest of the way to the feed ground. We pulled up on the feed ground with about 600 other elk. I held her down while Doug removed the hobbles. Once the hobbles were removed, I pulled the face mask off of her quickly and stepped back. She jumped up and tried attacking us again. She stood her ground and would not let either of us move back to our snow machines. Duke finally showed up to rescue us. He would end up breaking down a near-by dead aspen tree and fending off the angry cow with the dead tree while we returned to our snow machines. I learned something that day. When an animal feels endangered, they will stand their ground and protect themselves no matter what. Brad and I would be headed to the Arctic Cat repair shop south of Pinedale for a new hood and windshield. I would consider not using my personal snow machine for work in the future. The owner was used to seeing Game and Fish snow machines come in after an elk drive. Every time we would show up at his repair shop, he would run his fingers through his hair, shake his head and say, "Haven't ever seen that before, I'll have it ready for you by next week!" He would then walk off shaking his head!

Tim Baxley was having a heck of a time. Every time I would check my messages on my bag phone, Tim would have left a voice message. He would have to hike to the top of the mountain at North Piney to have any cell signal at all. His messages were usually broken and you could always hear the wind blowing in the background. Many of his messages came late at night because it took him so long to snowshoe to the top of the mountain to make the call. Listed below are standard messages that I received from Tim on a regular basis.

* "Hey Boss Man, my snow machine blew up and I'm stranded"

Scott C. Werbelow

* "Hey Boss Man, my new snow machine blew its engine."

* "Hey Boss Man, this is Baxley, the elk broke into the stack yard at Finnegan and blew out two sides of the fence when they left."

* "Hey Boss Man, I caved off two rows of frozen bales on my sled and broke my sled in half today, need some help, bring lumber, chainsaw, and bolts.

* "Hey Boss Man, could you please bring me up another tongue and double tree for my sled. Had a little wreck with the team today."

* "Hey Boss Man, my horse is lame, feeding with one horse and snow machine sled."

* "Hey Boss Man, elk walked over top of stack yard fence at North Piney, they are standing on top of the haystack under the hay shed roof eating hay. Horses walked out of corral today but can't go anywhere. Parked my snow machine on top of the outhouse today."

* "Hey Boss Man, can't keep up with shoveling snow out of the gates on stack yard. Team has to drop off a ten-foot drift to leave stack yard, broke another tongue and double tree today, please send help ASAP."

Tim was really struggling. He blew up the engine in his $200 snow machine. He borrowed another snow machine from the Game and Fish Department and blew the engine in it the very next day. He then borrowed another snow machine from his girlfriend's family and it wouldn't run. It was time for me to go visit Tim and see if I could get at least one of his snow machines running. As I drove through the small town of Marbleton, I observed Tim's old brown Ford truck parked in front of the Cat House. The Cat House was the name of a snowmobile dealership that sold and repaired Arctic Cat snowmobiles. I thought to myself, oh good Tim is here, I can visit with him and save myself a trip into the feed ground. He's probably getting his machine repaired. I walked through the front doors of the Cat House and Tim was standing at the front counter. He placed his credit card back in his wallet, turned around and smiled at me and said, "Hey, boss man, I just bought me a brand-new Arctic Cat Powder Special 600 on my gold master card. I'm sick and tired of breaking down. If I'm going to feed elk on two feed grounds, I need a reliable machine and I don't give a rat's ass what it costs me," I said, "Tim, you can't do that, that machine will cost you more than you will make this year feeding elk. Plus, you will be paying 24% interest on your credit card each month." Tim replied, "I know, I know, but I don't care anymore. I'm tired of snowshoeing in and out of feed grounds each day. I just bought me a brand-new good sumbitch." One thing about Baxley, he was always positive and happy. I helped Tim load his new sled. It was a beautiful sled. I may have been just a little bit jealous that I didn't have one myself.

About three days later I received a message on my bag phone that said, "Hey, boss man, this is Baxley, I had a little wreck with my new snow machine and I can't get the hood open to check my oil. I don't want to risk starting it until I can check my oil, because it was upside-down and the oil drained out of it." I felt sorry for Tim and immediately headed into North Piney feed ground to check on him. Tim had met with the previous feeder KC. KC showed Tim the new trail over Johnson Ridge. So, I would be taking the new trail into North Piney for the first time. This would be a shorter trail than going through the National Forest, but a more dangerous trail off the side of a steep mountain through heavy timber. It was storming again that day with limited visibility. I headed down the steep mountain into North Piney following the snow machine trail made by Tim and KC. About half-way down the mountain, I noticed a pine tree to my right that had all the bark missing from the ground to about five feet high. It looked like an elk or moose had rubbed its antlers on the tree and stripped all the bark off of it. Whatever had happened, it was fresh and the snow was all wallowed out around the tree about five feet deep.

I stopped my machine and shut off the engine to look at the tree a little closer. I could hear a faint yelling noise in the distance. I looked down towards North Piney feed ground and observed about 600 elk running in four different directions. I quickly grabbed my binoculars and focused on the elk that were running everywhere. I couldn't believe my eyes. Tim had hitched his snow machine sled behind a single draft horse and was feeding hay. He had about six bales of hay on the sled and was having a run-away with the horse through the herd of elk. Tim was wearing nothing but his white underwear garment with a red handkerchief around his neck. He had a coyote skin hat on, pink sunglasses, leather chinks and Sorrell lace-up snow boots. He was yelling at the top of his lungs, "WHOA, YOU, SUMBITCH, WHOA, YOU, CRAZY SUMBITCH!!" Even though he was having a run-away with his horse, he was still feeding hay off his home-made snow machine sled. I never laughed so hard in my life, and really wished I would have had a video camera that day.

I arrived at the feed ground just as Tim was putting his horse away in the corral. His brand-new Powder Special snow machine was parked on top of the outhouse with a smashed-in hood.

I pulled up next to Tim. He said, "Hey, boss man, top of the morning, do you want to come in for some corn?" I thought to myself, corn, are we having corn for lunch, I was kind of hungry. I replied, "Corn, sounds good, let's have some!" Tim led me into his trailer house. He had cleaned it up about as nice as it could be. I sat down at the table located in front of the trailer house. Tim grabbed a Styrofoam cup and placed it in front of me. He then grabbed a clear mason jar full of a clear liquid and poured my cup about half full. He said, "Try some of this shit, just made it the other day." I smelled it. It smelled like it might burn as fuel in my snow machine. I was actually surprised that it didn't melt the Styrofoam cup. I took a sip, it pert'-near killed me! I blew it out my nose on the table and said, "DAMN, TIM, you could use this as fuel in your snow machine if it ran anymore!" Tim said, "Come on, man, you don't like that shit?

That's the best batch of corn that I have ever made!" I said, "It may be good corn, but I'm more of a whiskey drinker." I honestly couldn't drink the rest of the glass, it pert'-near killed me!!

I asked Tim what had happened to his new machine. Tim replied, "Shit, boss man, I was trying to break trail up that steep damn mountain to go home. I had both feet on the running board, hit the "Loud Lever" and headed up the mountain out of control. I could see a pine tree coming up, but I didn't want to stop in fear of getting stuck. So, I just held on wide open and smacked into that damn pine tree. When the dust settled, my new snow-machine had hit the tree and peeled all the bark off the trunk. The snow machine was standing straight on end with the tree like it was trying to give the tree a big ole' hug!" He went on to explain, "I tried to pull the machine off the tree and it tipped over upside down. All the oil drained out from somewhere. I finally got it started and limped it home. It's sitting over there on top of the outhouse with no oil and I can't get the hood open to fill it back up.

I went outside and looked at the machine. The hood on the machine was trashed. The front bumper was bent so badly that the hood wouldn't open. After some creative work with a pry-bar, we were finally able to open the hood and add oil to the machine. Tim thanked me from the bottom of his heart. I asked Tim why he was feeding with only one horse today. He told me that one of the sorrel geldings had become lame and could not get up in the corral. I went out and looked at the horse. The horse was down and couldn't get up. This was one of the young matched Belgium's that I was so fond of. I looked at the horse's feet, but could not see anything visibly wrong with him. Tim had named the team of horses Lucky and Rooster. They were such a matched team that Lucky went on the left and Rooster went on the right when hitching them up. This was how he was able to remember which one went on which side each day while hitching them. Looking at that poor young horse lying on the ground made me sick to my stomach. We would need to get a vet into the feed ground and get him healthy again. Tim's girlfriend Patty worked as a Vet Technician for local veterinarian Brent Dean. I would need to visit with Dr. Dean and see what he could do for Lucky. Tim had a spare horse, but just had not hitched that horse with Rooster yet to see how things were going to work out. I told Tim that I would work on getting some help for Lucky and be in touch with him.

I contacted Dr. Dean. He recommended putting Lucky on very high doses of penicillin. Tim's girlfriend Patty told me she was going in to see Tim over the next few days and would bring him the penicillin. A few days went by and I received another message from Tim one night that said, "Hey, boss man, Patty was supposed to come see me today and she never showed up. I'm worried that something may have happened to her. We had had another horrible storm. As soon as I received the message, I loaded up my personal snow machine and headed for the parking lot into North Piney. I called Brad on the way to see if he would go with me as the weather was horrible and something may be wrong with Patty. Brad agreed to go. He would meet me at the forest boundary on the Middle Piney Road. I figured I may need a good snow machine to get through the deep drifted snow, so that's why I grabbed my personal machine.

I met Brad at the forest boundary. Patty's vehicle was parked in the parking lot. By the looks of the tracks in the snow it appeared that Patty headed to North Piney feed ground through the forest boundary and not Johnson Ridge. This worried me deeply. This was not a place for a woman, let alone anyone, to travel during a blizzard. I thought to myself, oh dear, Patty may have been caught in a blizzard, got stuck and froze to death. It was nearly dark the visibility was poor and large snowflakes were falling down sideways. Brad and I unloaded our machines and headed down the badly drifted road. It was difficult to see but after several miles I could see something in the trail ahead. It was a snow machine that was drifted in, parked in the middle of the trail. My heard sank, was this Patty's machine? Would we find her dead in the trail somewhere? We stopped and checked out the snow machine. It appeared that the drive belt was burned up. It also appeared that the parking brake was locked on the machine. I thought to myself, did Patty have her parking brake on when she left the parking area, burned a belt and decided to walk into the feed ground. The feed ground was a good 3-4 miles away.

We continued on down the trail. I could see something lying ahead. As I got closer it was a bag of red potatoes. I gathered the potatoes and continued on. My heart sank that we were going to find Patty dead in the trail. Froze to death. After about another mile we came across a gallon of milk. I gathered that up as well and continued on. About another mile later I could see something dark lying across the trail. It looked like a dead body. My heart sank again. As I approached it, it was a set of saddle bags stretched across the trail. Inside the saddle bags were several bottles of penicillin. I thought to myself, this was Patty and she is walking into the feed ground to see Tim. Hopefully she made it, Tim's trailer was still several miles away and the snow was deep. We soon arrived at the feed ground and knocked on the door of the trailer. It was now dark out. Tim opened the door with a huge smile and said, "Hey, boss man, did you gather up all of Patty's belongings on the way?" Patty jumped up and smiled. She said, "I didn't think that I was going to make it. I carried stuff as long as I could, but finally became too weak to carry and dropped stuff off in the trail as I went."

I explained to her that she had left the trailhead with her parking brake on, and that's why she had burned up her belt. She was very embarrassed. I couldn't even imagine carrying a bag of potatoes, gallon of milk and saddle bags in the deep snow as long as she did. She was very lucky to be alive. Tim offered us another glass of corn. I declined but Brad had to try some. Brad said, "WOW, that's some good stuff right there!!" I told Tim to give Lucky some heavy doses of penicillin and keep in touch with me. Brad and I left in the dark, thankful that Patty was still alive.

Tim would continue to give Lucky high doses of penicillin daily. While on high doses, Lucky would get up and walk around the corral but could not put any weight on his right rear leg. If Tim took him off penicillin for even one day, Lucky would lie down and couldn't get up. This went on for several weeks with no improvements. I finally called Dr. Dean and asked him if he would snow machine into North Piney feed ground and look at Lucky. Dr. Dean agreed. Except, the day that he decided to snow machine into North Piney, it was an absolute blizzard. He spent the whole day lost and never made it into the feed ground. I wondered what this bill was going to come to. Dr. Dean eventually made it into the feed ground several days later and examined Lucky. He called me later that night and told me that he couldn't visually see what was wrong with the horse, but he felt like Lucky had something stuck in his hind foot. Dr. Dean said, "I know it would be nearly impossible to get that horse out of there, but I need to x-ray his hind foot if we are ever going to save him."

My first thoughts were, there is no way we will ever get that horse out of the feed ground. The snow is simply too deep. The horse was young and beautiful. It would be an absolute shame to let that horse suffer anymore and die at North Piney feed ground. My heart told me that I would need to figure out a way to get that horse out of the feed ground and get him some help. I waited for a warm day when the snow was good and wet from melting. Brad and I broke a trail over Johnson ridge with our snow machines. We went back and forth on the trail many times to pack it down and make it wide with our snow machines. I then waited for it to get below zero at night, knowing the snow machine trail would set up like concrete. The snow conditions would have to be perfect to get Lucky out. I called Tim and told him to give Lucky twice the recommended dosage of penicillin as we were going to walk him out of the feed ground and get him some help.

A few days later the temperature dropped to -30 below at night. I called Tim and told him to get up before daylight and try to lead Lucky out. The journey would be about five miles up and over a large mountain top. If we went out the bottom it would be nine miles. I told Tim that I would head that way in the morning with my snow machine and meet him somewhere on the way out of North Piney. I loaded my snow machine into my horse trailer and headed that way early the next morning. I finally made it to the top of the ridge and could not believe my eyes. Tim was riding Rooster bareback with nothing but a halter and lead rope. He was dragging Lucky behind him with a lead rope. Joy, the spare horse, was just following behind them with no lead rope. When Tim saw me, he said, "Hey, boss man, had to bring all of them out because Joy wasn't going to stay in there alone. I was so proud of Tim, he was nearly half way out with Lucky. Maybe we were actually going to pull this off.

Soon, Lucky became very tired and could no longer make the journey. He would lay down in the snow machine trail and could no longer get up. The trail had started to thaw out and Lucky had been falling down to his belly in deep snow. Rooster was also falling through the packed snow machine trail and falling down to his belly. Tim got off of Rooster and tied Lucky's lead-rope to Rooster's tail. He got behind Rooster and slapped him on the butt and yelled "GET UP ROOSTER!!" Rooster dropped his head and began pulling Lucky on his side down the trail. Rooster would fall down belly-deep in the snow and Tim would yell, "COME ON ROOSTER, OK, PULL, PULL, PULL!" Rooster gave all that he had and finally became exhausted to the point that he could pull no more. Tim hooked Joy to Rooster and yelled, "GET UP, GET UP!" The two horses pulled and pulled and started heading down the last hill towards the horse trailer. Those draft horses knew they were saving Lucky's life and they never gave up. It was the most amazing thing that I had ever seen.

We finally reached the parking lot where the horse trailer was located. Both Rooster and Joy were completely lathered up. Steam was rolling off their warm, sweaty bodies. Lucky lay on the ground on his side and looked at me like he just wanted to die. We unhooked all the horses and tried to figure out how we were going to get Lucky into the horse trailer. Lucky could not get up. Tim and I would end up hooking a come-a-long to Lucky's lead rope and winched him into the trailer one-click at a time. I thanked Tim for his good work. Tim climbed back on the back of Rooster and headed back into North Piney feed ground leading Joy.

I wasn't sure if they were going to make it back into the feed ground or not, because the snow had become soft and the horses were dead tired. I couldn't worry about that, I needed to get Lucky to Dr. Dean's office. I was glad that I had hauled a spare horse into North Piney so that Tim had another horse to feed with.

I soon arrived at Dr. Dean's office in Pinedale. I explained to him how we got Lucky out. Dr. Dean could not believe it. He knew exactly what we had to go through to get that horse out, because he had been lost up there in a blizzard all day and knew what we were dealing with. We tied a rope to Lucky's good hind leg and hooked the rope to something solid. I pulled the horse trailer forward and dragged Lucky out of the trailer. I then used the winch mounted on the front of my game and fish truck to drag Lucky into an outside corral. Dr. Dean said he would give Lucky a few day's rest and some antibiotics and get him into an indoor stall where he could x-ray the bad foot.

A few days had passed when Dr. Dean called me and said, "Scott, you have to come down to my office and see this x-ray!" I quickly went down to Dr. Dean's office. Lucky had stepped on a rusty spike nail about eight inches long. The nail went up through his hoof and was stuck in his leg. Whenever Lucky tried to walk, he bent the nail over. The rusty spike looked like an eight-inch candy cane stuck inside of his leg. Dr. Dean performed surgery and removed the spike from Lucky's foot. He told me that it was going to be a long recovery and that Lucky would need to be doctored daily for about two months. I hauled Lucky to the corral at the office and began doctoring him daily.

Tim called me late that evening and told me that he had made it back into the feed ground. Apparently, the snow had become so soft that the horses could no longer go and had played out. He had to build a fire in the trees and wait for the snow to freeze. As the temperatures dropped and the snow became frozen again, he was finally able to move on. I told Tim the story about Lucky, Tim could not believe that Lucky was still alive. It had been a long day. I curled up on the floor under my desk in my sleeping bag in the office and fell asleep. I laid there wondering what tomorrow would bring.

Chapter 7

FROM BAD TO WORSE

I needed to find a place to rent, but there was just nothing available. I was tired of sleeping on the floor in my office. One of my elk feeders told me that he had heard that a rancher by the name of Kathy Miller was looking for a ranch hand. The job apparently paid $600 per month and came with a small house up Horse Creek near the Green River. I would need to find time to stop in and visit with her to see if she might be interested in hiring my wife, Lana. I was just so busy with work that I couldn't seem to ever catch my breath. All I did everyday was react to the crisis of the day. I was still concerned about my future with the Game and Fish Department. I had been competing with nine other wardens on the Reservoir Crew for a permanent game warden job. Had this all gone away? Did this feed ground manager job change my path to becoming a Wyoming game warden?

I finally built up enough courage to call my previous Casper supervisor Terry Cleveland. Mr. Cleveland answered the phone and seemed excited to hear from me. He asked me all about my new adventures in Pinedale and the feed ground program. I told him that I had been extremely busy, but was still having fun. I asked him if taking this job was going to change my path of becoming a Wyoming game warden. Mr.

Cleveland replied, "Scott, you keep working hard and keep a good track record and things will work out fine for you." He also said, "You never know, maybe this feed ground manager position will become permanent for you someday. That will put you ahead of the rest of the competition for a permanent job." I then asked him if I needed to turn in all my law enforcement equipment or if I could still do law enforcement work. He replied, "I will check on that and get back with you." I felt relieved after talking with Mr. Cleveland, but there were still some unanswered questions in my head.

I hung up with Mr. Cleveland and checked my voice messages. I had a message from Tim Baxley that the elk had walked over the stack yard fence at Finnegan and blew three sides of the stack yard fence out when they left. Now it sounded like we no longer needed an elk feeder at Finnegan as the elk were just feeding themselves. Tim also said that it was a horrible blizzard up there. He had slept in his truck at the forest boundary last night because he couldn't see to get into either feed ground. I became very worried about Tim because I knew he would try to get into each feed ground today and feed the elk. I decided I had better head that direction and help him out. It was an absolute blizzard in Pinedale. I couldn't even imagine how bad it might be up on the mountain where Tim was feeding. I loaded up my snow machine and headed that direction. The roads were horrible and the visibility sucked. I stopped at Brad's warden station in Big Piney to see if he would go with me. No one was home.

I arrived at the forest boundary. Tim's old brown Ford truck was completely snowed in. It was a blizzard at the parking lot, but it looked even much worse at the top of the mountain where I would have to travel over. We had built a new snow machine trail over the top of a steep mountain to get into Finnegan, so that the feeder didn't have to go through the cranky landowner's front yard every day. It was a tough trail in good conditions. You had to cross Middle Piney Creek, which was open water with large boulders. As soon as you got across the creek you would have to climb a very steep hill. If you got off the existing snow machine trail you were stuck. I could see fresh snow machine tracks in the snow headed towards Finnegan feed ground and not North Piney feed ground which was located in the opposite direction. So, I figured Tim had headed for Finnegan. I was worried about him. He was the kind of guy that if his snow machine broke down, he would still snowshoe in and get the elk fed. With blizzard conditions this would be very dangerous.

I crossed Middle Piney Creek through the open water and started up the steep mountain. I looked to my left and observed a snow machine upside down in the creek below me. All I could see was the track sticking out of the deep snow around it. I couldn't stop to look at it closer or I would become stuck. I figured Tim had wrecked his snow machine trying to climb the steep mountain and it had rolled off the mountain and into the creek. I also figured Tim would still try to hike into the feed ground to get the elk fed. I was worried now even more than before, that Tim would become lost and freeze to death in the blizzard. I headed up the steep mountain. As soon as I hit the top of the mountain the wind had to have been blowing over 40 miles per hour. I literally could not see anything, including the old snow machine trail that I was on. The storm had dumped about three foot of fresh powder and then the wind came up and created the worst blizzard that I had ever seen.

I was currently sitting on a bare ridge with a lay down electric fence strung across the ridge. I had a lone pine tree which stood about forty feet tall on my left. I could barely see the large pine tree in all the blowing snow. At this point I knew where I was and would remember that large pine tree if I became disoriented. I knew if I continued south towards Finnegan that I would encounter deep snow and no visibility. I sat there for a few minutes debating what I should do. I had been across this flat several times. I knew it was about one mile across a flat and then the trail went into some thick timber. I thought to myself, if I can just get across this flat and into the thick timber, I can make it. Once I'm in the timber the wind won't be as bad and I will be able to see the trail. Besides, Tim is caught out here somewhere and may die if I don't find him.

I put the visor down on my helmet and hit the "Loud Lever." I could not see anything. I couldn't even tell if I was moving or not! It was just white out. All I could see was white! I didn't dare stop or I would become stuck in the three feet of fresh powder. The wind was blowing so hard, at times I thought it was going to blow me off my snow machine. My throttle was wide open and my headlight was pointing straight in the air from breaking a trail in the deep snow. I knew it was flat sage brush country all the way across the open flat. I was not concerned about hitting any rocks or deep gullies. I just needed to make it to the heavy timber and I would be fine. About that time, I hit something hard and came to a sudden stop. I flew over my handle bars like a rocket. The landing was soft and I was not hurt. I lay there in the deep snow and looked at my snow machine. I could barely see it in the blowing drifting snow. All I could see was its red tail light sticking straight up in the air. I had hit a deep hole and my machine was standing straight on end with the hood and headlight completely buried under the snow. I waded in belly-deep snow back to my machine. I dug all the snow out around my hood and noticed each ski was bent back and sticking straight up in the air along the side of my hood. I hoped that they weren't broken, I had never seen a ski in this position before. I had fallen into a large sink hole. I had no idea where I was because I had never seen this hole before.

I dug for about twenty minutes and finally got the snow machine completely turned around. The three-foot trail that I had broken in the deep snow was already drifted back in. I couldn't even see the track that I had just left twenty minutes ago. It dawned on me at this point, I need to get the hell out of here before I die. There should not have been any deep holes across the flat, meaning I was lost. Hopefully I could go back the same direction that I had just come from and locate the large pine tree and bare ridge with the lay down electric fence. I took off wide-open, but couldn't see anything! I kept looking for the large pine tree. I was now praying Lord please help me find the lone pine tree and get me the heck out of here. I looked left, I looked right, no pine tree! Had I already passed it? I headed to my right looking for the tree, no tree. I then headed to my left looking for the tree, no tree! Shit, have I already passed the tree? I thought to myself. I couldn't let off the throttle or I would become stuck. If I got stuck there was no way I could hike all the way out with the snow being belly-deep on me.

I finally went against my better judgment and turned the snow machine around to go back and look for the lone pine tree. I never found the tree, and now I had no idea what direction I was headed. I was just happily going wide-open in a blizzard when I could not see anything but white. There were times when the strong winds would almost blow me and the snow machine over on its side. The situation was so bad, I chuckled to myself and thought Swerb you have really done it this time. You have no food, no water, no portable radio, no lighter, and nobody knows where you are today. Real good Swerb, you, dumbass!! Even if I had told someone where I was, they wouldn't be able to find me. You simply couldn't see anything! I became very afraid. I thought to myself, what if I drop off into a canyon and don't even know it. What if this storm doesn't pass for several days? How will I stay warm? How will I get out of the wind? What if I get stuck and have to walk? I don't even know where I would walk to?

I finally came across a fence. The fence posts were sticking about three inches above the snow. I could tell there was a gate in front of me. The fence post had a bright orange no trespassing sign barely sticking out of the snow mounted on top of the post. I decided to stop for the first time. I had never seen this gate or this bright orange no trespassing sign before? I thought, where in the hell am I? I sat on my snow machine trying to figure out what to do. I decided, worst-case scenario, I could dig a deep hole in the snow to get out of the wind. I could gather up some dead sage brush, pour some gas out of my tank on the sage brush and light it with my spark plug. I could pull the spark plug out of the engine and leave it hooked to the plug wire. Pull the starter cord to create spark and, Walla, I would have a warm fire. I had never had any of these kind of thoughts before but I was desperate. It looked like the fence was headed downhill. I decided to follow it. The fence had to go somewhere on private property and maybe the storm would let up if I got to a lower elevation?

I left my snow machine parked and walked over to the fence. The snow was over waist deep. I grabbed the top barbed wire with my snow machine gloves on and pulled myself one step at a time down the side of the mountain. I traveled about a mile and became completely exhausted from wading through the deep snow. I sat down on a log and almost started to cry. I was lost and in a very bad situation. I said a prayer to God and asked him for guidance on how to get out of this situation. About that time the wind let up for just a few minutes and the fog lifted enough for me to see a short distance down-hill. I recognized a creek bottom below me with heavy willows in the bottom. The only creek in this area was Middle Piney Creek. I thought to myself, if that's Middle Piney Creek, then that's north. At least I now know what direction to travel to get back out of here! I waded back up the fence line to my machine. It was a little easier walk this time because I had already broken a trail with my body.

Once I reached the snow machine I was back into the blizzard. Heavy winds and no visibility. I sat on my machine for over two hours trying to figure out what to do. Two hours sitting in 30-50 mile an hour winds seemed like eternity. If I decided to stay, I may die! If I decided to leave, I may also die! I decided I would die trying and not sitting. I knew which direction I needed to travel to get back to my truck, I just needed to be able to do it. I fired up my snow machine, put my face mask down and hit the "Loud Lever." I could see absolutely nothing and I was going wide-open. Quite an experience if you have never tried this before! I looked over to my left and could see a bare hill with a lay down electric fence. THANK GOD, I thought, I know where I am now. Pretty quick I found the lone pine tree as well. I headed straight down the steep mountain and crossed Middle Piney Creek. I was so thankful to be alive, but where was Tim? Was he stuck somewhere dying in the blizzard?

I pulled my snow machine up to my truck. From out behind my

Scott C. Werbelow

truck came Tim walking with snowshoes on. His gray cat was following him, I would never forget this sight. Tim had a long beard with icicle's hanging from it. He was wearing a coyote skin hat with his pink sunglasses on. He had wool pants and sweater with snow stuck to the wool. He was wearing knee-high lace-up snow boots with leather chinks to protect his legs while feeding hay to elk. He smiled. I could see his teeth through his thick beard. He said, "HEY, BOSS MAN, WHERE IN THE HELL HAVE YOU BEEN?" I replied, "LOST, LOOKING FOR YOU!" Tim said, "Hell, you drove right by me in the blizzard. I was yelling at you and waving my arms and you went right by me." I asked, "Where were you?" Tim replied, "Standing right next to my wrecked snow machine in the creek!" Tim said, "I hit the ole Loud Lever coming out of the creek bottom and she got away from me, rolled down the hill and landed upside down in the damn creek." I don't know how I missed him but apparently, I did. Tim said that he was just getting ready to snowshoe into North Piney to feed the elk. He wanted to ride double with me. I told him we needed to get his snow machine out of the near-by creek. He said, "Oh, Hell, don't worry about that damn thing, it's upside down, out of oil and gas. I will mess with it another day!" I replied, "No, I'm here to help you and you need a snow machine that runs, so that you don't have to snowshoe into both feed grounds every day.

I ended up helping Tim get his machine out of the creek and running again. It was quite a job, but we prevailed. We then headed into North Piney across Johnson Ridge. Tim had marked this trail very well one day after he had been lost on Johnson Ridge. I told Tim to mark all of his snow machine trails with willow branches to prevent him from getting lost. Tim had cut down about thirty pine trees, all of them over ten feet tall and stuck them in the snow on the left side of his trail. The trail was very well marked to say the least. I'm not sure the Forest Service would have been very happy with him if they knew about it. We arrived at the feed ground. I noticed Tim had even planted pine trees from his trailer house to the outhouse. I laughed at Tim, he said, "Don't laugh, I got lost one night

206

headed to the shitter. I won't do that again!"

We ended up digging out the stack yard gates to get them open. The eight-foot-high gates were completely drifted in. The elk had been walking over the eight-foot-high elk fence on the east side. The snow was so deep that the elk were able to walk on top of the snow and stand on top of the hayshed and eat hay under the roof of the shed. I would need to get some fence supplies hauled into both feed grounds and repair fence soon. After digging out the stack yard gates, the team of draft horses would have to drop straight off a ten-foot-high drift with a loaded sled of hay. Once they hit the bottom of the drift, they would have to climb straight up another six-foot-high drift to leave the stack yard. The team would hit the second drift so hard, that they would break the double tree almost every time they blew through there. I had already replaced four double trees on Tim's feed sled in the past week. I told Tim that we needed to shovel all the snow out of there to prevent broken double trees. Tim just laughed and said, "Well, you better have a strong back, a weak mind and a good shovel because you will have to do it every day." I told Tim that I could not find enough new double trees to replace one every day, so it would need to be done.

We harnessed up the team and headed them towards the stack yard. They didn't work very well together using the spare mare named Joy. She didn't want to do any of the work except help hold up her side of the tongue up. Tim was sure missing Lucky. Hopefully both horses would stay sound or we would really be in trouble. We loaded the sled light so that the horses could deal with the steep and deep snow drifts leaving the stack yard. We got to the top of the drift and Tim said, "WHOA!" The team stopped. Tim looked at me and said, "You better sit down and get a good grip on something. This is going to be a real tank slapper, maybe the best carnival ride you have ever been on." Tim sat down on the hay bales behind him, braced his feet up against the front wooden rack on the sled. He wrapped both lines around his hands tightly and said in a deep voice, "Rooster, Joy GET UP!!" The team of horses dropped their heads and

Scott C. Werbelow

Game and Fish employees shoveling snow off roof of hayshed.

headed off the steep ten-foot-high snowdrift at a dead run. They didn't want the loaded sled to smack them in the butt so they tried to out run it. And they didn't slow down a bit going up the other side of the drift in fear that they wouldn't make it over the drift. Tim was correct, this was a carnival ride. I would never have guessed that you could get a team of horses with a loaded sled over those drifts, but he did.

Tim slept in his truck again that night and hit Finnegan first thing in the morning. We got out of there after dark. Man, what a day! I was thankful to still be alive after being lost all morning. I stopped by Brad's

Frosty Hittle breaking trail into Muddy feed ground during a blizzard.

house to tell him my near-death story. He poured me another fine Jack on the rocks and listened to my story. He was upset that he had missed me that morning and that I had to go through all of that by myself. I told him that he didn't miss anything and that he was lucky that he didn't go with me. I told Brad the story about the elk getting in the stack yard at both feed grounds. He offered to help me repair the two stack yards over the next few days. I returned home late again, slept on my office floor and had not had time to visit with Kathy Miller about a ranch job for Lana.

I woke up at 5:30 AM and snow-machined out to Soda Lake to load up some treated ten-foot poles and several roles of woven wire to repair the stack yards. I had to make several trips with the body sled that we used to haul the cranky old cow to Franz feed ground. I stopped by Brad's for a cup of coffee and a breakfast burrito. We soon headed to Finnegan feed ground. It was a blue-sky day. I really wanted to go back and see where I had gone wrong on the trail the previous day and follow my tracks to see everywhere that I had gone. I asked Brad to get the sleds loaded up with posts and wire while I ran up the hill quick to look at my tracks in the snow. I reached the top of the hill by the lone pine tree and observed where I had hit the large sink hole. If I had stayed more to my right, I would have been fine but I was off course just enough to hit the hole and get lost. The amazing thing was that I followed my snow machine tracks to see everywhere that I had gone in the blizzard. My tracks went up and down several deep canyons. I didn't even know if I was going uphill or downhill. I can't believe that I didn't get stuck down in one of those canyons. I was truly thankful to be alive. I observed tracks all over that mountain driving aimlessly in the whiteout.

I returned back down the mountain to Brad. He was loaded up and ready to go. Brad looked at me and said, "You expect me to pull this loaded sled across that creek and up that steep mountain?" I said, "Yes, Sir, you can make it, go ahead of me!" I really didn't think that Brad could make it, but I wanted to see him try. Brad hit the creek with a full head of steam and quickly got stuck in the creek ahead of me. He stood up on his seat so that his feet wouldn't get wet. He flipped up his visor on his helmet and yelled, "I TOLD YOU THAT I COULD'NT MAKE IT!" I replied, "Hold tight buddy, I'll be right over!" I blew by Brad in the creek showering him with ice cold water. I hooked a tow-rope to his machine and pulled him out of the creek. We stopped on the other side of the bank and Brad said, "Nice, now my feet are all wet!" I smiled and said, "That's why I wanted you to go first." Brad and I were starting to develop our good friend relationship. I told Brad that I would have to pull him all the

Tim Baxley driving Kent and Doug.

way up the steep mountain with the sled load of poles. We had a heck of a time getting into the feed ground. We had to make several trips, but we made it. Brad and I repaired fence while Tim started to harness the draft horses Kent and Doug.

Tim had forgotten the horses' bits in his truck that morning. Tim always took the bits out of the bridle and warmed them for the horses, so they wouldn't have to put a cold bit in their mouths. I asked Tim if he wanted me to run back to his truck and grab the bits. Tim replied, "No, it's too far and we have work to do. I will fix them up with some homemade bits." Tim reached into an old rusty tool box and pulled out two 9/16 box end wrenches. He wired them into the bridle as bits, smiled and said, "They will only fight them for a minute and then they will be just fine." I had not ever seen that done before. He was right, the horses fought them initially. When Tim was done feeding, he assisted us with repairing the fence. It took us all day, but we finally got three sides of the stack yard repaired. Tim invited us over to the "Brown Turd" trailer for some whole made corn. I tried another sip but couldn't get it down. I ended up blowing it back through my nose and pert' near died. Brad just laughed and called me a Wussy. I just laughed and said, "At least I didn't get stuck in the creek and get my feet wet first thing this morning." Brad laughed and said, "Oh Man, you set me up on that one!"

Brad and I were becoming really good friends. We had done several elk drives together and a lot of hard work on the feed grounds to keep them up and running. I really liked working with the game wardens in the Pinedale region. Everything we did was a team effort and everyone helped one another with anything that needed done. We all worked long hard hours to accomplish all the work that needed done on a daily basis.

The next morning Brad, Tim, and I loaded our snow machine sleds with ten-foot posts and rolls of woven wire and headed into North Piney feed ground. We ended up attaching the ten-foot poles to the top of the existing fence poles that were sticking about one foot above the snow. We hung up two more rows of woven wire and had the elk fenced out of

Brad Hovinga and I with team of horses.

the stack yard. We spent another several hours digging out the gates. Tim got tired of digging the gates out each day, so he would just raise the gates up out of the deep snow. I'm sure in the spring of the year once the snow melted, the gates would be hanging eight feet in the air. Tim had pushed two rows of hay bales off on his sled while loading. The bales were heavy and frozen. They hit the sled so hard that the sled broke in half. We would also repair his feed sled that day. I was starting to think that Tim could screw up a railroad tie with a rubber mallet. But we truly loved the guy for his great attitude and bubbly personality.

I was so busy moving problem elk to feed grounds, repairing broken stuff and hauling draft horses to feed grounds that I hadn't even

Scott C. Werbelow

Brad and I loading hay bales.

been to all the feed grounds yet. Brad would take me out and show me the Bench Corral feed ground north of Big Piney. We used a game and fish truck and flatbed trailer to feed at this feed ground. Bench Corral was the lowest elevation feed ground. The snow didn't typically get that deep, so a truck was used to feed instead of draft horses. I would end up stealing the tailgate off that truck and putting it on mine since I didn't have one. The Bench Corral or (Muddy) feed ground as locals called it was the last feed ground created by the department. I had learned that the department used to have several moose feed grounds as well. The feed grounds were created to keep moose out of rancher's hay stacks. There were over a hundred moose fed each winter on these feed grounds. The department had just recently shut them down prior to my coming to Pinedale. The local ranchers loved them because they kept the moose out. The department was concerned about the cost to operate them and disease issues, so it was decided to close them.

I returned back to the office in Pinedale to check my messages. One of the BFH Biologists said he was headed up to Green River Lakes feed ground and would show me how to get up there if I wanted to go with him. I was happy to follow him up there and finally get to meet the elk feeder named Todd Stearns, who I had heard so much about. We left the trail head in a storm. The snow was piling up fast. Our ride would be about 15-20 miles up a groomed snow machine trail. We arrived at the feed ground and there were several hundred elk standing on the feed ground. The BFH Biologist took me up to the little elk feeder cabin to meet Todd. I thought the little cabin was really cool, nestled back in the trees with smoke coming out of the stove pipe. I loved the smell of pine wood being burned in a wood stove. Todd invited us in and made us a pot of coffee. Todd was a quiet man and a good listener. He did more tuning in than broadcasting. After visiting with Todd for a short time, I could tell he was very intelligent about the area and the elk. He spoke with a very soft tone and was very polite. Todd had been feeding at this feed ground for years. He rode for the Green River Cattleman's Association in the summer and fed elk in the winter. He would stay in a cabin owned by the association in the summer and the small cabin owned by the department in the winter. Todd owned a snow machine and a Subaru car and that was about it.

I overheard Todd tell the BFH Biologist that he felt it was time to start throwing out some hay to the elk. He felt the snow was deep enough and that the elk were ready to be fed. The biologist disagreed with Todd and explained that a certain number of elk needed to be on the feed ground for a certain period of time and with at least sixteen inches of snow present for a certain amount of time. I did not understand any of this and had never heard this sort of logic before to start feeding elk. Todd disagreed with the biologist, smiled and said, "It's time to start feeding!"

I shook Todd's hand and told him it was a pleasure to meet him. I could tell that the biologist was upset, I just wasn't sure why. Maybe I needed to read that red three-ring binder titled "Feed Ground Operational Plans" that Bernie had given me weeks ago. We made it back to the office. The biologist approached me and said, "Scott, I need to visit with you if you have a minute?" I said, "Sure, what's on your mind?" The biologist said, "I was reading through the Feed Ground Operation Plans and we have not yet met the criteria for feeding elk at Green River Lakes. The plan calls for sixteen inches of snow on the level and least three hundred elk on the feed ground for ten consecutive days. We only have fourteen inches of snow and the elk have only been there for five consecutive days. I simply can't recommend starting feeding at this time." I smiled at him and said, "If you want to wait another five days and two more inches of snow to start feeding those elk that is the most ridiculous thing that I have ever heard. If we don't gather them now, they may move down country and we may risk losing them." He replied, "Yes, but that is not what the plan calls for." I said, "I don't know who put this cookbook plan together for feeding elk, but you can throw it in the trash or use it to wipe your ass! Those elk need fed now, and I will notify Todd to start tomorrow." The biologist turned and stomped out of the room. My blood pressure was up.

I would need to visit with Ron and Bernie about this in the morning.

I sat down tired in my office (bedroom) and started reading the plan. The Operational Plan had requirements for all twenty-two feed grounds for when to start feeding elk. The department was trying to save money and reduce the dependency of elk on feed grounds. The plans also recommended getting elk off feed earlier at each feed ground. After reading the plan, I had violated every feed ground plan so far by starting feeding elk too early. We were already chasing elk every day on our snow machines, trying to get them back to feed grounds. If I had not started feeding, we would have elk strung from hell to breakfast on cattle feed lines on private property all over the county. I thought I was doing good things for the department. Come to find out I was creating enemies among my fellow employees. I just didn't know this until it was brought to my attention that day.

I visited with Bernie early the next morning and told him what had happened. He had a large Cuban cigar in his mouth. He pulled it out and said, "If Todd Stearns says it's time to start feeding the damn elk, then it's time to feed the damn elk!! Head up there and get him started today! If they don't like it, they can throw their damn cookbook plan in the trash!" I agreed with Bernie and was glad to have his support. I snow-machined into Green River Lakes and helped Todd feed the elk. Todd and I had a great visit. I really respected this man. He was the real deal. He invited me into his little log work shed and showed me some beautiful elk antler chandeliers that he had made. Todd was very talented at many things. I looked forward to spending more time learning from him.

I finally got a minute to stop by Kathy Miller's house and meet her. She had just got done feeding her cows with draft horses and a sled. She used a four-way hook up, meaning she fed with four draft horses all harnessed together. She was in the process of unharnessing all the horses when I pulled into her front yard. She had heavy winter clothes on with a scotch cap and earflaps pulled down over her ears. Her face was bright red due to the cold weather, she had frost on her eyebrows, and frozen snot dripping from her nose. She was a short, stocky lady. I parked my truck and approached her slowly as she was hanging horse collars in her unheated shop. The front large green fiberglass door on the shop had a large hole about 2'x3' knocked through it in the lower right corner. I would later learn that the famous bucking horse named Copenhagen Skoal had kicked that hole in her garage door.

Kathy turned around and looked at me in my green Game and Fish coat with the antelope shield on my left arm. I quickly said, "Hi, are you Kathy Miller? My name is Scott Werbelow." She replied in a deep voice, "Yeah, what brings you here?" I explained to her that I was new in the area and that I had heard that she was looking for a hired man. I told her that my wife Lana was looking for a ranch job and that she was a really good hand. Kathy said, "Yeah, well have her come talk to me if she is interested. The job comes with that little white house over there yonder and pays $600 a month." She was very short with me. I felt like she didn't care much for the Game and Fish Department. I was short on words, I said, "Yes ma'am, I will have her get in touch with you. Do you have a phone number that she can call you?" Kathy responded, "I would rather meet her in person." I said, "Ok, have a great day!" I left the area feeling like this gal was tired and needed help badly. I don't know how many cows she was feeding daily, but she was worn out and cranky.

I would call my wife Lana later that night and tell her about the possible job offer. She seemed excited about it, but would need to travel over five hours to meet with Kathy on her one day off per week. This would mean that she would have to spend about ten hours driving in one day on slick roads over south pass. She was not happy about that, but I was ready to be living in a house, even if it wasn't much and I missed my family. Lana traveled over and met with Kathy. Kathy offered her the job immediately and told us we could move into the house anytime. This was the best news that I had heard in a long time. I didn't have any time off to help Lana move. Maybe she could just bring over the bare necessities, and we could get moved in. Hell, all I needed was a bed and some wood for the wood stove and I would be happy. Lana showed up and we both went over and looked at the house. It was small, two bedrooms and one bathroom. It was kind of cute on the inside and would be easy to heat with the large wood stove in the front living room. The house sat on a large parcel of land surrounded by willows with the Green River right out the back door. We couldn't ask for a better location. Maybe Kathy would let me go fishing sometime. I would be happy to sleep on the floor in a sleeping bag in front of the wood stove after what I had been through over the past few months.

Lana headed back home that day. We were both excited, even though she had a long drive back home in the dark. She told me that she would quit her job laying gas pipe line and get started moving over in the next few weeks. I moved in immediately and couldn't have been any happier to get out of my office. I borrowed the feed ground chainsaw and cut up a bunch of Cottonwood around the house to stay warm until we could get some good pine wood to burn. Lana told me that she would also haul some good pine over that she had at our cabin in Shell. She was hoping to be moved in before Christmas, which was only a few weeks away.

The snow kept falling. We had elk on private property all over the place. It seemed like we were moving elk nearly every day. Brad called me almost daily needing help to move elk off the Hughes place, Fear place, Michelson place, and many others. We were having record numbers of elk on feed grounds due to the deep snow conditions. Elk that typically wintered out were showing up on feed grounds and private property. Some elk were in areas that we couldn't move due to deep snow conditions. These elk were co-mingling with cattle and feeding right off cattle feed lines. We would end up getting a kill permit to remove a small group of bulls that were getting into a hay stack on the Cottonwood Ranch. We could not move the bulls to the Bench Corral feed ground no matter what we tried they wouldn't go. This became very controversial with the public, as they didn't want to see us killing large bulls just because they were in a damage situation.

We would move a group of about one hundred elk nearly every day from the Hughes place to North Piney feed ground. The BFH crew had done a habitat improvement project below the North Piney feed ground several years prior. These elk were lured into the habitat improvement area nearly four years earlier and had never been to the North Piney feed ground. The snow got so deep that the elk could no longer winter out there. The elk didn't even know where the feed ground was, and we would be trying to move them through deep snow up county to get them there. We actually got them on the feed ground twice. They ran right through six hundred other elk and kept going, only to return to private property the very next day. We had so many elk displaced from feed grounds that we finally asked for additional assistance from other game wardens all over the state to help us move elk. I never saw so many stuck snow machines in willow bottoms in all of my life.

Brand new Powder Special 600.

All of the wardens were riding under-powered snow machines and getting stuck often. I seemed to be the only one that knew this, because I had such a great personal snow machine and knew the benefit of having more horsepower. I ended-up writing a letter of justification to the assistant division chief to allow wardens to have at least a 600 CC machine. The request was soon approved. The next thing I knew Brad, Doug McWhirter and I were allowed to purchase a brand-new snow machine. We drove to Worland and picked up three brand-new 1997 Arctic Cat Powder Specials with a 600 CC engine and reverse. These new machines were the cat's meow. Dennis would no longer be blowing our doors off with his new purple liquid cooled panther, and we also had reverse.

Bernie called me in his office early one Monday morning. He asked me how I liked my new snow machine. I told him that I absolutely loved it. He asked me how the elk drives were going to North Piney feed ground. I told him that we nearly had the elk there twice last week and the lead cow turned and took the whole herd back to private property. I explained that I tried everything to turn the lead cow and she literally ran over the top of me on my snow machine. Bernie looked at me very seriously and said, "We don't need that crap, next time she does that, shoot her! We have spent too many man hours trying to move these elk. We have a kill permit and don't need to tolerate that anymore, just shoot her!" I was surprised to hear Bernie say this, but I agreed with him whole heartedly. I was tired of moving these elk. I would pack my rifle next time.

Bernie grabbed his cigar out of his front shirt pocket and licked the end of it a few times before stuck it in his mouth. He looked like he was in deep thought as he stared at the ceiling in his office. He looked at me, pulled the cigar out of his mouth and said, "We have so damn many elk off feed grounds, we are going to have to start spraying the willow bottoms for elk." I just laughed. Bernie did not laugh. Bernie said, "The reason that I called you into my office is to inform you that I have visited with Wildlife Administration and they have agreed to keep you as a commissioned game warden in the region. You can hang on to your law enforcement equipment and do law enforcement work as time allows." This was the greatest news that I had heard in a long time. I was very excited. Bernie then told me that they still weren't sure where my position was headed, because it was still under appeal from the guy that had been fired. I shook Bernie's hand and thanked him for the news. I left his office and felt like doing cartwheels down the sidewalk. I was so excited.

Brad called me and asked me if I would like to come down and see one of the biggest mule deer bucks on the winter range that he had ever seen before. I told him that I would head that direction and that I had some good news to share with him. We traveled south towards LaBarge Creek and took an oil field road to the west. I told Brad the news about me being a commissioned game warden. He was so excited for me. He stopped the truck and gave me a high five. He said, "Congratulations, Buddy!" We traveled a few more miles and found several trucks all parked together on the winter range. Brad said, "You don't go looking for this buck, you just look for trucks parked in the road. You will find this buck because people camp out on him daily waiting for him to shed his horns. This buck had been named "Popeye" because your eyes will pop out of your head when you see him. We pulled up to the group of trucks and I grabbed Brad's binoculars. HOLY CRAP!! I could not believe the size of this buck. He was standing with four other bucks that were around thirty inches wide. You didn't even look at the other bucks. Popeye had a spread of about forty inches and had freak points going everywhere. His horns were massive. This was the biggest buck that I had ever seen in my life.

We stepped out of the truck and visited with a couple guys from Big Piney who had been watching Popeye for quite some time. One of the guys had collected the sheds from Popeye the previous two years. As I was visiting with him, I noticed that he was wearing white tennis shoes in the middle of the winter with about eight inches of snow on the ground. I asked him why he was wearing tennis shoes in the middle of the winter. He told me that he had been training and running wind sprints, because he didn't want someone from Rock Springs to beat him to Popeye's sheds. Apparently, the previous year he ran from his truck to Popeye to grab a shed antler, and had beat another guy who was from Rock Springs in a full-blown sprint by about five feet to collect the shed antler. They almost ended up in a fist fight over the shed antler. He was not going to allow that to happen this year. He would watch the deer twenty-four hours a day, seven days a week until Popeye shed his antlers.

As we were standing there, Popeye disappeared into some tall sage brush. The man got in his truck and watched for Popeye through his spotting scope. Pretty quick I observed the guy sneak out of his truck low to the ground. He took off in a dead sprint towards Popeye. I looked over at another truck that was parked about one hundred yards away. A man jumped out of this truck and was sprinting towards Popeye as well. I grabbed my binoculars and noticed that Popeye was missing one of his

Many deer starved to death that winter.

antlers. The guy from Big Piney arrived at the shed antler first and jumped with joy. He brought the shed antler back to the truck and showed it to Brad and me. Brad snapped a photo of me holding the antler. I looked at Brad and said, "Man, this is some competitive antler hunting right here. The man from Big Piney would end up with both shed antlers again that year. The winter of 96-97 was very tough on the deer populations. Popeye was last seen in the spring of 1997 and looked to be in poor health. This would be the last year that Popeye was ever seen. It is believed that he died that winter. The man from Big Piney has been offered over $50,000 for the sheds belonging to Popeye. What a magnificent deer he was. I was glad I got to see him alive and even hold one of his shed antlers in my hand for a moment.

Deer trying to survive.

My wife Lana had made one trip to our new house with a horse trailer full of our belongings. It was nice to finally be sleeping in my own bed. Christmas was coming up in a few days. I would plan to take a few days off over Christmas and head back to Shell to spend time with both our parents and get another load of stuff. The day before Christmas, we were blasted with another bad snow storm. Lana was worried that we wouldn't make it back to Shell because of closed roads. I told her not to worry. I was a trained professional driving in deep drifted snow conditions. We loaded up Wes and Wendy and headed for Shell in our 1995 Ford Truck. The roads were bad between Pinedale and Farson but still navigable. Once we got north of Farson a few miles, there was a gate across the highway that had flashing amber lights and a sign that read "Road Closed." I looked at Lana and said, "This couldn't be any worse than the trip that I took into Finnegan feed ground on the day that I got lost." I drove around the road closed sign and gave it the onion as we went through a deep snow drift in the borrow pit to our right and back up on the highway.

I'm not sure how we ever made it across South Pass that afternoon. There were places that I couldn't see the highway at all. We were in a complete whiteout at times, hoping to see the next delineator post. I could feel my truck breaking through deep drifts. I was in four-wheel drive with the gas pedal mashed to the floor. A couple of times we almost came to a stop in the deep drifts. My knuckles were white as I clinched the steering wheel tightly. I would show no fear to Lana and the kids, even though I was scared half to death. We rarely ever wore our seatbelts back in those days. I told everyone to put their seatbelts on. I looked in the rear-view mirror at the kids. Their eyes were the size of silver dollars and they both had a concerned look on their face. They both knew if Dad ever said to put your seatbelt on, shit was getting pretty bad!! Lana looked at me as she snapped her seatbelt on and said, "I told you this wasn't a good idea!" I never looked at her and responded, "I'm a trained professional, ma'am, please latch your seatbelt and sit back in your seat and enjoy the ride." Nobody said a word all the way across South Pass, including me. I reached down and turned up the radio. There was a song playing "Don't worry be happy, Do-Do-Do-Do, Don't, worry be happy." This put a smile on my face, it could have been a scene straight from Christmas Vacation with Chevy Chase.

We finally made it across south pass and dropped off into a few different canyons. The wind was screaming but the visibility was better. There were drifts across the highway that were 2-3 feet deep. I kept the engine wound up and broke through drift after drift. Thank God it was downhill or we would have gotten stuck. It was actually a beautiful snow storm (blizzard) I was kind of enjoying myself. We were the only people on the road blasting through soft drifts. The only tracks in the snow headed home for Christmas. On that trip I nicknamed my son Rusty and my daughter Audrey after the characters in the movie Christmas Vacation. The nicknames still stick today. We would eventually make it safe and sound to spend Christmas at home with our parents in Shell. The storm persisted. I checked the weather daily and all roads were closed back to Pinedale for the next several days. I was getting worried about all the feeders and the problems that they may be facing daily.

On day five of our Christmas vacation, the road report said that the road over Togwotee Pass was open into Jackson. We loaded up the Ford with pine firewood, two cats, two dogs, two kids and any other crap that we could possibly shove in a hole somewhere. Both kids were sick with the flu. Wendy had a temperature of 104 degrees and a bad cough. We said our good-byes and headed for Jackson. The roads were horrible over Togwotee Pass. We arrived at Moron Junction right at dark to observe a long line of cars and trucks. The Park Service had closed the road due to poor visibility. A lady walked up to my truck and told me that the road would be closed for at least two hours. She said the drifts were so deep that they were trying to open the road with a large rotary blower. Great, the kids are sick and we are still several hours from home with more bad roads ahead of us all the way home, I thought to myself.

Wendy was crying, she was so sick. Wes said, "Dad, I think the cat just puked on my coat." The cats and dogs needed to be let out to potty. How do you turn a couple of cats loose in a blizzard and make them go poop? Even if you had a leash, you can't make a cat poop in a blizzard! Several hours passed, traffic in front of us was starting to move. We would end up following the rotary snow plow all the way to Jackson at about 15-25 miles per hour the entire way. We arrived in Jackson Hole at 11:00 PM and still had another hour or two of bad roads through Hoback Canyon to get home. We finally arrived safely at home at 12:30 PM. Our driveway was completely drifted in with three to four feet high drifts. I mashed the throttle headed for the front gate to our house. The truck dug down in the deep snow and we became really stuck right in our front yard. I looked at Lana and said, "Falla Lalla La, Merry Christmas, welcome home Punkin!" I was just happy to be home. I finally got a fire going to warm up the house and put the kids to bed. I poured a stiff whiskey and sat in my recliner by the wood stove. I just needed to relax for a minute. The bad roads home stressed me out with my family in the car. I wondered what kind of disasters at work I would have to deal with in the morning.

It had snowed several more feet since I left to go home for Christmas. It would be time to start feeding elk at Soda Lake. I snow-machined into the feed ground and mounted a Briggs and Stratton motor on the water well next to the horse corral. I gave the carburetor a couple squirts of starting fluid and she fired right up. Next thing I knew water was coming out of the Spicket and into the large water trough. It was so nice to have running water at a feed ground. Many feeders had to melt snow in a large metal tank with a propane heater each day to water their horses. You can't imagine how much snow one must shovel daily to fill a fifty-gallon water tank with melted snow to water a team of horses. Some feeders hauled water daily behind their snow machines on a sled. Other feeders chopped a hole in the ice each day if they had a creek near their horse corral.

I then snow-machined over to the old feed ground north of Soda Lake and caught Amos and Andy. These were a beautifully matched team of black Percheron's. Both horses were always easy to catch and dog gentle. I led both of them behind my snow machine back over to the new feed ground and placed them in the corral. This team had been feeding together for years. There probably wasn't much that this team hadn't seen over the years. I was told by others that this was the best team of horses that the department owned. I would call the feeder for Soda Lake when I got back to the office and get him started feeding. This feed ground had about 800 elk standing on it that day waiting to be fed. It also had some of the largest bulls that I had seen on any of the feed grounds. It was pretty

Amos and Andy.

impressive to watch the large group of big bulls enter the feed ground. There must have been over one hundred large six-point bulls. I would be excited to come back and help the feeder feed these elk and get a better look at all the bulls.

I headed out of Soda Lake feed ground down the main road. I looked up and a coyote was crossing the trail ahead of me. I sped up and hit the coyote broadside with my snow machine right on the main trail. I came to a stop and looked back. The coyote was lying dead right in the road. I had run over many coyotes over the years with a snow machine but had never killed one with one single hit. Usually, you would mash the coyote down in the deep snow several times and they would get up and run off again. Sometimes you would have to run over them so many times to kill them that you felt bad. I walked back and picked up the large white coyote off the road. I thought, man this is a nice-looking pelt, I can probably get about $75.00 for this one. I laid the coyote across my seat and sat on him. Just before I reached the parking lot where my truck and trailer were parked, I could feel something biting me under my right arm. The coyote was not dead and very much alive. I reached down with my right arm and put him in a head lock and tried to choke him off. It was all that I could do to hold on to him even though I was sitting on top of him.

He growled and snarled at me I couldn't get to my pistol because it was inside my snow machine suit. I grabbed my throttle with my left hand and kept him in a head lock with my right hand and continued down the trail towards the parking lot. When I reached the parking lot there was a family of four unloading their snow machines getting ready to go ice fishing at Willow Lake. I slid sideways into the parking lot next to my game and fish truck with the coyote in a head lock. I wasn't sure what to do, so I just stood up and let the coyote go right in front of the ice fishermen. The coyote jumped off my snow machine and headed right towards the family of four. They all headed different directions as the coyote ran by them. I got off my snow machine and walked over to them. I introduced myself to them and checked their fishing licenses. The father of the family said, "What the heck was that all about?" I told him that I had always wanted to give a coyote a ride on my snow machine. I didn't want to explain the gory details in front of his wife and kids. The man stepped back, laughed and said, "Guess you don't get to see that every day."

I then headed into Fall Creek feed ground to check on Kathy. I hadn't been up there in a couple of weeks to see her. She was loading her last load of hay when I pulled up to the stack yard. I was happy that I would finally get to feed with Kathy and look over her elk herd. She told me that she had just gained about three hundred more elk with the last snow, and that she was feeding over eight hundred elk. She had counted her hay inventory and was worried that we may run out of hay with the increase of elk numbers. Kathy was very meticulous with everything that she did. Each flake of hay was about four inches thick and she would throw a "Flake" of hay about every twenty feed to ensure that the elk were spread out and all the calves got to eat as well. She would spend the entire day feeding elk. Because she lived up there in a small camp trailer and didn't have anything else to do. When she loaded the small hay bales, all the knots in the strings had to be to the inside and knots up. This way she could grab her machete and quickly chop all the strings right behind the knots, and easily pull the strings off each hay bale without the knots getting hung up on the under-side of the hay bale.

We loaded up the last load of hay and took the team to the top of the hill where we could see the elk. Kathy stopped the team and said, "Bonnie, Clyde, WHOA!" She then looked at the elk and yelled, "HERE ELKY, ELKY, ELKY!! HERE ELKY, ELKY, ELKY!!" Pretty quick the elk started coming down off the hill towards us. Kathy got excited and said, "OH, look here comes Curly and Moe, I haven't seen them for several weeks." Curly was a large 7x7 bull with brow tines that dipped down instead of up. That is why she named him Curly. As the elk gathered around the sled, they started eating hay right off the feed sled. This is when I realized that Kathy had all of her bulls named and she knew every one of them by name. She had even named some of the cows. One cow starting eating hay off the sled right next to me. Kathy said. "Oh, there's Sally, I gave her a haircut yesterday, isn't she pretty!" I said, "You gave an elk a haircut?" Kathy replied, "Oh yes, that way I can tell Sally apart from all the other cow elk." Kathy's elk were the tamest elk that I had seen on any of the feed grounds. It was because she would spend the entire day feeding and talking to them. The elk loved her and so did her horses.

Sally with a haircut.

We got done feeding elk, watered and fed the draft horses. Kathy invited me into her small camp trailer for a cup of cider. As I approached the trailer, I noticed it was wrapped with black plastic around the base of the trailer. She had also lined the base of the trailer with hay bales to help insulate the trailer. There was also a frozen dead calf elk hanging off the trailer next to the front door with her elk tag on it. As we entered her trailer, Kathy pitched a wad of Copenhagen out of her lower lip and said, "Do you like my meat locker?" I said, "Yea, that's pretty handy, not very attractive, but handy!" Kathy said, "Yeah, it's very handy. Whenever I need a piece of meat, I just open my door and carve off a chunk, don't even need to wrap it and risk freezer burn." I stepped into the trailer behind Kathy. The inside of the trailer was really cluttered with boxes and stuff stacked everywhere. Kathy moved several boxes and made room for me to sit at her front table. It was cold and dark in the trailer. I could see my breath inside of the trailer. I noticed a small propane bottle with a burner on the top sitting in the back next to Kathy's bed. I asked Kathy if she was able to adequately heat the trailer with the propane heater. She looked at her thermometer on the wall and said, "Oh Yea, the warmest that I have been able to get in here is twenty-eight degrees." I thought to myself, twenty-eight degrees, that's below freezing!" Kathy said, "It's not that bad. You just have to dress warm and put an extra blanket on at night." I thought, Holy Shit, what a way to spend a winter. I thought sleeping on the floor in my office was bad, but then I remembered my trailer house with no heat.

Kathy poured me a warm cup of cider and fed me some frozen banana bread. I enjoyed visiting with Kathy. She was tougher than most men and loved feeding those elk. She wore a faded red scotch cap with the ear flaps down, safety glasses, and a turquoise neck scarf. She always had a large chew of Copenhagen in her lower lip and loved to spit. She had a bubbly personality and laughed and joked about everything. She kind of reminded me of Tim Baxley. They could be two peas in a pod, I thought to myself. Kathy asked me if it was alright with me if she brings her chickens up and puts them in the old abandoned house trailer that was parked underneath an old hayshed next to her. I told her that I didn't see a problem with that. I thanked her for her hospitality and left the trailer. I was concerned about the amount of hay she had left in the stack yard to feed over eight hundred elk for the rest of the winter. I walked over to the stack yard and counted all the hay bales. I did some quick math. It didn't look good. We were going to run out of hay the way things currently looked. This was very concerning to me. How would we ever open the road to haul hay in the winter time? How would we buy hay and be able to get a semi-truck to where the hay was located?

I returned back to my truck and had a message from Tim Baxley. It said, "Hey boss man, this is Tim, I'm concerned about running out of hay at Finnegan. I counted the bales today and it looks pretty bleak if we continue to have a bad winter." I thought, shit, this winter could get really ugly before it gets better!" I went back to my office and looked at Ron Dean's annual feed ground reports over the past ten years. I looked at the average number of elk on feed grounds and average number of days fed. I quickly learned that we were definitely going to run out of hay at Finnegan and Fall Creek feed grounds, even if we cut the elk back fifty percent on feed starting tomorrow. This concerned me deeply. It would not be an option to run out of hay on any of the feed grounds. Where would the elk go? They would all be in cattle feed lines and some may even starve to death. I was very upset with the previous feed ground manager. Why didn't he stock more hay into some of these feed grounds? Seemed to me it would be much easier to buy hay in the summer rather than have to open roads in the winter and try to find hay for sale. Hay prices would also be very high during a bad winter. What would it cost to open some of the roads where the snow was over five feet deep?

I would spend the next week checking hay inventories on all feed grounds and doing the math as close as I could, based on the numbers in the annual feed ground reports. I did not want to say anything to Bernie and Ron until I knew exactly what we needed to do. After some very thorough inventory counts, we would need to cut way back at Scab Creek, Green River lakes, and Jewett. If we cut back on feed at these feed grounds, we could probably make it through depending on how long the winter lasted.

I would soon meet with Bernie and Ron and discuss the situation with them. They both agreed that I should start looking for hay for sale in the area and get some bids on what snow removal and hauling was going to cost. I thought, the department is going to get screwed on this deal, it's not an option to run out of hay. Hay prices would be very high and anyone who had equipment large enough to open the roads would be pretty proud of their services.

I snow-machined back into North Piney to check on Tim and his hay inventory. Something was weird, all the elk were gone? Where could six hundred elk have gone? Tim came walking out of his trailer as I pulled up. He said, "Hey boss man, don't worry about my hay inventory, the elk done left in the night." I said "Where do you think they went?" Tim replied, "Heck if I know. They left hay on the feed ground and left sometime in the night. Looks like their tracks are headed down country." I told Tim that I would find them and let him know where they were at. I jumped on my machine and followed the large swath of tracks headed down country. I followed the tracks in the snow for about twelve miles and found the elk at Bench Corral feed ground. They had joined the Bench Corral elk and it looked like there were over one thousand elk on the feed ground. I thought, shit, now we are going to run out of hay at this feed ground as well. I headed back to Pinedale to visit with Bernie about the situation.

Bernie told me that the BFH crew was trying to eliminate some feed grounds to save money and spread elk out at lower elevations. It was decided the previous year to bait the elk from North Piney to Bench Corral. It apparently worked and elk had left North Piney following an alfalfa bait line all the way to Bench Corral. Once the elk were fed there for the winter, some area landowners and cattleman threw a fit about the increased elk numbers in the area. They felt like their cattle grazing allotments would be cut in half due to the increase in elk numbers utilizing this area in the spring and fall. They also claimed that the Game and Fish did all of this illegally while the BLM was on a furlough and nobody was around to stop them. They also claimed that the game and fish had trespassed across certain properties with their bait line. After a large blow up from area ranchers, the Game and Fish were ordered by the Governor to feed elk again at North Piney.

This was all new news to me. This would have been good information. This time we did not bait any elk to Bench Corral they just left on their own as soon as the snow conditions became very deep at North Piney. It's like the elk remembered getting fed at lower elevations and less snow accumulations. The trail that they took, was exactly the way that we had baited them the previous year. We lost trust with the local ranchers over this deal. Now they would accuse the Game and Fish of not feeding the elk at North Piney to get them to go to Bench Corral. They accused us of feeding the elk rotten hay so that they would leave the feed ground. They also accused us of baiting the elk again in the middle of the night to get them to Bench Corral. None of this happened, the elk simply left because they knew the winter conditions were much milder at lower elevations and they would get fed. Now these ranchers would not tolerate any elk on their property. Brad and I would spend nearly every day in January moving elk off private property in this area. I told Brad that I would continue to help him move elk in his warden district daily. But we were damn sure going to take at least a half of day off to watch the Super bowl.

I spent a great deal of time looking for any hay that was for sale. Most ranchers were hurting for hay due to the severe winter. I finally located about four hundred ton of hay on three different ranches. I actually had to ride my snow machine out into their hay meadows to look at the hay before I agreed to purchase it. I remember shoveling over four feet of snow off the top of the hay stacks, just to dig down and look at the quality of the top bales. Most of the hay quality really wasn't that good, but we couldn't be choosey at this point in the game. I got lucky and found a guy named Melvin who thought he could open all the roads into the feed grounds and haul the hay. He told me, "We can do it, but it's not going to be cheap. We also would need to borrow the Game and Fish's old straight truck to get into Fall Creek and Finnegan feed grounds." Our straight truck was located in the Quonset hut out at Soda Lake. We would need to plow that road open for about five miles just to get the truck out. I didn't think that truck had been used in years. Hopefully it would start and run. Melvin's trucks were all regular semis, with long trailers, too long to get into some of the feed grounds with a plowed road.

I met with my office manager Des and made many calls to Cheyenne to see what needed to be done to purchase this hay and get it delivered. This was one of the most complicated processes that I had ever seen in my life. The bean counters in Cheyenne wanted me to put the hay and hauling out for bid, because they thought we were being taken advantage of. The bid process would take 4-6 weeks. We didn't have the time. This was an emergency. Besides, there was no other hay available for sale in the area and nobody else that could open the roads and haul the hay other than Melvin. The process would end up at the director's level. Fiscal was told to process the contracts immediately. I didn't make any friends in the fiscal division once this process was completed. I even received some nasty emails from the head of purchasing in the fiscal division, because I had gone around her and her team of professionals. I didn't care about hurt feelings, we needed to get the job done.

We decided to open the road into Finnegan first. Melvin showed up with a huge grader that had a large V-plow mounted on the front of it and a large blade located underneath. He also had a large caterpillar to follow the grader and do the final clean up. The grader was chained up all the way around. We would need to take all the heavy equipment right through the cranky landowner's front yard and calving corrals. I was not looking forward to this conversation. I banged on his front door to let him know what was going on. Thankfully he was gone for several days and I got to visit with his wife. She wasn't pleasant but she told me that she would call him and let him know. She also wanted my phone number so that her husband could call me. I thanked her and gave Melvin the thumbs up. He dropped the front V-plow and headed through the landowner's corral system. About that time my bag phone rang. I didn't recognize the number but answered the phone. It was the cranky landowner. He didn't say hi or anything, he just screamed into the phone. "YOU BETTER KEEP THAT DAMN EQUIPMENT ON THE ROAD ALL THE WAY TO THE FEED GROUND! IF YOU GET EVEN TEN FEET OFF YOUR EASEMENT,

I WILL SUE YOUR ASS!" I thanked him for being so understanding. He hung up on me.

I caught up with Melvin and told him under no circumstances don't get off the main road and tear up a bunch of sage brush. Melvin said he would do the best he could, but I may have to get out in front of him and locate the road all the way into the feed ground. Of course, it was another blizzard that day and the snow was so deep and drifted that I didn't have clue where the road was located. I would end up digging holes all day with a shovel in front of the grader to keep him on the road. Some of the holes were over six feet deep. If I found sage brush that meant we were off the road and would have to change our direction of travel. Melvin was an awesome operator and he could feel the road with his blade most of the time. We would end up cutting through a large drift up a steep side hill.

Road plowing in Finnegan Feed ground.

The drift was taller than my Game and Fish truck. I couldn't believe that Melvin was able to keep plowing uphill and make it through.

Grader coming off hill in deep snow.

We finally arrived at the feed ground. Tim was feeding elk with his team, Kent and Doug, as we arrived. Tim yelled, "GOOD TO SEE YA, BOSS MAN!" I couldn't believe we had made it. I would have never guessed that we could even get the road open. This was the easy part. We would now need to plow the roads into the areas where the hay was located and get the hay loaded onto trucks and get the trucks into the feed ground. Melvin hired several other truck drivers to haul the hay from the ranch where the hay was purchased to an area close to the feed ground. They would then off-load the larger trucks onto the smaller straight truck owned by the department. We chained up this truck all the way around and loaded it with a track-hoe that had a "Ten Pack" attachment on the front for moving small hay bales. This attachment allowed you to grab ten bales at a time and move hay from one truck to another. This was the first time that I had ever seen an attachment like this, and Melvin was very good at operating it. He would sit in one spot and swing from one trailer to the other in a nice slow smooth action. He could completely load a semi-trailer with hay in about twenty minutes. I had definitely hired the right man for the job. He would then hook a large loader with a "Ten-Pack" on the front and pull the straight truck loaded with hay into the feed ground. Once at the feed ground, he would use the loader to unload the hay from the straight truck. To my amazement the whole operation went very smooth into Finnegan.

We then opened the road into Bench Corral. This road was easier to open due to flatter road conditions and not nearly as much snow. Melvin thought we could just load a larger truck with a pup and not have to off-load onto the smaller truck. He hired another man named Gene for this haul. Gene had hauled hay for the Game and Fish for many years and was a very experienced hay hauler. Gene's truck was not nearly as nice as Melvin's, but ran great. Gene was the type of guy who could replace a transmission, engine or clutch in his truck overnight and never miss a day of hauling. He knew his equipment well and was a damn fine mechanic. We purchased hay up the Cotton Wood Creek road near Bench Corral feed ground. Gene loaded up his flat nose semi- truck and pup heavy. I noticed all the tires were bald on Gene's truck. Gene looked at me and said, "Well, if we can get up Peterson-Hill I think we will make it just fine." Peterson Hill was a steep hill on the county road several miles away. It had packed snow on it and was very slick. I told Gene that I didn't know what I was talking about, but if it were me, I would chain up all the way around. Gene said, "Oh hell, I have enough weight for traction, I should be fine." I went ahead of Gene in my work truck and waited for him at the top of Peterson Hill. Pretty quick here comes Gene rolling down the road with black smoke pouring out of his smoke stacks. I thought to myself, if he is going to attempt that hill without chain's he is one crazy son of a gun! Gene made it nearly to the top and spun out. The load was so heavy that he couldn't hold the truck on the steep hill. He slid back down the hill backwards and jack-knifed the truck right in the middle of the steep hill.

Gene rode it out. I would have bailed out of the cab of the truck.

The truck nearly tipped over the pup was leaning hard in the downhill direction. Gene stepped out of the cab and started walking up the road towards me. He slipped on the ice and fell down in the middle of the road in front of me. He got up and said, "Damn, that hill is slicker than I thought." About that time another semi was coming from the other direction headed down the steep hill. I jumped out of my truck and ran towards the semi yelling "STOP, STOP!" The driver hit the brakes but it was too late. He was already headed off the steep hill. He went sailing over the hill and almost ran Gene over in the middle of the road. Gene bailed off the road into the deep snow as the large semi-truck came to a stop right next to him. This truck jack-knifed as well right in the middle of the road on a blind hill. I couldn't believe he got it stopped before plowing into Gene's truck. The driver jumped out of the truck scared to death. He told me that he was hauling some sort of hot sludge in his tanker. He said, "If this stuff sets up, I will never get it unloaded. I need to keep moving as soon as possible." I told him that I would do what I could. I went to the top of the hill and parked my work truck in the middle of the road with my hazard flashers on. I called Melvin and told him the situation. Melvin replied, "Oh Shit, I will send my caterpillar up as soon as possible."

It took nearly two hours for the caterpillar to arrive. By now we had cars and trucks backed up on both ends of the road. Aaron was the man's name operating the cat. He pulled it off the steep hill and hooked a large stretch rope to the tanker truck. Aaron poured the throttle to the cat and started backing up the steep slick hill. He had the semi-truck straightened out and headed up the hill. I couldn't believe he was able to pull that large truck up the hill backwards. Pretty quickly, Aaron lost traction and he and the semi were headed back down the hill towards Gene's truck. Aaron quickly stabbed his "Stingers" into the ground behind him. This stopped them from going back down the hill. He poured the throttle to the cat and worked his tracks back and forth in the ice and soon headed back up the hill. I'm pretty sure this was a very scary moment for everyone involved.

The large cat would slide forward and then trudge backwards, blowing black smoke out of the smoke stack. Finally, they made it to the top of the hill. He went back down and pulled the hay truck up the hill with about the same degree of difficulty as the first truck. I called Melvin and told him that everything was back to normal again. He said, "Boy this one is going to cost your department!" I replied, "It better not, it's not my fault that he didn't take the time to put his damn chains on in the first place." Melvin replied, "Yea, I suppose you may be right."

Hay truck stuck in the middle of Peterson Hill.

Scott C. Werbelow

Over the next two weeks we had hauled about four hundred tons of hay into Fall Creek, Finnegan, and Bench Corral feed grounds. I was worn out, but relieved that we weren't going to run out of hay. Other feed grounds were going to be close on hay. We would have to cut back and monitor hay use daily to make it through until spring. I could not believe that we were able to open roads and get all the hay bought and hauled. I don't remember what the final bill was on this little operation, but it was damn expensive. I was ready for this winter to end. I still was not sure where my job was headed. Would I someday end up as a permanent feed ground manager/game warden or would I end up back on the reservoir crew in the spring competing with nine other game wardens for a permanent job?

Hay hauling into Bench Corral.

Straight truck off-loading into Fall Creek.

Chapter 8

LATE WINTER / SPRING

I was learning my new job as a feed ground manager quickly. Every day was a new learning experience and generally came with a curve ball. It seemed like all I did was react to some sort of a crisis on a daily basis. It was nearly impossible to take a day off, because it was something every day. Lana was helping Kathy feed her cows daily with her team of draft horses. They were generally done feeding each day by late morning and then she was done for the day. She wasn't making much money but we had a place to live. She had placed both our kids in school in Pinedale. Wes would be in the second grade and Wendy in Kindergarten. Lana would get a part-time job working at a pet/feed store in Pinedale. It didn't pay much but kept her busy. Lana was a person that needed to stay busy.

Now that most of the elk were settled in on all feed grounds it was time to classify the elk on each one. This meant getting accurate counts of all elk on all feed grounds. This was generally coordinated by our wildlife biologists, BFH Biologists, and game wardens. Each feed ground would be scheduled for a certain date and a certain time. Game and fish personnel would arrive at the feed ground and help the feeder string out a long feed line. Once all the elk were on feed the feeder would run his team along the feed line and Game and Fish personnel would count the elk. Each

Scott C. Werbelow

Kathy and Lana feeding cows

person on the feed sled would have his own job. One person would count cows, another would count mature bulls, another would count yearling bulls, and another would count calves, leaving the final person to count total elk. I always volunteered to count total elk. For some reason I was just good at it and always wanted to know myself what the total numbers were, in terms of making sure we had adequate hay supply's. Sometimes the counts went smoothly and sometimes the elk wouldn't cooperate. We would have to keep counting until we all felt good about our final counts. Over time I became really good at counting total elk numbers. I could look at a herd of elk and tell how many elk were on the feed ground based on the size of the herd. I usually guessed pretty close to the actual numbers. Classifying elk didn't seem like much of a job, but the coordination effort was difficult to get people together because everyone was so busy with other things. I think the feeders generally liked it when all of us would

From L to R John Fandek, Duke Early, Doug McWhirter, Scott Werbelow

show up, because they had help feeding elk for that day. With 22 feed grounds it would basically take an additional 22 days out of your schedule to count elk. Sometimes the feeder would have to short the elk on feed several days in a row, so that we could get a good count on all the elk. Some elk were too wild to count, and we would have to hide in the stack yard until dark to get an accurate count. Other times the elk wouldn't come in to feed or completely leave the feed ground and not allow us to get an accurate count. Getting an accurate count allowed us to better set our hunting seasons each year, as we knew exactly what our total elk numbers were.

Most regions in the state would have to fly over their elk herds and count them from the air. It can become very difficult to count large numbers of elk in a fixed wing airplane. Especially when you get into herds of several thousand elk at one time. It becomes very difficult to break out cows vs. calves and yearling bulls vs. mature bulls when you buzz over them in an airplane. So feed grounds did allow for very accurate counts that really helped with managing the populations. We pretty much knew exactly what we had for elk numbers each year on the feed grounds. We would also fly the surrounding areas to count elk that were wintering out on native winter range. During the winter of 96-97 not many elk wintered out on native winter range due to very deep snow conditions. We also lost a high number of deer that winter due to the severe winter. Many of the rancher's stack yards were full of dead deer that winter. Mostly dead fawns. It seemed like during a hard winter we would lose our fawn crop first and then the older age class bucks and the does would die next. I guess this is what kept populations healthy and in check. Sometimes you can attempt to manage animals based on science with all the best information available, but you can never predict what Mother Nature is going to throw at you. Or what wildlife diseases may show up at any given time that affect wildlife populations.

I had a voice message from the Jewett elk feeder Donny Calhoun. Donny rarely called and was always very self-sufficient. His message indicated that he needed some medication for one of his draft horses that had colic. I traveled up to the Antelope Run Ranch the next morning to meet with Donny. I ran into the ranch manager as I was unloading my snow machine in his driveway next to his ranch house. He was very friendly and invited me into his house for a cup of coffee. We had a great visit and he said to let him know if he could ever help out with anything at the Jewett feed ground. He apparently fed elk at the Jewett feed ground years ago during the late 70's and early 80's. He told me horrific stories about feeding the elk in the winter of 1978. He said that winter was by far the worst that he had ever seen in his life in Wyoming. He told me to stop in for a whiskey or coffee anytime. I really enjoyed our visit and would take him up on his offer sometime.

I snow machined a short distance up to the feed ground and met with Donny at his little log cabin. As I walked towards the cabin, I observed a dead draft horse in the horse corral. Donny came walking out of the cabin and said, "You didn't get here in time, she died in the corral last night sometime, I recon." I felt horrible and told Donny that I was sorry I didn't get there sooner. Donny said, "It's a damn shame, she was one hell of a draft horse." I could see a tear in his eyes. We would end up hooking both our snow machines to the dead horse and drug her out away from the corral for the coyotes and birds to feed on. I would need to go back to Soda Lake immediately and find a spare draft horse for Donny to feed with. I wasn't sure how I was ever going to walk a horse into this feed ground as the snow was very deep.

I headed back to Soda Lake where I only had a few spare draft horses left. The road into Soda Lake was drifted back shut after we had opened it a few weeks earlier to get the hay truck out to haul hay. I rode my snow machine into the feed ground. I had a spare draft horse that I had received from Ron Dean late in the year. His name was Mark and his feet had not been trimmed. His hooves were horribly long and starting to split out. He really needed to be trimmed soon. I looked at his feet. They had to be at least ten inches in diameter. His tracks in the snow looked like huge pie plates. I had an idea. This horse's feet were so large in diameter that maybe I could walk him into the feed ground early in the morning. I would follow Donny's hard-packed snow machine trail from the ranch house to the feed ground. Hopefully, we could stay on top of the snow based on the circumference of Mark's untrimmed hooves. It would be like a horse wearing snowshoes. I went back to the office and hooked up my horse trailer.

It was -30 below that night. I woke up early and headed for Soda Lake with my horse trailer. My plan was to hike five miles into Soda Lake feed ground and lead Mark back to the horse trailer. Once I arrived at the snowmobile unloading area, I decided to try and drive on the hard snow packed trail into Soda Lake. The trail was rough from snow machines going back and forth over large drifts. I was able to pull the horse trailer on top of the snow-packed trail to within one mile of the horse corral. I

Scott C. Werbelow

Donny Calhoun with his team.

parked the truck and trailer alongside the main trail and hiked in to get Mark. I soon caught Mark and led him out to the horse trailer. I loaded him up and away I went. I met some snow machines in the trail on the way out that were headed up to Willow Lake to do some ice fishing. They pulled over for me and gave me the darndest look as I went by them with the horse trailer. I think it may have been the same family that had seen me earlier giving the coyote a ride.

I soon arrived at the Antelope Run ranch and unloaded Mark. The ranch manager loaned me one of his snow machines and I led Mark behind the snow machine into the feed ground. Mark never fell through the snow even once. The mission was a huge success. I helped Donny harness up his new team and hoped that Mark would work well with the other horse. Mark did as good as one could hope for and we didn't have any wrecks. We were able to get the elk fed with the new team without incident. Donny was pleased with his new horse and invited me into his cabin for some lunch and a cup of coffee. I stepped into the cabin. The cabin was warm, and the coffee pot was still on the wood stove. I looked around the cabin and observed thin strips of meat hanging on baling wire all the way around the inside of the cabin. The meat was dried and looked like beef jerky.

Donny poured me some very thick lukewarm coffee and asked me if I would like a sandwich. I replied, "That sounds good, Donny, thank you!" Donny pulled out a bag of petrified hamburger buns and cut a few pieces of dried meat off the baling wire hanging on the wall and made me a sandwich with no mayonnaise or anything. I bit into the sandwich and the dry bun exploded all over the table and onto the floor. I chewed and chewed and finally swallowed. It was the worst tasting sandwich that I had ever had in my life. I tried to wash it down with the sheep herder's coffee and damn near died. Donny asked, "How is your sandwich?" I replied, "Good, Donny, thank you very much, that hit the spot!" Donny smiled and said, "I kind of like that meat myself. It came off a coyote that I shot off the dead horse yesterday. It makes for some pretty damn good jerky in my opinion." I would soon learn not to eat lunch with Donny.

As the winter progressed, I learned from the BFH crew that all the elk feeders would need to vaccinate their elk for brucellosis. I had no idea that we vaccinated elk on feed grounds. Apparently, we had started vaccinating elk on a couple of feed grounds in about 1985. The test results showed that the prevalence of brucellosis in elk was going down on some feed grounds where we had been vaccinating and doing surveillance. Each feed ground had a round elk trap constructed of wooden posts and poles. The corrals looked like a round pen that you would train horses in. The fences were eight feet in height. The elk feeders would bait the trap at night with hay and set a trap trigger on the gate. Once the elk were in the trap feeding, the gate would trigger and slam shut on the elk. Game and Fish personnel would show up early in the morning and work the elk through an alleyway. Once the elk were in the alleyways, biologists

Elk being worked in round corral.

would draw blood and collar each elk with a unique number. The blood samples would then be sent to our lab and tested for brucellosis. Generally, we would need to test about thirty to forty adult cow elk to get an adequate sample size to determine the prevalence of brucellosis on any given feed ground.

Game and Fish personnel working elk

Calf elk leaving elk trap,

Scott C. Werbelow

The strain of vaccine used to vaccinate the elk was called Strain 19. In order to vaccinate the elk, the elk feeders were issued an air-powered gun that would inject a tiny bio bullet into the elk's rump. The bio-bullet would dissolve over time and the elk would be vaccinated. All elk feeders were to get 100% coverage on all cows and calves the first year and then focus on getting a 100% coverage on all calves each following year. The vaccine rifle was a two-part rifle. The top rifle was a paintball gun that marked the elk with orange oil base paint. Once the elk was marked with paint, the feeder would pull the trigger on the second rifle and vaccinate the elk with the bio-bullet. This was a very ingenious system. The elk feeders would mount a large air bottle on the front of their feed sleds to power the rifle. They would store the paintballs in a small cooler with a heat pack to keep the oil-based paint balls from freezing.

In a perfect world' the elk feeders would feed hay in a large circle and park their team of horses in the middle of it. They would wait patiently for the elk to start feeding in the small circle. Once elk were on feed, they would try and mark the elk with the paintball. If an elk was successfully marked, the elk feeder would aim for the rump and fire the second gun that delivered the bio-bullet of Strain 19. This gun was similar to a high-powered pellet gun, and would embed the soft white gel capsule (bio-bullet) into the soft tissue of the elk. Feeders would not vaccinate the elk unless it was marked with the orange paintball. Overtime, all elk marked with the orange oil-based paint had been vaccinated. The more elk that you vaccinated, the harder it became to find an elk without an orange spot. Feeders would do this until they felt all of their calves were marked and vaccinated. The vaccine did not prevent the elk from contracting brucellosis, but would build up the elk's immune system to prevent the elk from aborting their calf, which is the primary result of the spread of brucella.

You can only imagine the horse wrecks that took place from shooting a rifle from the feed sled behind the horses. The feeders would have to acclimate their horses to the sound of the air rifle for several days

252

before the horses would stand still long enough for the feeders to vaccinate the elk. This was very time-consuming for the elk feeders. Most of them had second jobs and just wanted to feed the elk and get on with their day. Vaccinating the elk would take hours of extra work and sometimes in very inclement weather. Sure, it was always fun for a while to shoot elk with a paintball gun, but it got old really quick when you were expected to vaccinate all of the elk or all of the calves. The feeders were to keep track of the number of calves that they had vaccinated each day. Once we classified the elk on a given feed ground, we could compare their numbers with the total number of calves counted that year. This was a top priority for the department and the elk feeders to get all elk vaccinated. We would eventually end up paying the feeders extra based on the number of calves that they had to vaccinate each year.

The BFH biologists would spend time hauling vaccination equipment to the elk feeders. They helped them vaccinate and repair equipment on a daily basis. The rifles needed sighted in and maintained to work efficiently. If the paint balls froze, they wouldn't break and mark the elk. If you pulled the wrong trigger on the gun, you may shoot the elk behind the shoulder with a bio-bullet instead of a paintball and kill her. The guns would shoot accurately up to about thirty yards. Some feeders did an excellent job vaccinating their elk and others not so much. It would be my job to ensure that all feeders were getting their vaccinations completed on each feed ground. I would even occasionally help them vaccinate their elk, or sometimes just hold onto their team of horses while they vaccinated.

The other issue that popped up was shed elk antlers on feed grounds. There was no written policy on what the elk feeders were to do with shed antlers on the feed grounds. The unwritten policy was that each feeder could keep one set of elk antlers of their choice. All other elk antlers shed on the feed ground itself were to be turned into the department. This had been very loosely enforced over the years. Many feeders actually turned in very few shed antlers. And most generally, the ones that got turned in were small rag horn antlers. This was becoming a very popular subject with the public, as elk antlers were worth a great deal of money. It was early spring and I had already encountered several individuals trying to sneak into the feed grounds to steal antlers off the feed ground. I quizzed some of the elk feeders about how things had been enforced in the past. Most of them agreed to turn them in if they were shed on the feed ground itself. But some felt that it was alright for them to pick up shed antlers from the feed ground in the surrounding areas.

Because of the controversy that surrounded this subject with the public. It was time to tighten things up and not allow feeders to pick elk antlers up near the feed grounds. I had heard several comments from the public that elk feeders were stealing all the shed elk antlers and there were none for them to find once the feed grounds opened up to the public on May 1. I would meet with Ron and Bernie regarding this issue. They both agreed that all feeders needed to turn in all antlers found on the feed ground itself. They also agreed that if the public was not allowed in the area of the feed grounds to pick up shed antlers, the elk feeders should not be allowed in as well. After the meeting it was agreed upon that all feeders turn in all antlers that were shed on the feed ground itself. At the end of the winter, all antlers would be collected by me and given to the National Elk Refuge, so that they could sell them at their annual elk antler auction in Jackson Hole each May. This didn't seem right to me. These antlers were worth a great deal of money and the Game and Fish paid half of the feed bill on the refuge each year which amounted to several hundred thousand dollars in some years. I would have to think more about this, I had no idea at this moment in time just how many elk antlers we would be dealing with.

I visited with all the feeders about this. Most of them were good with it. Some of them didn't agree with me at all. One feeder told me that if he had to quit picking up shed antlers, he would just quit his job feeding elk and sneak into the feed grounds and steal the antlers. He said he would make more money selling antlers than he ever would feeding elk. He said "Besides, we are out here working our asses off seven days a week, and

Bull elk with one antler shed.

Bull elk tangled up with shed horns from another bull.

we deserve some extra compensation because the job doesn't pay worth a damn." I told him if the public wasn't allowed into the closed areas, neither was he. End of conversation!

I showed up to the office early one Monday morning. One of the BFH biologists approached me and told me he had had a confrontation with one of my elk feeders over the weekend. Apparently, he went out to assist one of them with their vaccinations because he hadn't even started vaccinating yet. The feeder wanted to go home and quit for the day because the weather was bad. The BFH biologist told him that they needed to keep vaccinating the elk because the elk were starting to leave the feed ground for the year. This ended up in an argument about who actually worked harder, the feeder or the Game and Fish employee? The elk feeder would eventually tell the Game and Fish employee to get the F---ck off of his feed ground and never return again. The BFH biologist was very upset about this and wanted the situation handled immediately. He met with me and said, "If I'm not welcome on a feed ground by one of YOUR feeders, we have a big problem!" I told him that I would handle the situation.

I snow machined out to this particular feed ground to watch the feeder from a distance. I wanted to see if he was vaccinating his elk after he fed them. I observed him park his team on the feed ground and go antler-hunting for about one hour in the area surrounding the feed ground. He found several large elk antlers and stashed them in the hay under the hayshed. He left the area and didn't vaccinate any of his elk. This made me very upset. I went back to the office and visited with Bernie about the situation. Bernie felt that we didn't need someone working for us who couldn't get along with other Game and Fish employees. And we didn't need someone working for us that was stealing antlers and not getting his vaccinations done. I told Bernie that I had made up my mind and that I would snow machine in their first thing in the morning and fire him. Bernie asked me if I would like him to go with me in the morning. As I was thinking about my response Bernie replied, "That way he can only throw a pitch fork at one of us." I told Bernie that it may be good to have both of us involved.

The next morning Bernie and I headed into the feed ground. Bernie agreed to ride double with me on my snow machine, so that we wouldn't have to mess with hauling his snow machine. We had decided to find a place to watch the feeder from a distance to see if he had started vaccinating his elk yet or not. From a distance looking through my binoculars, it appeared that the feeder had someone helping him feed for the day. Maybe he was planning on vaccinating his elk after all. The feeder fed two loads of hay and parked the team of horses up a hidden draw on the feed ground. Pretty quick I could see both men antler-hunting on the ridge above the feed ground. They both collected a handful of large shed antlers and returned to the team of horses after about one hour. They hauled the elk antlers over and stashed them in the hay under the hay shed. Then they took the team of horses over to the corral and started to unharness them for the day. I looked at Bernie and said, "Let's go, I want to catch up with them

Shed elk antler on feed sled.

before they leave the feed ground, because I want him to get all his personal stuff out and not have a reason to ever come back."

We jumped on my snow machine riding double and hauled ass over to the horse corral. I was very focused on what I was going to tell the feeder when I arrived. Apparently, I was going a little too fast and hit a snow drift right in front of the horse corral. All I saw were both of Bernie's feet go straight into the air past each side of my helmet. Bernie was no longer along for the ride. He was lying flat on his back in the middle of the snow machine trail. I quickly turned around to pick him up. He was lying on his back, laughing un-controllably. How am I supposed to be all serious and fire an elk feeder when Bernie is lying on his back, laughing uncontrollably right next to the horse corral? I helped Bernie up and we both walked over to the horse corral a short distance away. The elk feeder smiled and said, "What brings the two of you in here today on such a bright sunny day?" I asked the feeder, "How is your vaccinating coming along?" He replied, "Oh, I haven't got started much yet, I'm headed to Arizona tomorrow for a couple of weeks and then I will hit it hard when I get back." He also informed me that he had a back-up feeder who would cover for him while he was gone. I replied, "Why don't you stay in Arizona as long as you would like, I will find a replacement to feed and get these elk vaccinated starting tomorrow."

He looked at me and said, "Wow, are you firing me? I have never been fired before!" I responded, "Well, I have never fired someone before, so I guess this is a first for both of us." Bernie said, "I think I will grab a bale of hay to feed the horses." Bernie then headed for the stack yard. I told the feeder to pack up all of his personal belongings and get out of the area. He was pretty upset and I think a little embarrassed. What I hadn't realized was he had skied in on a set of cross-country skis behind his friend's snow machine by being pulled with a rope. He gathered up his horse harnesses, collars, pitchfork, snow shovel, and hay hooks and wrapped everything around his neck before putting on his skis. He was having a heck of a time and fell down a couple of times. I told him not to worry about getting all of his stuff out, that I would haul it out for him. He grabbed the end of the lariat and told his friend to "Hit It" His friend punched the throttle on the snow machine and away they went. The feeder went left, then he went right, then he went down in a big pile with his personal belongings. I walked over to him and offered to help him up. He said, "NO, I got this!" He got himself up and away they went down the trail over the hill and out of sight. I walked over to the horse corral and noticed a pile of large six-point elk antlers stacked neatly in the corner. I don't think these antlers were going to be turned into the Game and Fish Department.

Bernie soon returned from the stack yard with a bale of hay for the horses. He was smoking a cigar and said, "Well, looks like that went well." Do you have someone lined up to feed and vaccinate these elk tomorrow?" I replied, "I do, her name is Lana." Bernie took a puff of his cigar, blew the smoke into the air and said, "Hmm.....I'll have to run this one by Wildlife Administration" I told Bernie that it would be difficult to find a replacement feeder on such short notice and that Lana was looking for work and certainly capable of the job. We headed back out of there on the snow machine, Bernie holding on a little tighter this time. I thought to myself on the way out, I hope Lana is up for the challenge. Maybe I should have talked to her first."

Bernie called me several hours later and told me that he had had quite a conversation with Wildlife Administration. They had decided that since Lana would be a contract employee, it would be alright for me to supervise my wife. They weren't happy about the decision but understood the need to have a feeder in place by the next day. I called Lana and told her the news. She was very excited and felt that she could still help Kathy feed in the mornings and feed the elk in the afternoons. I would spend the next two days helping Lana feed and getting her familiar with her new team of draft horses Amos and Andy.

I left on Friday to attend the Wyoming Game Wardens Association annual meeting in Sheridan. I had only attended a few of these meetings since getting hired. I loved attending this meeting. This was a chance to visit with and meet game wardens from all over Wyoming. I really enjoyed sitting down with some of the senior wardens and listening to all their crazy stories over the years. How some of those wardens ever survived, I don't know! We would have a banquet at night with a guest speaker and raffle ticket drawings. I was greeted by one of the administrators that night. He reached out and shook my hand and said with a laugh, "So, you fired an elk feeder and hired your wife, huh?" I wasn't sure how to respond to that comment. I just replied, "Yup, she will be one of the best we have ever had!"

The next day would be various speakers including Wildlife Admin. The best part was listening to presentations from other wardens about great poaching cases that they had recently made. I thought to myself maybe that could be me up there talking about a great case that I had made some day. Back then, the wardens would stay up for hours drinking whiskey and telling stories about their careers as a Wyoming game warden. One game warden would tell a story and the next one would try to out-do the previous story with a better one. I heard stories about handcuffing the poacher to their headache rack on their patrol truck. Black bears being darted and placed in the large metal tool box in the back of the trucks. They would take the black bear to a remote area and simply open the lid on the tool box and release the bear. There were stories about horse wrecks, snow machine wrecks, getting lost, and getting stuck. Most of the stories were about doing good ole fashioned game warden work and catching the bad guys. Many wardens would wake up on Saturday morning with a headache, including me, but it was worth it.

Big Piney game warden Brad Hovinga and I had traveled down to the meeting together. This was the first time that we really had a chance to just sit and visit about things not related to work. We really enjoyed one another's company and had a great visit during the long road-trip to and from Sheridan. Brad had shared with me that he had just recently been divorced. I could tell this was a tough time in Brad's life. I felt sorry for him, I couldn't imagine just waking up one day and everything you had together was suddenly gone. Brad dropped me off at the small house out on Horse Creek road. Lana pulled up just as Brad was leaving. Brad asked her how the elk feeding was going. Lana responded, "Pretty good until today. All of my elk are gone! I think maybe some antler hunters visited my feed ground last night." Lana then explained to me that all the elk were there yesterday (approx. 800 elk) and not a single elk today. Lana was mad. She had only fed for a couple of days and now all her elk were gone, most of them unvaccinated.

We said our good-byes to Brad. I was still supporting a pretty good headache from all our fun-filled weekend activities. I was upset that someone had possibly snuck into the feed ground and ran all the elk off. I hauled my suitcase into the house and changed my clothes into my red-shirt. I told Lana that I would be back in a few hours. I headed into Soda Lake feed ground with my snow machine and parked by the horse corral. There were no elk on the feed ground so I decided to hike to the top of Fremont Ridge and look for people or snow machine tracks in the snow. Once I arrived at the top of the ridge, I noticed snow machine tracks and people tracks. I decided to follow a set of people tracks down off the hill into some thick trees. A short distance later, I couldn't believe what I had found. There was a large pile of large six-point elk horns stacked up high next to a tree. There must have been at least twenty large antlers in the pile. I thought to myself, these guys have already made a large haul of elk antlers out of the area. They found so many antlers that they couldn't carry all of them during their first trip out on their snow machines. There was no other logical reason that they would have left such a large pile of antlers.

I decided that the antler thieves would soon return to claim their stash. At this time, there was no antler hunting season in place. The only violation that I had was if I actually caught them trespassing on our Commissioned-owned wildlife habitat unit. The antlers were stashed in the forest, which was a legal area for them to be in. But I knew based on foot prints in the snow that they had crossed our boundary fence and trespassed on Game and Fish-owned land to gather the antlers. This area was posted closed to human presence from January 1 thru May 1. I would have to actually catch them trespassing on our wildlife unit or I would have no violation. I quickly grabbed three large-six-point antlers out of their stash and strategically placed them on our unit where they could easily locate them if they returned. I then found a good hiding spot in the trees and waited for dark to come.

As the sun went down over the hills to the west, it became very cold very quick. I was looking down on the feed ground which was located about one mile away. There was not an elk in sight. These antler hunters had moved a large herd of elk completely out of the area. I started to get the chills and began shaking from the bitter cold. I had many thoughts going through my mind. Would they ever return? How would I prove that they had not trespassed on our unit? How many people would I be alone dealing with in the night? Shit, I forgot my ticket book and flashlight in my back pack that was strapped to my snow machine over a mile away. About that time, I could hear the faint sound of snow machines coming my direction on Fremont Ridge. I thought to myself, alright here they come!

From my hiding spot I could observe three snow machines coming my way with one person on each machine. They were all wearing snow machine suits and helmets, so I could not recognize anyone. They came to a stop about one hundred yards from the location where they had stashed the elk antlers. It was nearly dark. All three men took their helmets off and hung them on their handle bars. They were all wearing ski masks, so I still couldn't see much of their faces from my location. They all headed into the trees towards their antler stash. After several minutes two men came walking out of the trees with a huge armload of shed antlers. They carried them back to their snow machines and placed them in a pile on a sled that they had pulled behind one of the snow machines. They quickly tied the bundle of horns together and lashed them to the sled. I waited patiently for the third guy to come out of the trees. I wasn't sure if they had all of the antlers gathered or if they would return back for another load. My timing to contact them would have to be perfect, or they may jump on their sleds and leave the area before I could identify them. I was starting to get a little nervous. Where was the third guy?

A few minutes passed when I heard a noise below me. I observed the third man walking through the trees right below me. He was within twenty yards of my hiding spot. I patiently watched the man cross our boundary fence and enter the habitat unit below me. He soon found one of the antlers that I had previously stashed and picked it up. I thought to myself ALRIGHT, GOT HIM!! The other two men went back into the trees for another load of antlers. I quickly ran up the hill through the thick trees and circled back to their snow machines. I would be waiting for them at their snow machines when they all returned carrying antlers. The man below me, who had trespassed on our unit, came walking up the hill towards me carrying a shed antler. He looked up and observed me standing next to his snow machine. He must have seen my green coat with my bright gold badge. His first reaction was to quickly throw the elk antler over the boundary fence and hope that I had not seen him pick it up on our unit. He then turned and started walking away from me. I yelled, "GAME WARDEN, COME ON UP YOU HAVE BEEN CAUGHT." The man slowly walked up the hill towards me. Once he arrived, I asked him for his identification. He told me that he didn't have any on him. I then asked him for his name and he reluctantly gave it to me. I recognized the name, but had never met the man before. I then asked him for the names of the other two men. He reluctantly gave me that information as well. Two of them were brothers.

The man tried to tell me that he didn't pick any shed antlers up on our unit and was sorry for trespassing. He told me that as soon as he realized he was on our unit he headed back and crossed the fence back onto the forest boundary. The other two men soon arrived with another armload of antlers. The look on their faces was priceless once they realized a game warden was standing there in the dark. They both claimed that they had not trespassed on the unit, and all the horns that they had found were on the forest (public land) with no closures. I knew they were lying, but could not prove otherwise as I had not observed them on the Game and Fish owned land. I identified both of them. They were very nervous. I did not have my ticket book, flashlight or snow machine, so I told them I would catch up with them tomorrow. I allowed them to keep all the horns, as I had no proof of where they had found them. This made me sick to my stomach to watch them leave with the large load of antlers on the sled behind their snow machine. I explained to them that they had run all the elk off the feed ground due to their activity in the area. I also explained that I better not ever catch them trespassing on the unit or the feed ground ever again.

I would end up issuing a citation to the individual that I actually observed trespassing and picking up the antler. The only statute that we had on the books at that time to address this issue was titled "Failure to obey regulatory signs on department lands." I believe the fine amount for this violation was only one hundred dollars. It soon became apparent to me that this was a huge problem with the current value of elk antlers at the time. Many of our feed grounds didn't even have official closures depending on the land status that they were located on. Some of them were located on private property and some on State, BLM, and Forest Service lands.

My hike out of there in the night without a flashlight was interesting to say the least. I finally made it home and was proud to tell my wife Lana that I had caught the individuals that were responsible for moving the elk off the feed ground. She was happy that I caught them but not happy that I was not able to confiscate the antlers that they had gathered. I was just happy to finally be in my own bed without a headache. I would meet with Bernie and Ron in the morning and explain the situation to them. The elk did later return to the feed ground for a short time. Lana was able to get most of them vaccinated before they left for good.

After meeting with Bernie and Ron the next morning they both felt this was a big problem. Bernie requested me to review all of the current feed ground closures that we currently had in place. He also wanted me to meet with all state, local and federal agencies and work with them to eventually get a "No Human Presence" closure on all feed grounds. This would be a huge and time-consuming project. Not to mention very confrontational with the public. Word got out on the street that I had fired a feeder for stealing elk antlers and had written others citations for stealing antlers from feed grounds. The elk feeders soon learned that I took this issue very seriously and they were to turn in all shed elk antlers that were collected on their feed grounds during the spring of each year.

I soon learned that a big part of my job would be getting draft horses out of the feed grounds once elk had left and traveled to higher elevations. At many of the feed grounds the elk were gone but the snow was still too deep to drive into the feed grounds with a truck and horse trailer. I would end up spending nearly two weeks walking horses out of feed grounds and putting them back at Soda Lake. The horses needed fed every day and the feeders would need to move onto other jobs. I was able to harness the North Piney team and herd them the nine miles out with my snow machine. The snow was deep and tough but we made it.

Tim called me and said the elk had left Finnegan and he was ready for the horses to be hauled out. Even though we had opened that road to haul hay earlier, the road had drifted back in. I was able to drive part way in with my truck and horse trailer and ride my ATV into the feed ground. I harnessed both horses and tied their lead ropes to the back rack of my ATV to lead them out. I had them about half way out when I heard a very loud "BOOM" to my right side. Both horses grabbed their asses and went racing by me. One on my left and one on my right. This sudden urge of "horse power" caused the rear end of my ATV to shoot straight in the air which pitched me over my handle bars between the two running horses. The ATV flipped upside down and landed in the middle of my back. When the smoke cleared, the horses were dragging my department issue ATV upside down and backwards down the middle of the road. Both of them bucking and farting at the same time. Thank God the lead ropes finally broke and freed the horses leaving the ATV upside down in the middle of the road.

Thankfully I was alright, but couldn't figure out where the loud "BOOM" noise had come from. Finally, I located a yellow propane Zon-Gun hidden in some tall sage brush right off the road. Brad had put this device there to prevent elk from coming down to the neighbor's cattle feedlines during the night. This device was set to make a loud BOOM noise about once an hour. It would have been really nice if Brad would have clued me in on this bit of information before leading the draft horses out. The horses finally quit running once they reached the horse trailer and stopped. The ATV was tough for me to get flipped back over on its wheels by myself, but I finally managed. The handle bars were bent and the front and rear racks were damaged, but other than that she was cherry. Just another day with the Game and Fish Dept. We had a late spring storm that dumped about two feet of snow in one night. Many of the elk started returning to the feed grounds. This had me concerned as several feed grounds were nearly out of hay, including the ones that we had already hauled hay into a few months ago. A heavy snow load on the Dell Creek hayshed roof came crashing down in the middle of the night. The feeder was unable to get his team of horses through all the debris caused from the collapsed roof. We would need to put together a team of Game and Fish employees immediately and clean up the mess so the elk could be fed by the end of the day. Thank God we had a snow cat with a plow that made the work for us much easier. I returned back to my truck to check my voice messages. Frosty Hittle, the feeder at Muddy feed ground had just called and left me a message that about half of the roof on his hayshed blew off during the high winds in the night. I thought to myself, how will, I ever keep up with all the maintenance by myself this spring and summer on all of the feed grounds.

My next message was from Kathy at Fall Creek feed ground. I

Collapsed hay shed at Dell Creek.

pushed the button and listened, "Hello, Scott, this is Kathy." In a very loud voice. "Hey I got two large bulls locked together on the feed ground. It looks like their horns are tied up in baling twine. One bull is down and can't get up. Could you call me back and maybe come up and dart this bull with something to put him down?" I thought to myself, shit I'm tired, it's been a really long day shoveling snow off the collapsed roof at Dell Creek. I don't even have time to get up there before dark. I called Kathy back as soon as I had service. She said the elk were still locked together and she was worried the one bull that was down was going to die. I told her that I didn't have time to come up with the dart gun. And to be honest, I had never darted an animal before and didn't have a clue what drug to use or how much drug it would take to put down an elk. I also didn't know where the dart gun was located or how any of the equipment even worked.

I told Kathy to duct tape a sharp knife onto the end of her pitchfork and try and get close enough to cut the twine loose without putting herself in danger of the bull that was still standing. She laughed and said, "OK, I'll give it the ole college try." I told her good luck and to call me when she was done to let me know how it went. About twenty minutes went by and my phone rang. I picked it up and heard heavy breathing on the other end. In a loud voice I heard, "HELLO SCOTT, THIS IS KATHY. Hey, I got the elk free but the one bull charged my team of horses and we had a runaway!" The team left the feed ground and plowed into a grove of aspen trees. The hay sled is stuck tight between two aspen trees and the horses are in belly-deep snow. I'm going to need your help to get the sled free!"

I told Kathy to hang tight, that I would grab a chainsaw and get headed that way. She said, "Hang tight! I don't think that will be a problem, I'm not going anywhere." With a giggle at the end. I would have to hook up my snow machine and find my chainsaw. There was no way that I would make it all the way up there before dark. I should have just gone up and darted the elk earlier I thought to myself. I soon arrived at the feed ground. Kathy had already got the horses and sled free from the aspen trees when I arrived. She had found a carpenter's saw in her trailer house and cut down two large aspen trees with that damn dull saw. She had just got Bonnie and Clyde put away in the corral and invited me into her trailer for a cup of cider. She cleared an area for me to sit and went about telling me the whole story. She said the knife and pitchfork worked great. But once the bull was free, he charged right at the team of horses that were standing on the feed ground. She said, "Those damn horses aren't afraid of elk, but I don't think they have ever been charged by an elk before either."

She said the horses whirled hard to their left away from the charging bull elk and grabbed their asses as they headed across the feed ground. The feed sled hit a couple of large boulders and hay bales went flying in both directions off the sled. The more hay that flew in the air, the harder the horses would run. Why they headed for the isolated grove of aspen trees is anyone's guess? We finished our cup of cider and Kathy said "Oh, by the way, you need to come check this out while you are here." She grabbed a flashlight and I followed her out the door. We walked a short distance down the hill to the old house trailer that was parked under the old hayshed. She kicked the door open and shined her light inside the trailer house.

I had never seen so many dead chickens in all my life. She had finally got all her chickens moved up there and had put them in the old trailer house as her chicken coop. A bobcat saw the chickens through the front picture window of the trailer and decided he wanted a snack. The bobcat flew through the picture window and killed every chicken in the old trailer house. Kathy was just sick that she had lost all her chickens and she wanted to kill the bobcat. I walked through the trailer with a flashlight and found dead chickens and chicken feathers in every room of the trailer. This would have been quite a sight to watch in person. I couldn't believe that the bobcat had actually jumped through a picture window. I was hoping that the bobcat wasn't still hiding inside the trailer house somewhere. This brought back memories of when my dad had lowered me into a deep dark hole to get the live bobcat out of his trap when I was a young child.

I would spend the next several week's walking horses out of various feed grounds and hauling them back to Soda Lake for the spring. I would also spend time gathering shed elk antlers from all the feed grounds. Some of the feeders had already hauled the antlers out of the feed grounds and had them stored at their homes so that they wouldn't get stolen from the feed grounds by antler hunters. You should have seen the look on several elk feeders face when I showed up at their home to collect the shed antlers. I don't think this had ever been done before by any Game and Fish personnel. At first, I thought it was pretty cool to get to handle and look at all the different elk antlers that had been shed on feed grounds. By the end of the spring, I had handled so many elk antlers that I didn't care if I ever saw another one. It became very time-consuming to get them all gathered up. More bulls had shed on the feed grounds that winter due to deep snow conditions that didn't allow bulls to leave the feed grounds early and shed somewhere else.

Several elk feeders told me that winter was the most shed horns they had ever found on their feed grounds before.

I had all of the shed antlers stored in a locked storage unit. It was a pretty impressive pile to say the least. I asked Ron Dean what I should do with them. He said in the past they had always hauled them up to the National Elk Refuge and given them to refuge personnel to add to their pile and sell during their annual May auction on the Town Square. I soon loaded up all the antlers in the back of my Game and Fish truck and headed for Jackson. Once I arrived at the refuge, I spoke with the refuge manager. He explained to me that they have a large auction once a year in May and sell all of their antlers that are picked up on the National Elk Refuge. He explained that 20% of the sales go to the Boy Scouts and 80% of sales go to the National Elk Refuge. I asked him if the Game and Fish Department spends money to feed the elk on the National Elk Refuge each year. He explained to me that yes indeed, the Game and Fish pays 50% of the total feed bill spent on pellets each year. The total feed bill on the refuge the previous year was about $300,000 dollars. Meaning the Game and Fish Department paid about $150,000 of that bill. I then asked him if there was any way that the Game and Fish Department could receive a credit on their feed bill from the sale of elk antlers at the auction each year. He ran his finger through his hair and said, "Yea, possibly."

I told him that elk antlers were worth a great deal of money and that I had a large pile of them in the back of my truck. I also told him that I would like to see the proceeds from the sale of elk antlers go back into the feed ground program somehow. He told me that he would make some phone calls and get back to me. He helped me unload the antlers and we weighed them together for total poundage. I believed the pile of antlers weighed over 3000 lbs. We placed the pile of antlers into the National Elk Refuge pile and I headed back to Pinedale.

Patrol truck loaded with elk antlers.

On my return trip to Pinedale somewhere near the little town named Bondurant, my radio dispatch was trying to call me "GF-84, Pinedale." I answered, "GF-84 go ahead with your traffic." I received a report from SALECS that someone had reported a sick cow elk on the west side of the highway about two miles south of Bondurant. Heck, I was very close to that location. I responded to dispatch that I would look for the sick cow elk, as I was in the area. I went up and down the highway several times searching for the sick elk but could not locate her. I finally got out of my patrol truck and walked along-side the highway to look off a steep bank that I could not see very well while in my truck. There she was straight below me about thirty yards away lying next to the highway right of way fence.

It looked like she had been lying there most of the winter. She had an area about twenty feet in diameter tromped out in the deep snow right next to the fence. She looked extremely emaciated and her ears were both drooped down along-side her neck. She didn't even have the energy to stand up anymore. I thought to myself, I wonder how long she has been lying here starving to death. I walked off the steep embankment to get closer to her. When I was about ten feet from her, I decided to put her down with my 9mm Beretta pistol. I carefully aimed at the back of her head, fired my pistol as she was facing away from me. My bullet struck her right where I was aiming, except she didn't immediately die. She was lying there kicking all four legs back and forth and flopping her head from side to side. I was getting ready to shoot her again when I heard a noise on the highway above me. It sounded like brakes screeching from a large truck or something? I quickly looked up, only to see a large yellow school bus that had stopped at the edge of the road, directly above me.

The cow elk was still kicking and flailing around. I could see several young kids looking through the small windows on the bus. They had their little faces pressed tight up against the window on the bus, using their hands to put around their faces to block the glare from the sunshine. It looked like several of them were crying, I could hear one of them yelling something at me. About that time the bus driver came running down the hill towards me, waving both arms in the air and yelling and screaming at me. He yelled, "OH MY GOD, WHAT HAVE YOU JUST DONE?" I explained to him that I had just shot the cow elk because she was starving to death and needed to be put down. He screamed, "THE KIDS AND I HAVE BEEN FEEDING HAY TO HER ALL WINTER LONG, AND NOW YOU HAVE JUST KILLED HER!!" I replied, "Sir, I'm sorry to hear that, please stand back as I need to kill her again." I couldn't stand the thought of all the kids watching this poor elk suffer. I pulled out my 9mm and shot her in the head again. Do you think this elk would die? Heck no! She just kept kicking and flopping around while the bus driver continued to yell at me.

The bus driver was finally tired of chewing my butt and headed back up the hill towards the bus. He stopped, turned around and said, "What are you going to do with her ivories?" I said, "I don't know, do you want them?" He said, "Hell Yea I Want Them!" I quickly removed the ivories from the now dead cow elk and gave them to him. He shook my hand and thanked me as if he was no longer upset with me. There were probably a few kids on the bus that day that may have been scarred for life watching that poor elk die. I would use better discretion in the future before I ever put down another animal along a major highway.

I did end up receiving a call several days later from the Refuge Manager. He told me that he had spoken with the higher up and they had agreed to credit the Wyoming Game and Fish Department's annual feed bill each year based on the average price per pound each year. I was very excited to hear this news. It wasn't that much money in the grand scheme of things, but at least it was going back into the feed ground program in some manner. The elk feeders would be happy to hear the news. That particular year generated approximately $30,000 in revenue in antler sales. I believe this process has still been in place for the past twenty-five years.

The elk feeders had worked hard seven days a week all winter long. I decided it would be fun to have a potluck dinner celebration at the local bar in Pinedale. The owners of the bar were very receptive to the idea and they were able to get Budweiser to donate a keg of beer. I don't think anyone from the department had really ever appreciated the elk feeders for their efforts before. All the elk feeders on 22 feed grounds were invited. The turnout was huge and everyone brought their spouses. Many folks that worked for the Game and Fish also participated. The elk feeders had a great time meeting others and sharing crazy stories about things that had happened to them while feeding elk during the horrible winter months and deep snow conditions. Kathy even got up and sang everyone a song. It went something like "HERE ELKY, ELKY, ELKY!"

Black Butte elk feeder John Fandek was presented with a large metal sculpture of elk being fed on a feed ground for all his dedicated years of service feeding elk. John continues to feed for the department today, with over 43 years of service. The annual elk feeder party continued each spring for many years. This was a time for all feeders to get together and unwind a bit and celebrate another year of hard work, taking care of western Wyoming's treasured elk herds.

Elk feeder welcome party sponsored by Budweiser.

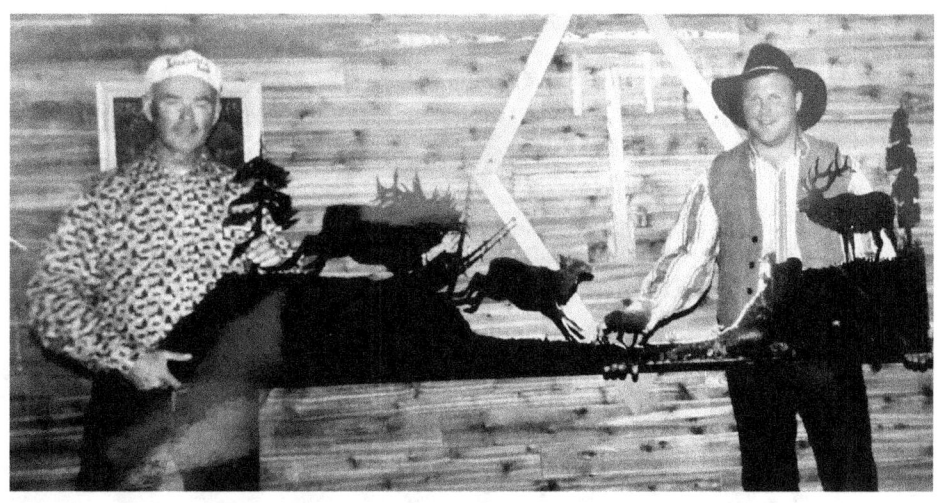

John Fandek receiving metal sculpture at elk feeder party.

Kathy singing "Here ELKY, ELKY, ELKY".

I would spend the next several months performing feed ground maintenance on all of the feed grounds. I had to clean the horse manure out of each horse corral with a tractor and a front-end loader. I had to haul all the twines and wires that held the small bales together from each feed ground. Most stack yard fences and horse corrals were in great need of repairs. It was a very busy summer trying to keep up with all the maintenance. Many feed grounds were in need of additional hay sheds to store hay under to prevent hay from spoiling while sitting outside and getting rained and snowed on all year. Several hayshed roofs blew off that spring and summer and needed new roofs.

After completing all my hay inventories, I met with Ron Dean to discuss hay purchasing. Due to the severity of the long winter, we had fed more elk on average than in most previous years. Ron and I would need to purchase roughly nine thousand tons of hay that summer and fall. The majority of this hay would have to be in small squares in order to feed with a team of horses and hay sleds. Between the two of us, we had over fifty hay producers and at least six hay haulers that we would contract with that summer. I think we bought nearly every small bale of hay that was for sale in Lincoln, Teton, and Sublette counties.

Purchasing hay was a big job. I would spend hours at night talking on the phone with hay producers, bickering about hay prices. I soon learned that the Game and Fish Department purchased so much hay in the area that they set the hay prices for the entire area. People would not sell their hay to anyone in the area unless they got at least what the department paid. If the department paid too much for hay, the locals were mad because they couldn't buy any hay for less than what we paid. The other difficult thing was that we needed to have all our hay contracts in place before the hay was even produced. Producers wouldn't know how much hay they could produce until after the growing season was over. They didn't want to come up short on their contracts or they would be penalized. They also didn't want to agree on a price for hay until they knew what the market was doing and how much they were able to produce.

Cheyenne headquarters could not pay the producers until the hay was in the stack and inspected for certain moisture and protein requirements. It also took about 6-8 weeks to get a hay contract processed with all the needed signatures. Once an invoice was received from a hay producer it would take approximately 45 days for the producers to get paid. All of this combined made purchasing hay for the elk feed grounds a very difficult and tedious process.

I would spend the majority of the summer and fall testing hay for quality, weighing hay bales to determine average weights to compensate producers fairly and performing maintenance projects on all feed grounds. This new job as feed ground manager/game warden proved to be much busier than I had ever imagined. Thank God for my office manager Des who handled all my hay hauling and purchasing contracts!

Chapter 9

FALL OF 1997

Fall was coming quick and I was getting very excited about the upcoming hunting season. This would be my first fall hunting season in the Pinedale area. I had a lot of country to learn. I knew the area pretty well due to all the feed grounds that I managed in the area, but I had not been back in the high country or wilderness areas on horseback to learn any of that country yet. Lana had recently gone to work for a cement contractor pouring cement to earn some extra money in the fall. She asked me to start looking for a new house that we could buy and own. She wanted at least 10 acres in the country with a horse barn. This was going to be tough for us to afford let alone even find as real estate in this area was getting pretty expensive, and there was not much to choose from.

I had not yet been through the twelve-week law enforcement academy, nor had I heard if my job was going to become permanent or not? I was worried that if my job got reclassified and became a permanent position with benefits, that I may not even be able to put in for the position if the department opened it up for a lateral transfer. Basically, I was a contract employee and would not be allowed to apply for a permanent position unless no one else applied and they re-opened the position. I still wanted very much to become a permanent game warden with my own district. I wasn't sure about the feed ground manager position. My heart was set on becoming a permanent game warden someday. There were currently no open warden positions in the entire state and it didn't look like any other wardens were going to retire anytime soon.

Big Piney game warden Brad Hovinga called me one evening and asked me if I would like to go on a day ride with him up North Piney Creek. I had never been up there before and was excited to get my new horse out and see some new country. I agreed to go with him and would meet him early the next morning at his warden station. I had just bought a new paint horse that I named Norton. I hadn't even ridden him yet, and had no idea how well he would perform in the mountains. I guess this would be a good trip to see how well he would do.

It was a beautiful and warm blue-sky day. The leaves on the aspen trees were starting to turn bright orange, red, and yellow and were absolutely stunning to look at. Brad told me we would be taking a short but steep ride up Long Hollow and should be back to our patrol truck by noon. It was going to be a good trip to try out my new horse and get him some exercise to prepare him for the fall hunting season. I had decided to pack light with no lunch or coat due to the fact we would be returning to the truck soon. We soon headed up the trail. The trail was steep and rocky. Norton was full of piss and vinegar the first mile and soon calmed down. Now he was just focused on breathing and making it to the top of the steep mountain without tripping and falling down. We finally reached the top of the mountain several hours later. What an absolutely stunning view we had with all the pretty fall colors in the aspen trees.

Brad jumped off his horse and grabbed his binoculars. He was looking down into a very steep canyon below us. North Piney Lake was so far away it looked like a small blue dot on the landscape. As Brad was looking through his binoculars he said, "That's North Piney Lake way down there. Bernie is camped above the lake somewhere." Brad then looked at me and said, "Do you want to ride down there and see if we can find Bernie's camp?" I replied, "Well, let me think about it for a minute. The horses are tired, we have no food, no coats, if we drop down into that canyon the horses will be too tired to climb their way back up the mountain, YEAH, let's do it!! Brad smiled and said, "Sounds good buddy let's go!"

We dropped off the steep mountain trail. The trail was so steep in places we both got off and led our horses. In some areas the trail had completely disappeared and we had to bushwhack our way through heavy timber and steep rocky ridges. It took us approximately four hours to reach the bottom of the canyon and hit the main trail into North Piney Lakes.

The legendary Norton.

The horses were lathered up and exhausted. It was late afternoon as we continued up the trail with the sun in our faces. North Piney Lake was absolutely beautiful as we rode along the edge of the lake. We stopped for a bit and gave the horses a nice drink of water. The sun glistened off the deep blue color of the water as the gentle breeze made small white caps across the lake. According to Brad, this lake was full of nice healthy cutthroat trout and was a very popular fishery for local anglers during the summer months. We continued on up the trail through the thick pine trees for about a mile. Brad was leading and turned around in his saddle to say something to me. He said, "I think Bernie camps somewhere in this area and he should be around somewhere?" I thought it would be pretty cool to surprise visit our boss way back in the middle of nowhere on horses.

We rode a bit further and noticed a white teepee tent set up in the trees on our left. Brad said, "I think that is Bernie's camp right there." I noticed several bottles of expensive bourbon sitting on the ground at the edge of the tent. I told Brad, "I don't know if this is Bernie's camp or not but it looks good to me, I'm thirsty." Brad said, "Sounds good. Let's tie these horses up and wait awhile to see if Bernie returns to camp. We were pretty sure it was Bernie's camp, so we decided to have a little pull off the bottle and taste some expensive bourbon. I had never tried "good" bourbon before. I had always drunk some form of cheap Canadian whiskey. I took a pull off the bottle and could feel it burn all the way down to my stomach. It actually tasted pretty damn good to be honest with you.

It was about 5:00 PM. The sun was just setting over the mountain to the west. I felt a little chill run through my bones as I had left my coat back at the truck. I was also feeling a little hungry as I hadn't eaten anything all day long. Brad said, "Let's grab a bottle of that bourbon and do some horse training. My horse has never been picketed before." I said, "Sounds good, my horse has never had hobbles on before." We led the horses over to a small meadow full of belly-deep grass. Brad pulled out a rope and a hobble out of his saddle bags and attached the hobble to the front leg of his horse. He then tied the end of the rope to a nearby tree. I

Camp for the night.

then led my new horse a short distance away and put a set of hobbles on both of his front legs.

Both horses seemed content with grazing in belly-deep grass and neither one of them attempted to even take a step for quite some time. Brad and I sat down on a couple of tree stumps that had been sawed off and passed the bottle back and forth a few times. Brad looked at me and said, "I think it's time for a fine Cuban cigar, ya want one?" I said, "Heck yea that sounds really good right now." Brad walked over to his saddle bag and pulled out a zip lock bag with several cigars in it. He pulled a knife out of his pocket and neatly cut the end of the cigar off. He then pulled a lighter out of his front shirt pocket, lit me up a cigar and handed it to me. "He said "Enjoy. That will be the best cigar you have ever smoked." I thanked him and said, "Well, today is a pretty special day, expensive bourbon and fine Cubin cigars." Brad said, "Yea, probably a little better than your Lord Calvert and Swisher Sweets."

I laughed as I took a puff of the fine cigar. About that time, I heard a loud farting and snorting noise. Norton my horse had finally tried to take his first step with the hobbles on and blew a gasket. He hadn't learned how to "hop" with hobbles yet and took off in a full-out run. He ended up face-planting in the dirt and rolled over a steep embankment face first out of sight into a thick willow bottom below us. Meanwhile, Brad's horse spooked at Norton taking off like a bullet and decided to do the same thing. When he hit the end of the rope it tripped him face first and all four feet went straight into the air. The rope had broken and Brad's horse went face first off of the same embankment. One moment we were both sitting on our stumps smoking a fine cigar and all of a sudden both of our horses were gone! We jumped up and the horses were standing below us in the thick willows. We slowly walked down the steep hill to try and catch them. I approached Norton and whispered, "Easy boy, easy boy, everything is going to be alright." Norton tried to run and took another step and fell down in the willows. I got him caught and took the hobbles off and led him back up the hill into the grassy meadow. I put the hobbles back on him and he never tried to take another step. Brad led his horse back up to the meadow and put the picket back on the front leg. His horse never tried to take another step. I looked at Brad and took a pull off the bottle of bourbon and handed it to Brad and said, "Good deal, I think our horses are now broke to be hobbled and picketed." Brad took a swig of

Scott C. Werbelow

bourbon and said, "Good deal, I'm getting a little cold. Maybe we should build a fire and wait for Bernie to return.

It was now dark and starting to cool off a bit. We soon had a roaring bonfire which felt very nice, since I had no coat to warm me. Brad told me that he was getting really hungry and wondered if I had brought any food along. I told him that I didn't think so, but I would check my saddle bags to see if I could find anything to eat. Brad said, "I would check inside of the teepee tent for some food, but I'm not even sure this is Bernie's camp?" I'm not quite sure how we got ourselves in this situation but we did. We were not going to ride out of there in the night and we had no food or warm clothing. Would we end up sleeping by the fire all night? Or would we possibly invade another person's tent to stay warm. It was getting late and still no Bernie? Brad looked at his watch. It read 9:30 PM. The bottle of expensive bourbon was nearly empty. Had we drunk someone else's bourbon? I walked over to my saddle and checked my saddle bags for food. Low and behold I found a small bag of baby carrots. I thought, thank God, these carrots are going to be delicious! I yelled to Brad in the night, "WE ARE IN LUCK BUDDY, I HAVE A BAG OF BABY CARROTS!" Brad replied, "Thank God, buddy, give me some of those damn carrots." I gave Brad the bag of carrots and before I knew it, he had eaten every one of them. He threw the empty bag in the fire and said, "Thanks for the carrots buddy. That hit the spot." He then took another pull off the bottle of bourbon to wash down the carrots. The fire was starting to die down and we were getting ready to invade the empty teepee for the night. About that time, I heard a loud voice in the timber above us yell, "HELLO IN CAMP!" this scared the shit out of me. I could not see who was coming towards us in the thick trees. Could this be the owner of the bottle of bourbon that I was holding in my hand? Would I be shot in the heart from someone in the trees for invading their camp and drinking their expensive bourbon? Whoever it was, was coming towards us in the night. We could not see anything beyond the dim light of the campfire. We could only hear footsteps as the person stepped on broken branches and pine cones scattered on the surface of the ground near us.

Brad quickly threw a handful of small branches on the fire for more light. I grabbed for my pistol to make sure I still had it on me in my pancake holster on my hip. The man entered the light of the fire. He was wearing a round brimmed cowboy hat. He had blood trickling down both sides of his face between his nose and his cheek. His forehead had a large knot on it with an open wound that was still spewing blood. As the man got closer, I recognized this man as Bernie my boss. Thank God it was Bernie, I thought to myself. Bernie seemed surprised to see the two of us sitting at his campfire late at night. Bernie's first words were, "Have either of you guys seen Woodrow my mule? He knocked me off under a tree branch several miles from here." We explained to Bernie that we hadn't seen his mule all evening. I told Bernie that he had a pretty good knot on his head and was bleeding. I handed him the nearly empty bottle and apologized for drinking his expensive bourbon. Bernie giggled and said, "Not a problem at all, that's why I brought several bottles." He then laid his head back and poured some bourbon on his open wound and took a large swig of out of the bottle. "AHH," he said, "That hit the spot."

Bernie was in the mood to party. We opened another bottle of bourbon and passed it around the fire. He didn't know that we hadn't eaten all day, except for Brad and the baby carrots. We told him that we rode in to see him, and just got a little hung up around the campfire. We decided to wait for him to make sure he was alright. He told us that he was riding along the trail in the dark and suddenly came off the back of his mule. He thought a tree branch had swiped him across the forehead when he came off the mule. He also laughed and said, "Shit, I'm even missing one of my spurs." We told stories for another hour or so and decided to go to bed. Bernie offered his teepee to Brad and me to sleep in. It was going to be a tight fit, but this would be much better than sleeping on the ground by the fire. We entered the teepee tent and tried to get settled. Bernie had an extra sleeping bag and offered it to Brad. I would sleep on top of horse blankets and cover myself with an old dirty canvas pack mantee.

Bernie with his fine Cuban cigar.

I had just started to fall asleep when I heard Brad frantically try to un-zip his sleeping bag. He un-zipped his sleeping bag and the zipper holding the tent flap shut, almost simultaneously. Out the door he went like a flash. Pretty quick I could hear the loud sounds of Brad puking outside of the tent. I don't know how to spell the sounds of someone puking loudly, so please use your imagination on this one. Brad finally quit puking for just a moment, and I heard an elk bugle. The bull elk was answering back to Brad every time he puked. I always thought that you needed to be somewhat skilled and talented to call in a bull elk, but that's not the case. Once this bull elk bugled another bull elk bugled in the opposite direction. Pretty quick Brad had three separate bulls bugling and heading for our camp. Within a few minutes it sounded like the bulls were right in camp. Their bugle was very loud and very close. This was one of the coolest sounds a hunter can ever hear at a close distance. I lay underneath my canvas tarp in the teepee and just giggled. Pretty quick Brad would puke again and all the bulls would start bugling some more. Finally, Brad crawled back into his sleeping bag and went to sleep.

The next morning Bernie woke us up early. He made us some horrible black sheep herder's coffee that tasted like something similar to diesel fuel. I looked over at Brad who was still snuggled up in his warm sleeping bag. He was as pale as a piece of white paper. I nudged him and said, "How ya feeling this morning, buddy?" He replied, "Not good at all. I think I may have food poisoning." I laughed and said, "Or maybe whiskey poisoning." Brad did not laugh. He was very sick. Brad rolled over and said, "Did you hear those damn bull elk last night? I thought one of them was going to hump me by the fire while I was bent over puking. I thought you had to be good to call in bull elk?" I laughed and said, "Oh yea, I heard it all very well." I told Brad to stay in bed for a while and that I would help Bernie make some breakfast. I stepped out of the tent and discovered little piles of baby carrots everywhere. Brad thought he had food poisoning? I started to think about it some and realized that those baby carrots had been in my saddle bag since the previous fall. They were over a year old. I didn't think carrots could ever go bad?

Bernie made up a pot of black pinto beans for breakfast over the open fire. The beans tasted like shit, but I didn't say anything because I hadn't eaten anything for more than a day. I'm sure a belly full of beans and bourbon was just what the doctor ordered. Let alone the syrup-thick black coffee. I did everything I could to get a bowl of beans down and chased it with a slug of cold coffee. I offered Brad some beans, but he was still in the tent sleeping. He replied with a wince, "No thank you, will you please saddle my horse? We need to get out of here." I saddled up both our horses and told Brad his ride was ready. Brad staggered out of the tent. I told him to be careful and not to step in any baby carrot piles. He didn't laugh. Bernie and I helped Brad onto his horse. Bernie said he was going to walk out ahead of us and look for his mule and his spur. We went a short distance down the trail and I could hear Brad puking off his horse behind me. I turned around in my saddle to see Brad holding onto the saddle horn with both hands and puking down the side of his horse. Poor guy. That would suck and it's a long ride back home. I thought to myself.

We had ridden about two miles from Bernie's camp when we came across a lone pine tree next to the trail. Bernie was still walking in front of me when he stopped and said, "I think this is the spot where Woodrow brushed me off last night." I got off my horse and helped Bernie look for his lost spur. We looked everywhere and nothing! Finally, Bernie walked underneath the tree and looked up and said, "AH HA, here it is." He reached up high into the tree and pulled his spur out of the tree branch. Near as we could figure, Bernie had hit his head on a tree branch while riding, which caused his feet to both go straight into the air. His spur hung up in the branch as he went off Woodrow completely upside down. It's a wonder that it didn't kill him! Bernie headed back to camp, and Brad and I rode the rest of the way out to our truck with Brad puking all the way. Brad would end up getting diagnosed with food poisoning and I would end up telling Brad sometime later that those baby carrots were over a year old. To this day, I don't know if Woodrow ever came back to camp or if Bernie hiked out? Brad and I did return to that same camp spot over a year later and all the piles of baby carrots were still there. Nothing would eat them! I was just thankful that Brad had hogged all the baby carrots that night.

It was good to get out in the mountains with Brad and ride my new horse Norton. He actually did pretty well on that trip. I had been bogged down with purchasing hay for feed grounds, building new hay sheds, replacing hay shed roofs that had blown off, repairing horse corrals and stack yard fences. The maintenance work on feed grounds was overwhelming for one person. I would end up contracting with several contractors to perform some of the larger jobs such as new hay sheds and extending existing hay sheds to hold additional hay, so that we wouldn't run out of hay again during a bad winter. I did as much law enforcement work as I had time for, which wasn't much. Not as much as I would have liked. Lana and I had doctored Lucky's foot at my house for several months. He was now back out at Soda Lake and fully recovered. This was the young draft horse that had stepped on the large rusty nail.

Cheyenne (Fiscal Division) was giving us fits with hay purchasing. They felt that hay producers were gouging Ron and I and taking advantage of us. When in fact, Ron and I were able to purchase hay far cheaper than someone could in Cheyenne. Fiscal decided that they would bid the hay out. This meant that hay producers would have to send in a bid for how much they were willing to sell their hay for and how much tonnage they were going to provide. The hay producers didn't like this idea. They teamed up against fiscal and all of them sent their bids in twice what hay prices were worth. It got so bad that fiscal had them re-bid the process again. They all came in even higher with their prices the second time. By the end of the process, our attorney for the Department was doing the hay purchasing, trying to avoid law suits. At the end of the process the department would end up spending more than $300,000 over what Ron and I could have bought the hay for. Fiscal also wanted us to have a contract in place for any service provided that was over $150.00. The contracts would take nearly 6-8 weeks to process before you could have any of the work completed. So, if a road or culvert washed out and you weren't able to get a hay truck into the feed ground, you would have to wait 6-8 weeks before you could complete the work. This made it impossible to get any emergency work done.

The other difficult thing was fiscal required three bids on anything over $500.00. So, if I needed to purchase a draft horse, I would have to get three bids. How do you get three bids on a horse that you are wanting to purchase? They also wanted to know how many draft horses we had on all 22 feed grounds. They even sent us a Wyoming State Property sticker with a number on it for each horse worth more than $500.00. Ron told the head of fiscal that those property stickers wouldn't stick on a horse's ass for very long. Ron and I would actually start breeding and raising our own draft horses just to keep fiscal out of it. At times we would have a draft horse or two that either needed to be put down for old age or sent to the canners. At that time canners were paying as high as forty cents per pound. We had draft horses that needed to be put down due to old age, and they were worth four to eight hundred dollars depending on what they weighed. Canners would use this meat to make dog food.

I became so frustrated with the process that I would sell canner horses for cash. I would put the cash in a coffee can under Des's desk and saved it until I had enough money to pay cash for a new draft horse. This worked really well for several years until Bernie observed Des pay someone cash for a horse in the office one day. Bernie confronted me and said, "You probably should consider getting rid of the coffee can full of cash used to purchase draft horses." That was the end of the good ole days of purchasing draft horses for the department.

It was a Friday afternoon at 4:55 PM. I had just shut my computer down to go home for the day. The telephone rang at the front office. Office manager Des Brunette answered the phone. I over-heard her say, "Hello, Hello, are you alright?" Des then transferred the call to me and said "Swerb, can you please take this call, I can't understand this lady at all. I picked up the phone and said, "Hello, this is Scott, how may I help you?" I could hear the sound of a lady's voice cutting in and out of signal. It was difficult to understand her. It sounded like she was crying. The lady was trying to explain to me that she was being stalked by a mountain lion. She was crying and screaming and told me that she was in a tree and that the mountain lion was at the base of the tree. I quickly asked her what her location was, and she replied in a loud tone "NYLANDER CREEK!" I then heard the terrifying scream of a mountain lion in the background. This sound was so loud that it gave me goosebumps when I heard it. The line went quiet. I said, "HELLO, HELLO, can you hear me?" HELLO, HELLO, are you there?" The line went silent, I had lost contact with this woman. I sat there with the phone still against my ear in silence. I thought to myself, "Oh my God, did this lion just kill her? Or did her phone just die? Hopefully she will call back in a few minutes?"

I jumped out of my chair and told Des that I needed to head up Nylander Creek very quickly. I quickly explained to Des what was going on, and blew out the front door of the office. I jumped into my patrol truck and screamed down main-street in Pinedale with my red and blue lights on and my sirens blaring. I headed west out of town at a high rate of speed. I only knew of one Nylander Creek and it was a long ways away. Probably at least an hour's drive traveling at a high rate of speed. All I could think about was the terror in the lady's voice and the sound of the mountain lion screaming in the background. Even if I got to Nylander Creek, how would I ever find this lady? I passed a couple of cars at a high rate of speed. Other cars were pulling over ahead of me and letting me around them. I looked down to see how fast I was going. Shit I'm also out of fuel! My gas gauge read about one quarter of a tank. I was already well past town and didn't have time to turn around to get fuel. The governor on my truck cut me off at 94 miles per hour. I hit the county gravel road headed up Cottonwood Creek and drifted around every corner nearly sliding off the road several times. I was literally taking every corner just as fast as I could without sliding off the road.

Questions were racing through my head. Should I grab my shotgun or take my M-14 rifle? Do I have my bear spray? I soon arrived where Nylander Creek crossed the county road at the base of the Wyoming Range. Parked off the road was an older Dodge Dakota pick-up truck with a camper shell on it. I slid in behind the truck hoping this was the lady's truck. I grabbed my mic to tell our dispatch SALECS my location and what I would be dealing with. Every time I keyed the mic, all I would hear was a loud BEEP. Crap, I don't have any radio or cell phone service at this location. I decided to honk my horn and run my loud sirens for a bit to let the lady know that I was in the area. I had no idea how far she was from her truck, or which direction she may have traveled. I didn't even know if this truck was associated with the women whom I had spoken with approximately one hour earlier.

I exited my truck and looked for foot prints in the snow near the truck that was pulled off the road. Thank God, there was snow on the ground. I could see fresh foot tracks in the snow that headed up a main trail along the creek to the north. I quickly grabbed my department issue 12-gauge shotgun and loaded it up with slugs and double-aught buckshot. I alternated every other shell thinking that if I needed to shoot this mountain lion it would probably be at close range, based on the circumstances. I loaded a slug for the first round. I also grabbed my canister of bear spray and made sure my 9mm Beretta pistol was locked and fully loaded. I headed up the steep trail with my shotgun locked and loaded and the safety on. Once arrived at the top of the hill, the trail went through some thick pine trees. I slowed my pace as I walked through the thick trees looking to my left and then to my right as I walked, listening for any kind of sound from anything.

A short distance into the thick trees, I heard a loud screaming noise to my left. This startled me. I quickly looked to my left to see a woman crying and screaming as she ran towards me. She was screaming, "OH THANK GOD, OH THANK GOD!!" as she nearly knocked me down with a huge hug. I didn't know if I should be more afraid of her or the mountain lion? She cried and hugged me and kept saying, "Thank you so much!" I asked her to breathe deep and try to calm down and tell me what had happened.

She claimed that she was walking along the trail through the thick trees and smelled something dead. She looked over to her right and observed what looked like a dead calf elk that had been buried near the trail. She soon realized that this could be the cache of a mountain lion or a bear, so she stopped and pulled her bear spray out of her backpack and headed down the trail away from the cache. As she was walking away, she had a feeling something was following her or watching her. She slowly turned around to see a mountain lion crouched down on its belly stalking her about twenty yards away. She became scared and tried not to panic. She held her back pack high over her head to look bigger and slowly walked away facing the mountain lion with her bear spray in one hand and her back pack in the other. She said she didn't yell or scream, but just calmly told the mountain lion to "Go Away."

She worked for the Forest Service and had spent quite a bit of time in this area before. So, she knew there was no cell phone service in the area except one tiny spot out on the end of a ridge. She kept walking backwards and the lion kept following her. She claimed the lion stalked her for nearly one mile before she reached the end of the ridge. She was afraid to try and stand in one spot and focus on trying to make a phone call while the lion was stalking her. She knew lions could climb trees, but she felt safer up in a tree above the lion. Once she climbed the tree the lion stood at the base of the tree and screamed at her. She had worked with other department employees before and had the phone number to the Game and Fish office stored in her contacts. Once she made the call, she had very limited service and the lion continued to scream at her. After several minutes on the phone, her battery went dead and we lost contact. She thought about using her bear spray on the lion, but felt she was never really close enough to give it a good blast of pepper spray. She said that most of the time the wind was blowing towards her face, and she didn't want to risk getting a face full of bear spray.

The lady claimed that the lion never tried to climb the tree, just sat at the base and growled and screamed at her. She was hoping that eventually the lion would leave the area on its own but it never did. She had sat in that tree over an hour waiting for me to arrive. She said, "Once you showed up and honked your horn and turned your sirens on, the cat got up and ran off into the trees to the north." That's when she jumped out of the tree and was trying to get back to her truck before the lion returned. She was still afraid that the lion might find her and stalk her again on the way back to the truck. That is why she was so excited when she saw me walking through the trees. I escorted her back to her truck safely.

I then hiked back into the timber and found the cache that the mountain lion had made. From a distance, it looked like a dead calf elk that had been dead for a few days. The lion was standing next to the cashed elk calf growling at me. I had convinced myself that if the lion tried to stalk or charge me, I would kill it. We didn't need a mountain lion stalking people in the mountains even though it was only trying to protect its food source. It is not normal lion behavior to stalk people and scream at them while sitting in a tree. I quickly raised up my shotgun when I observed the lion standing there under a tree branch. He growled at me but made no attempt to charge or stock me. I decided to back out of the area and leave him alone to his meal. I returned back to Daniel Junction running on fumes, but I made it. This was a good lesson for me to always try and have adequate fuel supply in my truck in case I ever received calls of this nature again.

It was time to sit down and do my contracts to hire all the elk feeders again. It looked like all my feeders were coming back for another year. I would end up hiring only one new elk feeder that year and that was Mike Stevie for Soda Lake feed ground. Mike was tall and thin. He was an avid hunter and guide. He shod horses during the spring and summer months and guided hunters all fall for his brother Todd Stevie, who was an outfitter in the Upper Green River area. I hadn't met Todd yet but I

Mountain lion guarding cashed elk calf.

had heard some interesting stories about him from others. I was looking forward to driving up to his outfitter camp someday soon and meeting him. His brother Mike called him "Roundy" Apparently Todd was a large man with a temper and took little crap off anyone who stood in his way. Mike had a nickname of "One Beer." I'm not sure what that stood for but maybe I would find out someday. One beer had a high energy level and was always happy. He had a great attitude about life and was a hard worker. One beer had already fed elk on Soda Lake as a substitute feeder for the previous elk feeder for several years. He knew the ropes very well and required very little supervision. He was also an excellent hand with horses. I was looking forward to working with Mike. He seemed like a great guy. Also, Cheyenne headquarters wasn't very excited about me hiring my wife Lana back to feed on Soda Lake. It worked in an emergency situation, but this was no longer an emergency.

Mike Stevie "One Beer" with his team.

I was still pretty new to the community, but I was meeting new people every day. I drove into the Fayette Ranch to meet the ranch manager Chris Soderberg. Chris seemed like a great guy with one of the most unique personalities that I had ever observed in my life. He was a true cowboy and a hard worker. He offered to let me snow machine through the ranch anytime to get up to Fall Creek feed ground. This would save me many miles and time traveling back and forth to Fall Creek. We sat on the tailgate of his truck and visited for quite some time. I learned that he had a poker game at his house every Friday night. I even got an invite to come play sometime. I was very excited about this as I loved to gamble and was really missing a good poker game. Chris had a very unique sense of humor and came up with some of the most off the wall and colorful haywire jokes that you had ever heard in your life. Most of the time it would take me about ten minutes to get one of his jokes, and then I would laugh for days thinking about them once I figured them out. I was really looking forward to spending more time with Chris, especially at a high stake's poker game. I wasn't sure what games they played or how much they played for but it sounded really fun to me.

Before I knew it, it was opening day of antelope season. Brad had invited me to come down to his warden district and check antelope hunters in hunt areas 88 and 89. I was excited about this. I really enjoyed checking antelope hunters because the country was wide-open sage brush for as far as you could see. This made it easier to observe hunters from a distance actually kill their antelope. You knew who shot the antelope, if they were wearing orange, and if they shot from the vehicle or public road. I always enjoyed parking on a high hill somewhere in the middle of nowhere and just watching antelope hunters hunt.

Opening morning I decided that I would work the Bench Corral feed ground area because I had some feed ground maintenance to do. I pulled off highway 189 and headed into Bench Corral. There was a small camp trailer parked right off the highway. It was about 5:00 AM and I could see a light on in the small trailer house with people moving around.

As I drove by the trailer a man stepped out and waved at me in the dark. I waved back and he said, "Would you like to come in for a cup of coffee?" You just have to love Wyoming and Wyoming hunters. This man had never met me before and I had never met him before and he just invited me in for a cup of coffee. I hadn't yet had any coffee so the offer sounded pretty good to me. I parked my truck in front of his trailer and introduced myself by shaking his hand and telling him my name. He said, "Pleasure to meet you, Scott, come on in, my wife has some fresh coffee brewing."

I entered the tiny 15' trailer house and sat at a tiny table with a kerosene lamp whistling above my head. His wife introduced herself to me and poured me a hot cup of coffee. She was wearing a fluorescent orange coat and a fluorescent orange winter stocking cap. The steam rolled off my coffee cup and rose upwards and twisted around the hot burning lantern above. The man joined me at the small table while his wife continued to get ready for their hunt. He offered me a home-made cinnamon roll right out of the oven. I accepted and we had a nice visit as I finished my cup of coffee. I thanked the man for his hospitality and told him that I'd better make a mile and get back to work. I stood up from the table and heard a very loud "BOOM" right behind me. This had to have been one of the loudest noises that I had ever heard before in my life. His wife's .243 rifle had just gone off in her hands as she was standing next to me. Thank God that she had her mussel pointed in a safe direction. The bullet pierced through the ceiling of the trailer house and no one was killed or injured. I looked at the lady. The terror in her eyes looked like she had just seen the worst thing imaginable. She and her husband apologized profusely for the mishap. They both felt absolutely terrible. I knew I didn't need to lecture them and add insult to injury. I said, "Thank you so much for the coffee and cinnamon roll and thank you for making sure your muzzle is always pointed in a safe direction. Please enjoy your day and be safe out there." I shook their hands and thanked the good Lord that I was still alive as I left the trailer. That is an example of how easily your life can end at any given moment.

I jumped into my patrol truck, said a short prayer and couldn't believe that I had almost died and it wasn't even day light yet. I very humbly headed down the rough two-track road to start my day. It was late morning I came around a sharp corner in the road and observed a truck with Kentucky plates headed my direction. I hadn't checked a single hunter yet that morning. I stopped in the road and rolled my window down. I said, "Good morning, any luck?" The heavy-set man replied, "Yep, I got a couple of them." I jumped out of my truck and looked in the back of his brand-new power stroke diesel Ford. I observed a doe and a fawn antelope dressed out in the back of his truck. I said, "Congratulations, do you have your license on you?" He quickly handed me a license that was valid for a doe or fawn antelope. I said, "Ok, do you have another valid license for the second antelope?" He replied, "What do you mean? I have a doe/fawn license that is valid for both of them." I replied, "No, your license is only valid for a doe or a fawn antelope, not both of them!" He replied, "I thought a doe/fawn license was valid for a doe and a fawn antelope so if you shot the mama, you wouldn't orphan the fawn." I had never heard that one before. I explained to him that his license was only valid for a doe or a fawn and not both of them. I ended up citing the man for taking an antelope without a license and seized the fawn antelope. Now I would have to donate the shot-up fawn antelope to someone on my needy list. The man was not very happy with me and I was not very happy with him.

It was early afternoon. I came across a brand-new silver Ford truck with California plates. I pulled over as the man drove up next to me. I jumped out of my truck and looked into the back of his truck. I didn't observe any dead antelope in the back. The roads were very muddy that day and this guy was tearing the hell out of his brand-new Ford truck. I asked the man if he had had any luck. He responded, "Yes, it's in the back of the truck!" I had just looked in the back of the truck and saw nothing. I said, "Where in the back of the truck is your antelope?" he replied "In that small cooler under the tool box." I looked under the tool box and indeed there was a small red and white cooler under the tool box. The cooler was only big enough to hold a six-pack of beer and maybe a half bag of ice. I opened the small cooler and it was full of boned-out meat from a fawn antelope. I checked the man's license and everything was good. I couldn't believe that someone would drive 2000 miles, tear up their brand-new truck in the deep mud and shoot a fawn antelope? There could not have been more than fifteen pounds of meat in his cooler! This small cooler of meat must have cost that man at least hundreds if not thousands of dollars. If you were to add up all the expenses of traveling out to Wyoming, buying a non-resident license, meals, motel room, gas and all other expenses, this man could have bought and paid for a nice beef cow and filled his entire freezer for what he spent on that small fawn antelope. I guess it's all about the experience and the hunt, right?? Sorry, if I offended anyone. There is nothing wrong with shooting a fawn antelope for the meat, probably pretty tasty, just expensive!

I would end up meeting up with Brad later that day. I shared my stories of nearly being shot in the small trailer house that morning and about the man who had killed two antelope on a doe/fawn license. He just laughed and told me a story of a time when he stopped a hunter to check his license. The hunter thought that it was illegal to have a loaded firearm in his vehicle. As Brad approached the vehicle the man was trying desperately to unload his firearm. The rifle accidentally went off and the bullet exited the side of the vehicle off of the engine block sending bullet shrapnel into Brad's ankle bone. He hadn't told me that story before. I said, "Man, between poisonous carrots and accidental discharges, you are lucky to be alive today, buddy!"

Brad and I had met at the Bench Corral feed ground. He helped me hook up the spare trailer used for feeding elk and we loaded up all the twines. I figured I might as well get them hauled out while I was in the area. The road was pretty muddy, but I thought I could make it out. I was wrong and became very stuck on the way out. As a game warden it was always embarrassing to get stuck. As another game warden always found great pleasure in taking a picture of you being stuck and sharing the picture at the annual game warden's association banquet. It was always pretty entertaining seeing different pictures of warden's getting stuck each year. Most of the time you would look at the picture and say, "What was he thinking!"

Found a soft spot.

Elk seasons were now open in the upper Green River area. I decided to run up the river, do some feed ground maintenance on the Green River Lakes feed ground, and meet local outfitter Todd Stevie for the first time. I was a little nervous as I pulled into his outfitter camp in my green patrol truck. By the look on Todd's face (Roundy) he was a little nervous to see a green Game and Fish truck pull up in his camp as well. For some reason, I felt like he hadn't had many positive experiences with the Game and Fish Department in the past. It took a great deal of courage for me to knock on the door of his cook tent. Todd opened the door and said "Come on in, would you like a cup of coffee?" I said, "Thanks that sounds great." As I entered the cook tent several people left the tent suddenly. Almost as if they didn't care much for game wardens. Roundy poured me a stiff cup of coffee and introduced me to his very lovely wife Bev, also known as Ellie May. She was an attractive woman and very polite. I introduced myself to both of them and shook their hands. Ellie May offered to feed me breakfast. I was hungry and accepted the offer.

Roundy and I actually hit it off pretty good and I kind of liked the guy contrary to what I had heard about him previously. He was very honest and didn't hold anything back. You never wondered what was on Roundy's mind. He told you straight up. I appreciated his honesty and he respected my opinions. We hashed out several big issues over a cup of coffee. Ellie May served me one of the finest breakfasts that I had ever had before. Roundy and I talked about poachers, scab outfitters, and laws regarding outfitting in the wilderness without a guide. I told Roundy that I thought it was a bunch of bullshit that you needed an outfitter to hunt in the wilderness in Wyoming as a non-resident hunter. I said, "Anybody in the whole world can enter the wilderness legally to hike, fish, take pictures, trap or whatever the hell they want to do but they can't legally hunt big game animals without an outfitter? That sounds like a racket to me!" Roundy sat back and laughed and said, "Yea, you may be right, but because of that law you have fewer non-residents hunting in the wilderness, which makes for a more quality hunt for residents.

While at his camp, Roundy introduced me to his whole family including his step-brother Billy. Billy's nickname was "Billy Buck." Billy was quite a character and guided for Roundy in the fall. Billy Buck and I had a great conversation. We had a lot in common and we both loved to gamble. Billy Buck told me that he played poker on Friday nights with Chris Soderberg. I told him that I had been invited to play and was excited to join their game sometime in the near future. I didn't want to wear out my welcome so I stood up and shook all their hands and told them that

Roundy enjoying a nice Cuban cigar.

I was happy to meet them. Roundy gave me a firm handshake and said, "Stop back in when you have time for dinner, whiskey, and a cigar. These were my kind of people.

I left the Thompson Outfitter camp feeling like I really needed to return another time and get to know Roundy a little better. I felt like we had a lot in common and that our beliefs on many topics would align. I headed a few miles back down river and stopped in at the Green River Lakes patrol cabin. This was a cute little log cabin nestled back in the trees off the main road. The cabin was used as a patrol cabin for wardens in the fall and an elk feeder cabin for Todd Stearns to stay in during the winter months while he fed elk on the Green River Lakes feed ground. As I pulled up to the cabin, North Pinedale game warden Duke Early was unloading his ATV. Duke was the type of guy that was always happy to see you. He looked up with a big smile and said, "Hey Swerb, how are you doing today?" I responded, "I'm doing great Duke, how are you on this lovely fall day?"

I visited with Duke for a few minutes. He told me that he had to run up towards Gunsight Pass and look at a dead cow that a grizzly bear may have killed. The Game and Fish Department reimburses cattle producers for any losses that they may have from grizzly bears, wolves, mountain lions, and black bears as long as we can confirm that the cows or calves have actually been killed by a trophy game animal. Once a grizzly bear kills a calf, it's very important that we look at the carcass within 24 hours before it becomes completely consumed by the bear or other predators.

There is a large organization called the Green River Cattleman's Association. This is a shared allotment on the Forest where several large cattle producers all put their cattle on during the summer and fall months. It is a shared allotment that may run 5000-10000 cattle each year. The cattleman's association hires riders to tend to the cattle and move cattle to various different pastures to prevent over-grazing. The riders or cowboys are the ones that generally find the dead cattle and report them to Game and Fish Department personnel. Once we get the call, it becomes a high priority to look at the carcass before it becomes completely consumed. Often times there is only a hide left for us to look at. If we have a hide, we gather it up and soak it in water until it becomes soft and we can stretch it out and examine it for tooth puncture wounds. Generally speaking, grizzly bears almost always kill calves by biting them on the top of the back in the wither area. Once we observe tooth puncture wounds in this area on the hide, we generally confirm that the calf or steer was killed by a grizzly bear. Once confirmed, we fill out a wildlife affidavit indicating ownership of animal killed, date, time, and location of animal killed. At the end of the year, once cattle are off the allotment, cattle producers submit a damage claim to the department to get reimbursed for their losses.

With all that said, not to get caught up in the weeds on that whole program. Duke was headed up to try and locate a dead calf to determine if it was killed by a trophy game animal or not. He invited me to go with him. I had not seen any of that country before and was very excited to ride along with him. I also had a department issue ATV in the back of my truck, because I was going to try and spend some time learning new country and checking elk hunters that day. All the roads in this area were extremely rough and required an ATV to get to most remote locations. We soon had our ATV's unloaded. We left the cabin crossed the Green River and headed north up Pinion Ridge. The road was steep and rough and the river crossing was fairly deep in a few spots. I actually floated down stream for a short distance as my ATV tires were no longer touching the ground in the swift water. The upper Green River basin and Green River Lakes is one of the prettiest areas that I have ever been blessed to spend time in.

We soon made it to the top of the ridge and located the dead calf. The calf was about half consumed and there were grizzly bear scat and tracks around it. The calf was also bit in the withers. This one was pretty easy to confirm as killed by a grizzly bear. It's always a little eerie

Duke and Dennis with first grizzly bear caught in the Upper Green.

walking into those kill sites because you know the grizzly bears are either still feeding on the dead calf or pretty close by. We would always have our shotgun loaded with slugs and our bear spray on the ready. At this point in time, this would be the first confirmed grizzly bear kill in the Upper Green area. Duke and members of our bear crew had set a leg hold snare the previous day to try and catch the offending grizzly bear. They were successful and caught a very large boar grizzly bear. I was fortunate to be with Duke that day and get the opportunity to work a sedated grizzly bear.

Duke asked me if I wanted to see some new country while I was up there. He told me he would take me to Gunsight Pass and show me around. We finally arrived at Gunsight Pass. What an absolutely beautiful area this was. The leaves on the aspen trees in the lower country were a brilliant yellow, red, orange, and green in color. The high peaks were snow-capped. We were currently sitting at over 10,000 feet in elevation. I took a few pictures with my Kodak camera. Duke said, "Hey, while we are in the area, I would like to show you a secret game warden trail that will take you off this mountain without having to go all the way back the way we just came." I was excited to see this trail. I was always game to learn secret game warden trails. Especially from a man who knew that country inside and out. After a short distance we dropped off the mountain on what looked like an old jeep trail. The trail was very narrow and grown in with trees and various shrubs. Some places it was nearly impassable due to large boulders and rock slides that had blocked the trail for many years. The trail was very steep with few switchbacks to take you down off the mountain.

We hadn't come across any elk hunters all day. I was focused on following Duke down the steep mountain trail with white knuckles gripping my handle bars. I looked to my right and caught a glimpse of a white wall tent set up back in the trees about seventy-five yards from the trail. I was traveling kind of fast and just barely got a glimpse of the tent. It was almost like someone was trying to hide their camp. We traveled about another mile and Duke came to a stop. He turned around on his ATV and shouted, "Anyhow, this is how you get off the mountain if you stay on the trail. I think we better turn around as it's getting late and trail is getting worse." I asked Duke if he wanted to stop and check that wall tent on the way back. He said, "What wall tent? I never saw anything on the way down." I told him that it was tucked back in the trees and hard to see from the trail. Duke said, "Yea, let's stop and check that camp. I'll follow you." I headed back up the steep rocky trail nearly almost all the way back to the top of the mountain. We finally arrived at a location where we could see the wall tent behind some trees. We parked our ATV's and shut off the engines. I grabbed my binoculars and looked at the wall tent. I couldn't see anyone stirring around, nor could I see any horses or ATV's. It looked like maybe nobody was around.

Hunter's wall tent.

Duke and I decided to walk over and check the tent out. The tent flaps were tied shut indicating that there was probably no one around. I banged on the tent flap with my hand and yelled "HELLO IN CAMP!" I heard some rustling around noise coming from inside of the tent. Pretty quick a man opened the door. His hair was standing on end and his face looked like he had just woken up from a nap. There were three men in the tent and they had all been napping. We introduced ourselves as Wyoming game wardens and asked to see their licenses. They all three produced a very coveted 95 type 1 bull elk license. This was considered a trophy area for bull elk, this license was very hard to draw for non-residents. All these men were from Alaska. They were trophy hunting for a large bull elk. I figured if they all drew the license, they must have entered the draw as a party application. This means that the party organizer's name goes in the draw one time and if he draws, everyone in his party gets the license for up to six people. I looked at the hunting license closely and noticed a long number that shows they had applied as a party of four people. I wondered where the fourth hunter may be. The men were all very nice and friendly. We stood out in front of their wall tent and visited for nearly an hour. Finally, one of them said, "How did you guys get here anyway?" Duke laughed and said, "On our secret game warden trail over there," as he pointed towards our parked ATV's. One guy laughed and said, "You got to be kidding me. We had to park clear at the top of the mountain and pack all our stuff down here to camp." I finally asked them if there was a fourth hunter in their group. They told me that yes there was and that he was still out hunting somewhere. We finally said our good byes and walked back to our ATV's. I told Duke that I sure would have liked to talk to the guy that was still out hunting. I just had a weird feeling about the whole deal. Why would this guy be out hunting by himself when all of his buddies were back at camp napping?

We were sitting on our ATV's getting ready to head out when I noticed a man walk out of the trees and into a small meadow near the wall tent. Could this be the fourth hunter? I told Duke that I wanted to visit with that man and check his license. Duke and I quickly headed across the meadow to intercept the man before he arrived back to camp. Once we caught up with him, we startled him because he didn't expect to see two game wardens come out of the trees in the middle of nowhere. I quickly introduced ourselves as Wyoming game wardens and asked him for his license. I noticed his hands were shaking and covered in blood as he reached for his wallet to show us his hunting license. I looked at his license and asked him if he had killed anything. He replied, "No, I haven't even seen an elk today." I then asked him, "Where did the blood come from on your hands?" He laughed and said, "Oh, I came across a man down off the mountain below us that had two elk down and he told me that his buddy was sick with multiple sclerosis (MS) and had to return to camp to get his medication. The man was very tired and by himself so I helped him dress out both elk." This raised a red flag to me. It sounded like maybe this man down in the trees somewhere had shot both elk and there was never another person with him?

I asked the man if he could draw us a map to better explain the location of the two dead elk. This man was amazing, he drew us a very detailed map of how to get down through the trees to the meadow where the dead elk were lying. Without this man and his detailed map, we would have never been able to find this spot. We thanked him and jumped onto our ATV's and headed back down the steep trail for approximately one mile. We parked the ATV's and took off walking through the thick timber searching for a small open meadow. It took us about one hour to finally find the correct meadow. When we arrived, we found a dead cow elk that had been gutted. She was lying out in a small meadow near some large white bark pine trees. I looked her over carefully and determined that she had been shot one time behind the shoulder. I also found a hunting license stuck in her ear. The license had been filled out correctly and the name on the license was Frank from Cheyenne. I looked over and noticed a calf elk lying dead about thirty yards from the cow elk. The calf was not gutted nor was it tagged. It appeared to me that the calf had been shot in the guts. It also had a bullet hole in its head. It appeared to me that someone may have shot the calf in the guts and it lay down to die. Someone walked up to it and shot it from close range right between the eyes. This wasn't making any sense to me? The Alaskan hunter told us that he had helped the man dress out two elk? Only one elk had been dressed out? Was there another elk that we weren't finding?

I told Duke that I smelled a rat and suspected that Frank had killed both elk and there was never anyone with MS involved in this picture. Duke replied, "I suspect you may be correct, but how are we going to prove it since both elk have been shot through and through and there is no bullet to match to anything?" I said "You are right, unless we interview the guy and get a confession we really don't have much here." I then told Duke that they will be returning at some point in time to pack the elk out. Maybe we should hide in the trees close by and try and overhear their conversation when they return to determine what happened. About that time, we could hear the sounds of ATV's coming up the trail. They were very close! I looked at Duke and said, "Quick, follow me, let's hide in that patch of trees over there." Duke and I quickly ran a short distance to look for a hiding spot that was close enough to the dead elk that we could hear their conversation when they returned. I found where a large spruce tree about three feet in diameter had fallen over years ago and brought up its whole root system with it. I dove over the top of the tree and landed on the ground lying flat to the ground, face down. About that moment I felt the weight of Duke land right on top of me and Duke is a large man! The only way that we could both be completely concealed was for Duke to lay on top of me. We were only about twenty yards from the dead cow elk in the meadow. I could look under the large trunk of the tree and actually see the elk from my location. I thought to myself, this is going to be perfect, except Duke is getting very heavy really quick!

There were two ATV'S involved. Both of them drove off the secret game warden trail right over to the cow elk in the meadow. They parked their ATV's right next to the cow elk and never shut the engines off. One man got off and pulled out his hunting knife and started cutting something on the cow elk. It looked like maybe he was trying to cut the front leg off at the knee joint. The men were talking, but I couldn't hear a word they had said due to the sound of the ATV's still running. About that time, I heard a branch snap right next to me. I thought Duke had moved around and broke a branch. Then I heard another branch break. I was hoping a grizzly bear was not stalking us being that close to a dead elk. I slowly turned my head to the right side and observed a hunter wearing a fluorescent orange vest and hat standing right over both of us. I was completely embarrassed. Here were, two Wyoming game wardens spooning behind a large dead tree in a very remote area. I was completely embarrassed. I rolled out from under Duke. He hadn't even seen the hunter yet. I jumped up and quickly asked the hunter if he was part of the group that had shot the two elk. He said that he was part of the group but was not present when the elk were shot. I quickly jumped over the tree and headed out to visit with the man who was cutting on the front leg of the elk. As the man was bent over cutting on the elk, I said, "How are you doing, sir?" in a deep voice. The man looked up at me and it startled him so badly to see a game warden, that he sliced his hand wide open with his hunting knife. The cut was really deep and bad. Every time his heart would beat, a stream of blood would squirt out of his hand. The man took out a red handkerchief from his pocket and wrapped his hand tightly with it.

Duke had now joined us and we both started asking the men questions. Frank told me that he had shot the cow and showed me his license. I asked him who had killed the calf. He told me his friend Dennis had killed the calf but had MS and had to get back to camp for his medication. I asked Frank where Dennis was and where was his license? He told me that Dennis was back at camp and that his license was right here in his shirt pocket. I looked at the license. It had not been filled out. I asked Frank why he had Dennis's license and why hadn't Dennis put it on his elk after he shot it before returning to camp? Frank told me that he forgot because he was feeling so badly. I also asked Frank why they hadn't dressed out the calf elk yet. He told me that Dennis was sick and was unable to dress out the second elk. I asked Frank if there were any other dead elk in the area. He told me no, only two dead elk.

Duke agreed to go back to their hunting camp with the other

hunters and find Dennis. While Duke was gone, I asked Frank a series of questions that I would also ask Dennis later on. I asked him how many elk were in the bunch before they shot. I asked him who shot first. How many times did they shoot? What direction were the elk traveling when they were shot? How far away from the elk were each of you when you shot? Frank was able to give me an answer on every question and I recorded his response in my pocket note pad. I would ask Dennis the same series of questions to learn if Frank was lying and to see if Dennis was even in the area when the elk were killed. I told Frank several times that I thought he was lying to me and that Dennis was not with him when he shot the second elk. Frank would not admit to doing anything wrong and was very adamant that he had only killed one elk. Pretty quick Duke showed back up. They had loaded Dennis on the back of the ATV and hauled him right to the kill site. I told Duke to interview Frank and I would interview Dennis.

Duke grabbed Frank and they both sat down on a log sitting next to each other. I could hear Duke asking him questions from a distance. I walked over to the ATV to visit with Dennis. Dennis had the shakes something horrible. He couldn't even get off the ATV and stand on his own. I helped him off of his ATV and held his arm as we walked over to a near-by tree. Dennis could not walk or stand without his cane. He leaned up against the tree and I introduced myself to him. He said he was not feeling good at all and really needed to get back to camp and rest. About that time, I heard Duke yell at me from a distance, "SWERB, Frank just passed out!" I looked over and Frank had passed out cold and was lying in Duke's lap. I think maybe he had lost too much blood and became lightheaded. Duke was now slapping Frank's face with his hand and yelling "FRANK, FRANK CAN YOU HEAR ME?" Frank finally came back to life and I heard Duke say "So, anyway you were telling me about your hunt, continue where we left off." Duke had gone right back into his interview. I looked at Dennis leaning against the tree shaking. We were in a bad situation with both of these hunters and it was nearly dark out.

Not to mention we were in the middle of nowhere. I looked at Dennis and said, "Dennis you need to listen to me very carefully. You need medical attention and your medication. Frank just passed out because he is about to bleed to death from a deep cut on his hand. We are a long distance from any hospital. I need to know that you did not shoot that calf elk and that you were not even present when this elk was killed. Dennis looked me right in the eye and stated, "I did not kill that elk and I was not ever here when that elk was killed." I thanked Dennis for his honesty and told his buddy to take him back to camp so that he could get some rest. I walked over to Duke and Duke said, "Swerb, I think we may have got things figured out over here. Frank thinks that when he shot his cow, that bullet may have passed straight through her and killed that calf. He thinks that he may be responsible for killing that calf." I replied, "He is damn responsible for killing that calf." I asked Frank for his driver's license and told the other man still standing there to go dress out the calf elk and get Frank home before he bleeds to death.

I borrowed Duke's citation book and issued Frank a citation for taking an over-limit of elk. I wish I could have issued him another citation for lying to the game warden. Frank signed his citation with his bloody hand and Duke helped him back to his ATV. I walked over to help the other man finish dressing out the calf elk. This was the man who had walked up behind Duke and me as we were hiding behind the tree. As soon as we were done dressing out the calf elk, the man looked at me and shook my hand. He thanked me for the work that we did day in and day out. He said, "But I gotta tell you, when I walked up behind the two of you lying on top of one another behind a tree in this very remote area. I thought to myself Oh my God, what has, Frank done now!!" He honestly thought that Frank might have killed both of us and placed us behind that tree in a pile.

Thank God Duke had remembered his ticket book and pen that day because I didn't have either. I hiked back up the hill and grabbed my ATV and brought it back down to load the calf elk. It was well after dark now.

Duke even had some rope in his back pack to lash the calf down to the rack on my ATV. One thing about Duke, it took him awhile to get going in the mornings, but he was the most prepared man that I had ever met. If you needed Visine, Aleeve, Pepto-Bismol, lash rope, hobbles, gloves, hat, shooting glasses, ear muffs, whatever you needed Duke always had it. I shook Duke's hand and said, "Good case. A lot of things had to come together on that one. If it weren't for us finding the Alaska camp because you were showing me the secret game warden trail, and waiting for the fourth hunter to return to see the blood on his hands, we would never have known that any elk had been killed in the area. If Dennis hadn't been so sick and Frank hadn't severely cut his hand because I scared him to death by hiding behind the dead tree, Frank would still be lying to us." Duke chuckled and said, "I can honestly say I have never had someone pass out in my lap while interviewing them before. And I don't know what you said to Dennis, but that was the quickest interview I have ever seen." I laughed and told Duke, "I told Dennis that they were both in need of immediate medical attention and he didn't have time to lie to me or someone may die before the end of the day." Duke laughed and said, "That was the quickest interview I have ever seen." I bet those hunters will never forget that day. They are probably still wondering where we came from and how we got there. And why were there two game wardens piled up behind a dead tree in the middle of nowhere?

I still think there was another dead elk in the area that we didn't find. I thought it was odd that the one hunter came walking down out of the trees from up above us. The one that found Duke and I together behind the tree. What had he been doing above us, and why wasn't he involved with the other two elk being shot? I have learned over time that sometimes you never learn everything, but just have to take what you can get. I should have gone back up and visited with the Alaskan hunter and had him show me where the two elk were that he helped field dress. Heck, maybe Frank had already hauled one elk back to camp and had it tagged with someone else's tag on his first trip back to camp. Who knows? It was late and we had a long, cold ride home in the dark on our ATV's. I was learning quickly that you never know what you are going to run into as a game warden, and you need to be prepared for anything that may come your way. We probably should have had a first aid kit with us that day too.

I really enjoyed working in the Upper Green River area. The country was absolutely breath-taking. I had decided that I was going to work opening day on October 15 when all the license types opened for the area. This would be a very busy day as this area was known for its great elk, deer and moose hunting. I would plan to stay in the rustic Game and Fish cabin on the night of October 14th so that I could get an early start checking hunters at first light on the opening day.

Green River Lakes.

I would end up going over to the Fayette Ranch one Friday night to play poker. I soon learned that God threw away the mold when he created Chris Soderberg and Billy "Buck" Gransden. All the players were a one of a kind. I couldn't figure out or trust any of them. The players consisted of ranchers, outfitters, and the president of a bank, an oil field consultant, and a damn game warden. This made for some pretty lively conversations. Every one of them were completely full of bullshit and knew how to bluff very well. I ended up having the time of my life, even though I donated to the cause. These were my type of people. I would plan to attend this poker game as much as possible. While at the poker game, Billy Buck told me that they were looking for an extra pool shooter to join their pool league team. Little did Billy Buck know but this was right down my alley and I used to be pretty good at the game. I happily told him that I would love to join their team. The team would play every Tuesday night and rotate through all the different bars in the area. Between the poker game and the pool league, I was starting to meet more people. I was really excited about joining the pool league and playing poker.

Chapter 10

THE DREAM

For those of you who read my first book Son of a Poacher, Wyoming Warden in the Making. You may recall the story about my grandpa Lyle lying in the hospital dying of lung cancer. He was in a coma and the nurses and doctors told the family that he didn't have much time left here on Earth. Close family were all standing around his bedside when Lyle opened his eyes and smiled. He said in a very faint voice, "I had a dream that I was playing basketball in a large gymnasium. The walls were painted bright white and there was a small door on one end of the gymnasium. I was shooting baskets by myself. Heck, I couldn't miss a basket from anywhere in the gym. It didn't matter if it was a full court or half-court shot, I couldn't miss a shot! I had never even played basketball before and I was having the time of my life making baskets. About that time the small door opened at the end of the large white room. A beautiful woman waved for me to come over to her. I started walking towards her. She was the most beautiful women that I had ever seen in my life. She was wearing a bright white dress that dragged on the gym floor behind her every step. She had the most beautiful smile and long black hair that flowed all the way down her backside. We walked towards each other and she smiled and grabbed both of my hands." She said, "Enjoy your time, Lyle, be prepared. We are coming to take you tomorrow." My Grandpa Lyle told us about that dream. He smiled, closed his eyes and went back into a coma. My grandpa passed away the next day. I was a young boy but I never forgot his words about the dream that he had that night. I believe this was an angel coming to be with my grandpa to comfort him in his final time on Earth.

Approximately fifteen years later, I suddenly awoke in the middle of the night. I'm a very deep sleeper and this never happens to me. I raised up in bed and had sweat running off my forehead and my hands were shaking. I had just had the most vivid dream that I had ever had in my life. It was so real, I had to reach over and touch my wife to make sure that this was only a dream. The dream scared me almost half to death.

I had a dream about a bunch of people standing on the bridge at White Creek Ranch near Shell, Wyoming. This was the ranch that my stepfather Martin owned when I was a young boy. There were about one hundred people standing on the bridge over-looking Shell Creek. Everybody was dressed nicely and most had a drink of some kind in their hand. It was very crowded with people and difficult to walk through the crowd. I was pushing my way through the crowd of people on the bridge and didn't recognize anyone. From out of nowhere a beautiful woman with long black hair wearing a beautiful long white dress stepped in front of me. I noticed a halo of light shining over her beautiful face. She had the most beautiful smile with the brightest white teeth that I had ever seen before. She was the only person on the bridge who didn't have a drink in her hand. As we were facing each other, she placed her right hand on my left shoulder, smiled and said, "Scott, be prepared, we are coming to take you next Monday. She smiled and was gone. I suddenly woke up in a sweat. Was this the same angel that had spoken to my grandfather? Was I going to die next Monday?

I woke up and went to work and couldn't quit thinking about this damn dream all day long. I never told my wife Lana about it. I'm not sure I had ever told her the dream that my grandpa had had just before he passed anyways. I kept thinking to myself, next Monday, next Monday, what in the heck is so special about next Monday? I quickly opened up my planner and looked at the calendar. Next Monday was October 15th, opening day of hunting season. I had planned to spend my time in the Upper Green River and stay in the patrol cabin. Was someone going to kill me on opening day of hunting season? Monday was almost one week away. I couldn't get this dream out of my head. Was it real? Was I really going to die on Monday? I never really ever wanted to know when I was going to die.

I even decided to maybe do some really crazy stuff between now and Monday. Heck, if I'm going to die Monday, maybe I should live on the edge a little more and push the limit. I awoke Sunday morning and started packing up for my trip to the Upper Green River patrol cabin. I would be staying in the cabin the night of October 14th by myself. My plan was to wake early before sunrise and cross the Green River at the bend in the river several miles downstream of where the cabin was located. I had crossed the river on my ATV at this location several times before. If you didn't pick the right path and stay on a sandbar, the river was very deep on both sides of the sandbar and you could be swept downstream. I decided that since I would be crossing the river in the dark before sunrise that I had better stop and look at the crossing in the daylight and make sure it was still passable.

I soon arrived at the crossing in my patrol truck on my way up to the cabin. I jumped out of my truck and walked over to the river. I studied the crossing very hard for several minutes. During the daylight, I could see the sandbar about one foot deep under water that I would need to stay on or I would be swept down the river. I knew I wouldn't be able to see the sandbar in the dark. I decided that if I centered myself up with the road and headed straight across the river until about half way across, I would need to veer to my left to stay on the sandbar. It didn't look that difficult in the daylight. The river was about thirty yards wide and the water was rolling pretty fast over the large boulders in the area. I would have never mapped out this crossing in the daylight if I hadn't had that damn dream. I was going to die tomorrow. I just didn't know when or how?

I decided that I would travel up to Todd Stevie's outfitter camp just up the road and say hi to everyone. I arrived there just before dark. This outfitter camp was located a couple miles up the road from the Game and Fish patrol cabin. Todd greeted me at the front door of the cook tent. He said, "Swerb, come on in and let Ellie May feed you some dinner. I felt like I knew Todd (Roundy) a little better now, so I jumped out of my truck, shook his hand and said, "That sounds good, thanks for the invite Roundy I really appreciate it." Roundy then introduced me to several of his hunters as one of the local game wardens. He pulled down a gallon size bottle of Crown Royal off a nearby shelf and broke the seal. He then grabbed a small glass, filled it up half full of ice and topped it off with Crown Royal. He placed the drink in front of me as I sat down at the head cook table. He said, "Drink up ole son, I'm sure you have had long day and are thirsty!" I didn't know if I should accept the drink or not as I was still wearing my red shirt and duty belt. I did have a soft spot for Crown Royal and it did sound pretty good. Would Roundy be offended if I didn't except the drink, I thought to myself. I decided I was probably going to die somewhere tomorrow anyhow, so I might as well go out with a bang! Heck, this might be my last dinner and drink, who knows!

The meal was absolutely awesome and the dessert was even better. Ellie May was a top hand in the kitchen to say the least. The non-resident hunters were really enjoying themselves listening to and telling stories with a Wyoming Game Warden, Roundy, and his guides. They would ask me questions about catching poachers and hunting big game in Wyoming. I would tell a story and they would laugh, pour another whiskey, and puff on their cigars. Everyone there was having a Big and Rich time and the large bottle of Crown was slowly disappearing. Roundy told me that he had some portable hand-held radios that he would communicate with his guides on, if they had elk down and needed pack horses. He asked me if it was illegal to use their portable radios to direct hunters to the elk from his base camp. I told him that currently there were no regulations in place to make this an illegal activity. I also told him that I had just received a portable scanner that I could use to scan the conversations on his portable hand-held radios. He laughed and said, "You're full of shit, you don't have a scanner that can hear us talk. Don't be pulling that game warden bullshit on me!" All the non-resident hunters laughed, I replied, "I'm not shitting you Roundy. I have one, so be careful what you say on your portable radios because I can hear every word." He poured me another drink and laughed. I really did have a scanner that I had just received from Cheyenne Headquarters. I just hadn't had time to try it out yet. Heck, I didn't even know how it worked or if it even worked.

The non-resident hunters soon went to bed in their wall tents outside. They were going to have to get up very early, eat one of Ellie May's famous breakfasts and endure a long horseback ride at first light in search of a bull elk. Billy Buck and his brother Mike (One Beer) pulled out a crib board and wanted to play some cribbage. I had become good friends with both of them. I had hired One Beer to feed elk at Soda Lake feed ground coming up in December or January. We played a few games of cribbage, laughed, and had a great time. I finally told them that I needed to make a mile because I had to get up early as well and make sure all the hunters were behaving themselves on opening day of elk season tomorrow.

I drove a short distance back to the Green River Lakes patrol cabin. It had started to snow lightly. I wondered what it would look like in the morning and how cold the temperatures would be. My plan was to leave the cabin on my ATV about one hour before daylight and head up Pinion Ridge. It would be about a 3-4 mile-ride to get to the river crossing at the "bend" in the river. I would need to locate the key to the cabin that was hanging on a piece of wire up in a tall lodge pole pine tree behind the cabin. I had a belly full of Crown Royal and no flashlight. This proved to be a difficult task. I finally located the key to the cabin by feel. I spent several minutes trying to feel for the key hole on the cabin lock on the front door. Finally, I was in the cabin. It was dark inside and very cold. It took me awhile to feel for matches in the dark to light the propane light above the kitchen table. I was excited to get the propane lanterns lit to provide some heat and light in the small cabin. I held the lit match up and "POP" the lantern lit. I wanted to build a fire in the wood stove to heat the cabin, but it was getting late and I would be asleep in my cozy sleeping bag before the cabin even warmed up.

I turned on the battery-operated AM radio that was located on the small kitchen table. The radio signal was not good. All I could hear were bits and pieces of a song that I had not heard before. I walked into the bedroom and lit a couple more propane lanterns that were mounted on the wall above the bed. The bed was so high up off the floor, I thought I might need a step ladder to get into it. I damn sure didn't want to fall out of it in the night. I might break my neck. I rolled my sleeping bag out and propped my pillow up against the wall to warm next to the lantern. I could still see my breath as the three propane lanterns hissed in the background. I noticed a small battery powered alarm clock sitting on the counter next to the small wash basin. I set the alarm for 4:00 AM. I slid my pancake holster with my 9mm Beretta pistol off my leather belt and laid it on top of the refrigerator. I went through my back pack to make sure I had everything ready to go for morning. Portable radio, extra batteries, ticket book, lunch, water, binoculars, new portable radio scanner, first aid kit, flashlight, extra gloves and warm hat. My back pack was absolutely stuffed. I don't think I could have even fit another baby snickers candy bar in there anywhere.

I untucked my red shirt and took my boots off. The cabin was starting to warm up a bit. I jumped up on the tall bed and started reading some 1970's outdoor magazine. Pages were missing, pages were torn in half and bent over. This magazine had been around for a while. It felt comforting to just relax for a bit. The crackling AM radio was now starting to drive me nuts. I jumped out of bed and shut it off for the night.

Now all I could hear was the sound of the three propane lights hissing in the background. I always kind of enjoyed the sound of a propane lantern hissing in the night. I jumped back into bed and lay there with my eyes wide open. All I could think about was how was I going to die tomorrow. Was the dream real? Was the angel real? I guess I would find out tomorrow. Now I was wound up and couldn't sleep.

I jumped out of bed, cut an empty plastic Gatorade bottle in half and filled it full of icicles that were hanging off the porch of the cabin. I then grabbed a bottle of whiskey and filled the plastic container about half full. My mind ran crazy as I sipped on the marinated icicles. I needed something to take the edge off and make me tired so that I could get a good night sleep. I finally shut the lanterns off. POP, POP, POP and the cabin became darker than the inside of a black cow. I lay in bed in dead silence. All I could hear was the ticking of the alarm clock that was now lying right next to my head. The time read 12:04 AM. I guess I had already survived the first four minutes of the day before someone was coming to take me away. I wondered if I would even wake up in the morning or would I go in my sleep?

The next thing I knew the little tiny alarm clock was doing its job bouncing along the window sill. It was so loud that I woke up pissed off and was frantically trying to get it turned off with no lighting in the cabin. The clock read 4:00 AM. I finally got one of the propane lanterns lit. The cabin was cold as hell and I could see my breath as I hopped around trying to get my pants on. I finally got fully dressed and warmed up a bit. I really wanted a fresh cup of coffee but I was not going to take the time to build a fire and make a pot of coffee. I ate a couple of granola bars and a piece of dried-up beef jerky. I dressed warm with the only clothes that I had. I knew the trip on the ATV was going to be cold until the day warmed up. I grabbed my backpack full of food and supplies and headed out the door. When I opened the cabin door, I could feel snowflakes hit me in the face. The wind was blowing slightly. I thought to myself, Shit, it was going to be a cold day. I hated riding my ATV in the cold. The cold wind would chill me right down to the bone. I strapped my backpack onto the front rack of my ATV leaving room for the headlight to shine. I always liked my backpack in the front where I could see it and not worry about it falling off and losing it somewhere.

I wiped the snow off the seat of my ATV. The seat was frozen harder than a brick. This was not going to be a very pleasant ride. The Honda ATV fired right up. It was always reliable that way, except it was one of the roughest riding ATV's that I had ever ridden before. I sat there in the dark wondering what I may have forgotten. Shit, I forgot toilet paper and I still needed to lock the cabin. I was soon on my way down the Green River Lakes road headed for the bend in the river to cross the river. It was snowing and the wind was blowing. I wanted to be to the top of Pinion Ridge by daylight. I arrived at the river crossing. This had me concerned that I would not be able to see the sandbar in my headlights that I needed to stay on to safely cross the river. I pulled up to the edge of the fast-moving water and shined my headlights to my left and right. Shit, I couldn't see anything of a sandbar, just fast moving water as the water rolled over large boulders in front of me. I could remember in my mind that I needed to head straight across the river until I was about halfway across and then veer slightly to my left to stay on the sandbar.

I sat there and stared at the fast-moving water in my headlights for several minutes. This little voice in my head said, don't do this, It's very dangerous! Had I ever listened to that little voice before? Hell no, I sat back and gave it the onion! Cold water was spraying over my handle bars and into my face. I had the throttle wide open. I was about to the middle of the river and veered to my left to stay on the sandbar. I must have veered too soon as I could now feel my ATV riding the waves and I was headed downstream very quickly. I kept the throttle wide open. I could not see anything except water coming over my handle bars and into my face. I was still headed in the right direction to get across the river, but I was quickly going downstream and my tires were no longer touching the ground beneath the water. I went up and over a couple of large boulders and nearly flipped over upside down. I just kept the throttle mashed and leaned hard to my right to prevent from tipping over and being swept down the ice-cold water in the night. I must have been swept downstream for approximately fifty yards when I could see a steep dirt bank coming up. Thank God, I was nearly across the river.

I could see the steep bank coming up quickly. It was about four feet tall and almost straight up and down. I had to make it or who knows how far down the river I would be swept in the strong current. I quickly decided that if I hit the bank and went over the handle bars, at least I will be on shore. I didn't even care what may happen to my ATV being swept down the river without me. I hit the bank hard and the ATV shot straight into the air. All I could see was my headlight shining straight above me with large snowflakes dancing through the air. I landed hard on my rear tires. The front tires came down hard and pitched me over the handle bars into a thick patch of tall willows. I was all right, the ATV was still running and upright on all four tires. I hadn't tried to get up yet, I just laid there in the willows shaking from being so scared of the thought of drowning in the ice-cold river in the dark by myself.

I finally got up I was soaking wet from my waist down and mostly wet from the top of my head down to my waist. I took my gloves off and felt my pants with my bare hands to feel how wet my clothes were. As I patted my rear end to see how wet my pants were, I noticed something that made my heart absolutely sink. I could not feel my pistol anywhere on my waistband. Shit, I had forgotten my pistol on top of the refrigerator in the cabin. Not only did I just survive the river crossing, but now I would have to go back and cross the river to retrieve my pistol and cross the river two more times to get back to where I currently was. I couldn't even imagine trying to be a game warden on opening day of elk season without my pistol.

I had to drive my ATV through the thick willows to get back over to the two-track road about fifty yards upstream. This was almost worse than fording the river. The willows were nearly eight foot tall and very thick. At times the willows were the only thing holding me up as the ATV tires were not even on the ground. I finally made it back to the river crossing with my headlights again shining across the river and no sight of the sandbar again. I sat there in the night and thought to myself. Oh yea, is this supposed to be how I die today? Now I have forgotten my pistol and will need to cross the river two more times! At this point I was so mad at myself I really didn't even care if I was going to die. I put the ATV in reverse, backed up about thirty yards. I put the transmission in second gear and gave it the onion. I'm pretty sure that I hydroplaned all the way across the river this time. I had to have thrown a wake of water over ten feet tall. Now I was really wet!! But I made it and was thankful for that.

I took the ATV back to the cabin and retrieved my pistol from the top of the refrigerator. I jumped back onto my ATV and headed back towards the river crossing. By the time that I made it back to the river crossing it was starting to get light. I pulled up to the river and I could see a truck across the river with its headlights on. Someone had crossed the river in front of me in their pick-up truck while I was gone getting my pistol. I grabbed my wet binoculars and watched them from a distance of about 200 hundred yards. I could see two men walking around in front of their headlights. It looked like maybe they were putting tire chains on the front tires of their truck.

I was hoping to be high up the mountain ahead of all the hunters before daylight, but that didn't happen. I could see well enough now that I was able to cross the river and stay on the sandbar without incident. I crossed the river and headed over towards the truck. As I neared the truck it was a baby blue Ford truck, probably about a 1976 model. It had Wyoming plates, but I did not recognize the county number on the license plate. I was pretty sure it was from somewhere in eastern Wyoming. As I pulled alongside the passenger side of the truck with my ATV, the two men had just jumped into the cab of the single cab truck. I sat there on my ATV looking over at the man who had just jumped into the cab on the passenger side. There was another man sitting in the bed of the truck. I had not even seen him until I pulled up next to the truck. He was wearing a black cowboy hat with a narrow strip of orange plastic wrapped around the top of his hat. I guess this was his hunter orange for the day. The man on the passenger side finally rolled his window down to talk to me. He could see that I was a game warden because I had my green coat with the antelope patch on my left shoulder and my bright shiny gold badge.

He rolled down the window and asked, "Where is your orange, BOY?" I replied, "In my pocket." He glared at me with his beady little green eyes and said, "Aren't you worried about getting shot BOY?" I replied, "No Sir, I'm not." He then squinted his eyes and stuck his head out the window towards me and said in a very soft tone, "Well, I would be worried about it if I were you, BOY." This really pissed me off. He basically just threatened me as a game warden and I didn't like being called "BOY." He rolled up his window and the truck started moving forward. I raced around him on my ATV and parked in the middle of the road in front of them. I got off and approached the truck as it was coming towards me. The driver pulled the truck up to where his front bumper was resting on the rack of my ATV. I walked over to the driver's side of the baby blue Ford truck and waited for the driver to roll down his window. He didn't roll down his window he just sat there looking straight ahead. I banged on his window with my gloved hand indicating that I wanted to speak with him. He looked like an older man wearing a cowboy hat. The hat was a faded grey in color with grease stains around the brim. He also had a thin orange plastic ribbon wrapped around the top of his hat for his florescent orange requirements. He had a grey beard and his face looked weathered like a Wyoming rancher.

He finally pushed me out of the way with his door and said, "My window doesn't work." I asked him if he was hunting elk. He replied, "Nope I'm just showing these guys around a bit. They are the ones with the license. I asked him what his name was and where he was from. He seemed hesitant to tell, so I asked him for his driver's license. He was disgusted with me that I was bothering him and holding up their hunting.

It was now daylight but just barely. I looked at his driver's license. His name was Adams and he was from Niobrara County. The man in the back of the truck stood up and asked, "Could we get going now?" I replied, "Yes, just as soon as you guys show me your elk license." The man jumped out of the back of the truck right next to me. He was short and skinny and was wearing cowboy boots. I looked at his license and he was from Kansas. He had a license valid for a cow elk only. I then walked over to the passenger side of the vehicle and banged on the window as this man had not yet offered to show me his license. He also seemed put out, but eventually pulled his license out of his wallet and handed it to me without looking at me. He also had a cow-only license and was from Missouri. I thought to myself, why is, an old man from eastern Wyoming all the way over here with two non-residents. Sounds to me like he may be doing some scab outfitting without a license and in the wrong area.

I was so upset with the Missouri man threatening me that I had decided right then and there that I would follow them in some capacity all day long. I would also call dispatch if I could ever get signal and run Adams to see if he had any prior violations. These guys were up to no good and had no respect for a Wyoming game warden at all. I told them to go ahead of me and that I would stay behind as to not get ahead of them and screw up their hunting. What they didn't know is that I would be bird-dogging them all day and make sure they did everything correctly. I moved my ATV and they went around me crawling their way up a steep, rough, muddy slope.

I sat on my ATV and became very cold. My pants were frozen and I could barely bend my legs. I didn't even have an extra pair of pants back at the cabin and I was not going to take the time to dry out as I needed to keep up with the baby blue Ford. I let them get a few miles ahead of me and I headed up the rough road behind them. I went for several miles and the wind was so cold that I couldn't take it anymore. I parked and walked over to a large boulder to stand behind and get out of the wind. I soon decided that I might freeze to death if I didn't build a fire and get dried out or at least warmed up. I quick made a fire ring out of small rocks and gathered up some dead aspen branches from nearby. Soon I had very nice fire and was thoroughly enjoying the heat of the fire. I looked down and my blue jeans had steam rolling off of them as they were slowly drying out. My backpack was soaking wet. I decided to dig out my brand-new scanner and make sure the water hadn't damaged it. It looked alright, but I hadn't even put any batteries in it yet to make it work. I fumbled around and finally got some new batteries in it.

I'm not much of a techno nerd and I hate reading instructions. It generally takes me about an hour and a half to watch 60 minutes. So, if I turn the on button on, the damn thing better just work! Besides I don't have time to be reading any instructions out here in the wind behind this damn boulder. I turned on the scanner and the second that the scanner turned on I heard something that I will never forget. I heard Roundy's voice saying, "GF-84, GF-84, do you have your ears on, son? Do you have your ears on son? We have poachers on the knob, poachers on the knob... over!!" I was nearly frozen to death but thought this was the funniest thing that I had ever heard in my life. I couldn't answer back, but I damn sure heard "Roundy on the Radio Show" for the next ten minutes. He kept saying something about a (Rusty Trombone.) I never did understand what all that meant. The fact of the matter, Roundy didn't believe that I had a scanner and he was testing me to see if I could hear what he had to say. What were the odds of me turning on that scanner at the exact second that I did to hear his conversation? The scanner worked very well and I was excited to try it out for a while. I couldn't wait to see Roundy again and say "GF-84, GF-84, you got your ears on, poachers on the knob, poachers on the knob."

I was just starting to warm up. It was still early morning. I could see the snow clouds start to lift and it looked like the sun may come out at some point in the day. I heard a loud shot to the north of me, and another shot, another shot. I quickly grabbed my binoculars. I could see a large group of about 300 elk headed up a steep mountain to my north.

Scott C. Werbelow

The elk were going in and out of thick trees, so it was difficult to tell just how many elk there were. I kept hearing shots but I could not see anyone shooting or any elk dropping dead in the large herd of elk. Finally, I located the shooter. He was standing on top of the mountain shooting down towards the herd of elk. He was wearing a full-body pumpkin suite (florescent orange) and shooting down into the large group of elk that were at least 600 yards away from him. I counted seventeen shots before the elk disappeared into the trees and went out of my view. This made me furious that someone would shoot seventeen times at over six hundred yards into a group of elk. I quickly put my campfire out and headed north on my ATV to cut the distance. I would need to hike up a steep mountain for over two miles to get to where this man was shooting from. All I could think about was, I wonder how many damn elk this man has shot and wounded or killed?

I drove my ATV as close as roads would allow me to this location and parked my ATV. I put on my heavy wet backpack and started my steep trek up the timbered mountain to check this hunter and see how many elk he had killed. I had left my scanner turned on and could hear it squawking in my backpack. I figured I had better stop and listen to it because maybe others were about to run into this same large group of elk. As soon as I got it out of my back pack, I heard a voice say "We just killed another one, that's three now. Oh, that's four, now we have five down." I could barely hear the voice over the scanner as signal was weak. But I could hear really faint gun shots to the north of me. My guess is someone else just got into the large herd of elk that this guy had just shot at. I sat down for several minutes to catch my breath and listen to the scanner some more. Near as I could understand, it sounded like two guys had killed at least five elk and they were trying to get more hunters in their camp to come up and tag all the dead elk. Party hunting in Wyoming is illegal. You have to shoot your own elk. I was so frustrated. There was not enough of me to go around. How would I ever find the location of where the five dead elk were lying, and how many elk had the guy killed that I was headed up the mountain to check on?

I continued up the mountain and finally got on the elk tracks from the large group of elk. The further up the mountain I hiked, I started to see blood in the snow where elk had been wounded. I followed several different blood trails of wounded elk but couldn't find any dead elk. I was nearly to the top of the mountain when I looked up and could see a man and a young child dressing out a cow elk at the bottom of a rock slide in front of me. I stopped to rest and grabbed my binoculars. Up above the man was another dead elk laying in a steep rock slide. This man and child had at least two elk down and several more wounded.

I hiked up a very steep slope to get to their location. My pants were still wet from my morning river crossing. I approached the man in the full pumpkin suit. This was the same man that I had watched shoot from the top of the mountain down at the herd of elk. He was a large heavy-set older man. He and the young boy were bent over dressing out the cow elk, and had not yet looked up to see me standing ten feet from them in the middle of nowhere. He was breathing extremely hard as he dressed out the cow elk. I could tell he was not in very good shape and the young boy only looked to be about twelve years of age to me. I looked straight above him and I could see another dead elk in the rock slide about 200 yards straight above us. The elk looked like a calf lying with its head pointed downhill. It looked to me like the calf elk was lying on top of its head with its neck bent straight backwards. All I could see was the body of the elk and not the head. Finally, I asked the man, "Who killed the calf elk above you?" He looked up and almost fell over backwards when he saw the game warden standing there. I had shocked both of them. He said, "My God where did you come from? Why are your pants wet?" I told the man that I had waded the Green River at first light this morning to come check his license. He seemed very surprised to see me. The man told me that his twelve-year-old son had shot the calf and that he had shot the cow. He was breathing very hard. I checked his license and helped him fill it out correctly. I told him that I was going to walk up and look at the dead calf elk. He said, "Oh absolutely, I will come up there with you!" I replied, "No, just stay here and finish taking care of this cow so that you don't have to make two trips.

I had not seen his son shoot earlier from the top of the hill and suspected the man had killed both elk, but would need to prove it. I headed up the very steep rock slide and noticed both the man and boy were following me up the hill towards the dead calf elk. I soon arrived and looked closely at the calf elk. The calf was still alive, I could see its stomach moving back and forth as it breathed. The man and son finally arrived. I asked the man, "Who killed this elk?" He quickly responded, "My son did, shot it right between the eyes at about six hundred yards and killed it deader than hell with one shot. It's his first elk!" I said, "Well, congratulations young man, but the elk is not dead yet." The father blurted out, "The hell, he ain't dead. He shot him right between the eyes with a 30.06." I said, "Well, look at his belly, he is still breathing." The man replied, "Well, he can't be very goddamn alive." The man grabbed the hind leg of the calf and pulled it downhill to expose the calf's head. As soon as he moved the calf, the calf kicked him right between the eyes and knocked him over backwards, sending him down the steep rock slide end over end. The calf jumped up and ran down the rock slide and ran right over the top of the man as he lay face-down in the rockslide. The calf stumbled and fell down a short distance from where the dead cow elk was lying. The calf had been shot in the head, but was still very much alive.

It took the man a bit to get back his wits and get back on his feet. He said, "Let me go down there and grab my rifle and I will put it down." I told the man that technically it would be illegal for him to shoot it and that his son would need to put it down. I walked up to the calf and told the man that I would just put it down with my pistol, so that the boy didn't have to shoot it at close range with a 30-06 rifle. The man agreed to allow me to shoot it with my pistol. The young boy came running up behind me and tried to pull my pistol out of my holster yelling, "LET ME SHOOT IT, I WANT TO SHOOT IT." I couldn't believe what I had just witnessed.

What twelve- year-old boy, or anybody for that matter, tries to jerk the pistol out of the game warden's holster and shoot it?" I peeled the little boy's hands off the butt of my pistol and told him to stand back while I put the calf elk down. The little boy stood to my left with his hands over his ears. I took a careful aim at the back of the calf's head and slowly pulled the trigger. "BAM." The calf elk died and I heard the little boy yell, "AHH." I looked over and the little boy had brain matter stuck to his forehead and cheek from the calf elk. He quickly wiped it off and started gagging. Sometimes things don't work out the way they are supposed to. I don't think the little boy ever did shoot the calf elk, but I didn't want to make a huge deal out of it. I would have to prove it and probably end up interviewing and interrogating the twelve-year old boy. I did not want to do this. I wanted this to be a positive experience for the young boy and his father.

I visited with the father alone away from the boy. I told him that he should be ashamed of what just happened that day in front of his son. I told him that I didn't ever see the boy shoot and that I suspected that he had killed both elk. I also told him how unethical it was to shoot seventeen times into a large group of elk at over 600 yards. I explained to him that I had already tracked three different elk with blood trails and that if I found any other dead elk in the area, I would be back to visit with him. He asked me the best way to pack the elk out due to the steep mountain terrain. I told him they would have to go out the same way they came in. I also explained that there was an old jeep trail below us, but it was closed to motorized vehicles and I had better not catch him violating the road closure packing his elk out. I went back down off the steep hill and tracked three more blood trails for several miles. I did not find any more dead elk, but knew in my heart that this man had killed or wounded several more elk and I was not happy about it. I had done so much hiking that my pants were nearly dried out by now.

I made it back to my ATV and turned on my scanner. Hopefully, I could hear more information about the men that had killed five elk. I was really wanting to find this area before they got all the elk tagged with other licenses and hauled out of the area. I also had not forgotten about the assholes in the baby blue Ford and really wanted to catch up with them again. About that time, I heard more chatter on the scanner. I heard a voice say, "Hey, I got a really nice four-point buck standing below me. Do you want me to shoot him for you?" The man on the other end replied, "I don't know have you seen any game wardens today?" The other man replied, "Nope." The other man replied, "Go ahead and shoot him then!" The first man came back on the radio a few moments later and said, "Got him, he's a nice one!" the man replied, "Good deal, where, are you at?" I got excited and turned up the scanner to listen closely. The man replied, "I'm just below where we were yesterday." That didn't tell me a damn thing! This scanner was starting to drive me absolutely nuts. There was poaching going on in the area and I couldn't pinpoint any of it.

I worked my way north to try and catch up with the large group of elk that I had seen earlier that morning. There was snow on the ground and I could tell which two-track roads had been used more than others. I started following the road that looked like it had the most vehicle traffic on it. Pretty quick I could see blood in the snow on the road indicating someone had killed an elk and hauled it out in the back of their truck. I started finding drag marks in the snow where people had dragged their dead elk to the road. I decided to park my ATV and go for a hike and follow some of the drag marks and people tracks. The tracks took me down into a small canyon off the main road. What I would found really upset me. I ended up finding nine different gut piles in the area. This was the area that two men had killed at least five elk. Well, no, it was at least nine elk! They had already had all the elk dressed, dragged, and out of the area. I was so upset with myself. I had missed out on all of this because I was dealing with the man and his son on the side of the steep mountain. I couldn't just ignore that situation. I didn't even make a case on that one, even though I suspected the man had killed both elk and probably had more elk lying dead somewhere. I was starting to feel like a real failure. I would spend more time in the area tomorrow morning to look for additional dead elk once the ravens and magpies found them. That is if I was still alive? It was afternoon and no angels had come to take me yet. The river crossing was pretty scary earlier that day. Maybe I had overcome that and actually survived what was supposed to take my life.

The sun had finally come out and it was a blue-sky day. I was really wanting to find a warm spot in an aspen grove and take me a good ole game warden nap in all the pretty fall colors. I was really tired between being cold all morning, long hikes, and getting only four hours of sleep. I decided to do just that. I hid my ATV in some trees and hiked back into a remote location and lay down to take a nap. I had just started to fall asleep when I heard a branch break behind me. It scared me. I thought maybe a grizzly bear was sneaking up on me. I slowly turned around and observed a hunter standing over me staring down at me. I don't know how long he had been watching me, and I could not believe that in all that country someone had found me napping. I looked up at him and made eye contact. He asked, "Are you a game warden?" I replied, "Yes, sir!" He replied, "Oh, thank God, I have been lost all day and could use some advice on how to get to the Green River Lakes campground". He told me that his friend had dropped him off on the Union Pass Road and was going to pick him up at the lower Green River Lakes. I explained to the man that he had a long hike ahead of him, but he could do it before nightfall if he hurried. I told him exactly how to get there from our location. He thanked me and took off running through the trees. I was a little upset that he had screwed up my nap but I may have possibly saved his life or at least him having to spend the night out with a campfire.

I lay back down and tried to fall asleep again. I was just about asleep when I heard a voice yelling, "DAD, DAD, DAD!" I turned around to see a young boy running frantically through the woods with no orange on and no rifle. I jumped up again and yelled at the boy from a distance, "Can I help you!" The boy looked at me and came towards me. He was crying and said, "Have you seen my father anywhere?" I explained to the young boy that his father had just come through about ten minutes earlier and was headed for Green River Lakes. I explained to the boy how to get to Green River Lakes and that his father was just ahead of him. The boy took off like a bullet headed off the mountain. I thought to myself, why didn't the father tell me that he had become separated from his son? What is wrong with people! By now I had decided that a nap was not in the cards for me today. I jumped back onto my ATV and headed back down country.

I traveled several miles and soon observed a set of tail lights come on about a mile in front of me. The vehicle had just topped a hill and stopped at an intersection in the road. I quickly grabbed my binoculars and checked out the truck. It was the baby blue Ford truck. I had finally found them again. I observed two individuals get out of the truck with rifles in hand. The truck soon went out of sight. I hit the loud lever and hauled ass towards them. I wanted to keep them in sight and try and figure out what they were doing. I just had a feeling that they were up to no good. I wanted to see which direction the hunters were headed so that I could watch them hunt. I soon was at the location where I had last seen them from a distance. I could not see any truck or any hunters. I turned left at the intersection and was traveling very slowly down a ridge to the west. There was a beautiful aspen stand to my right as I traveled down the road. Pretty quick I heard a loud "BOOM" over the sound of my running ATV. I quickly stopped the ATV and shut off the engine.

I could hear the sound of something rolling down the hill right across from me in the aspen stand. It was making a loud crashing noise like an elk rolling down the hill through dead trees or something. I looked up and I could see taillights again. Someone had hit their taillights right after the sound of the rifle shot. I grabbed my binoculars to look at the taillights. It was the baby blue Ford and it was stopped in a road about two miles away. I heard voices over in the trees a short distance away. I heard someone say, "Where is it?" I heard another voice say, "It should be right above you somewhere." I wanted to know who shot the elk, who was going to tag the elk, and if the elk was going to even get tagged. I only assumed that an elk had been killed. I looked up and the baby blue truck was turned around and headed towards me. I quickly ran my ATV off the road into a stand of trees and hid it. I wanted to hide somewhere close where I could still hear the men talking and possibly figure out who had killed the elk.

The blue Ford was getting close. I grabbed my backpack and took off running across an open meadow towards the aspen stand to find a place to hide in the trees. I quickly dove over some dead aspen trees that were lying in a pile. There was not much cover to conceal me, so I would have to lay flat against the ground face down. The truck pulled up and parked in the road right next to me, but I could not see it due to a small hill that was between us. The motor of the truck sounded loud as I lay there face down in the trees. I heard doors slam and voices close by. I was pretty sure that whoever was in the blue truck was going to head up into the trees to help the other hunters drag the dead elk out. It seemed to me that maybe they had portable radios, because why would the baby blue truck stop, and turn around the minute that the elk was killed and then return to the area where the hunters were dropped off. I felt like whoever was in the blue truck was going to walk right through the trees where I was hiding, and I didn't have a very good hiding place. I heard the truck's engine shut off. It became very quiet. I could no longer hear voices coming from anywhere including up in the trees where the elk had been killed.

I lay there face down in the snow for about ten more minutes. Nothing, nobody was talking anymore? Pretty quick I heard the sound of a truck start up and drive off. I quickly grabbed my scanner out of my backpack. I wished I had thought of that earlier. I turned on the scanner and heard a voice say in almost a whisper, "Be careful, game warden is in the area. We are leaving, will return later." The response came back, "10-4, if he finds us, we will deal with him appropriately, if you know what I mean." The scanner went quiet for about a minute when I heard the response come back, "10-4 just be careful and don't get caught, if you know what I mean." I thought to myself, holy shit, what are these guys up to? Did they see my ATV stashed in the trees? Did they see me run across the open meadow to hide in the trees? The scanner went quiet and so did everything else. I sat in my location for about twenty more minutes just listening for anything. The evening sun was shining bright and the fall colors in the aspens were vivid red, yellow, orange, and green. I never heard another noise. I thought maybe I was going crazy, because I knew I had heard the voices of two men right across from me in the trees. I knew I had heard the sound of a gun go off and the sound of something rolling down the hill a short distance away. Now there was nothing? Usually when someone kills something the hunt is over and all you hear are the sounds of happiness coming from the hunters followed by high fives and hand-shakes. This was not the case and very weird. Both men had a cow license. Why would everyone leave the area? What really had happened in the trees? I would soon find out.

I walked back to my ATV to make sure it was still there and hadn't been vandalized or missing. It was still there and all was well. I keyed the mic on my portable radio. I could tell it hit the tower by the way it sounded. Holy cow, I actually had some signal and could possibly call SALECS and check out this Adams guy a bit more. I was able to give dispatch his name and date of birth. I had written that information down when I contacted him earlier down by the river. It took dispatch awhile to get back to me. Finally, I heard, "GF-84 SALECS." I responded, "GF-84 go ahead with your traffic." "GF-84, can you call me please," I responded, "Negative I do not have cell service in this area." "10-4, GF-84 for your 10-43 (Information) Mr. Adams is a convicted felon for charges stemming from child molestation." I responded, "10-69 (meaning message received) thank you." I thought to myself, that's why the son of bitch didn't have a hunting license. He is a convicted felon and couldn't legally possess a firearm! I could tell dispatch didn't want to tell me this over the radio but wanted me to have the information. I told dispatch my location the best that I could and also told her that I would possibly be dealing with a violation with this individual. I didn't know what I would be dealing with, but I wanted them to know something about the situation that I was in.

I grabbed my backpack and portable radio and headed into the trees. I knew I wasn't crazy. I had heard voices, a gunshot and other noises in the area above me and I was going to figure it out. I walked through the trees as slow and quiet as I could, constantly looking and listening for anything. There were about three inches of snow on the ground, so it should be easy to find people or elk tracks. I would eventually make a large circle around the area that I had thought this all happened in. Nothing, I could not find a single boot track in the snow or a dead elk anywhere. I was starting to think that I was going crazy. I went back to the original place where I had started searching and where I thought I had heard the men's voices. I grabbed my binoculars and glassed up the hill above me. The colors of the aspen leaves were very vivid as the sun was setting.

I was just about to give up and get out of there when I noticed a very vivid red color in my binoculars about 100 yards above me. This didn't look like bright red aspen leaves but something else? I hiked up the steep hill to get a closer look. As I got closer to the bright red spot that I had seen from down below, I noticed the heart, liver and lungs of an elk hanging from a tree branch about eye level. This was eerie. Why would someone do that? I searched the area and soon found a dead cow elk that had been gutted out and covered up completely with large green pine boughs. I also noticed two sets of boot tracks in the snow that left the area to the north not the south of where the blue truck was waiting for them earlier. I wondered what was going on. Why didn't they tag the elk? Who shot the elk? Why did they cover it up and leave the area to the north? Why did they hang the liver, lungs, and heart in a tree by the windpipe? I decided I would get my questions answered, because I was going to hide near the dead elk and wait for them to return. My guess is that they had no intentions of tagging the elk. They were going to try and sneak it out in the night and they were going to kill as many elk as they could before they got caught.

Scott C. Werbelow

I hid behind a large rock about twenty yards from the dead elk. The longer I sat there, the more that I started thinking. The Missouri man threatened me earlier this morning when he asked me if I was worried about getting shot. When I replied no, he looked me in the eye and said, "I would be if I was you, BOY!" Then I heard them talking on the scanner and someone said, "If he finds us, we will deal with him appropriately, if you know what I mean." What the F—k is that supposed to mean? Are they planning on killing me? Should I really be hiding in the trees by myself right now with nightfall just around the corner? I turned my portable radio on and keyed the mic. BEEP, BEEP, I had no radio signal. Shit!! I became very cold as the sun disappeared behind the mountain. I actually made a bed out of pine boughs on top of the dead elk and lay down on top of her still-warm body. Her body cavity was still giving off some heat and much warmer than the snow-covered ground. I was determined to "bust" these guys because of how they treated me earlier that morning. As I lay there, I thought about the dream that I had had nearly a week ago. Was this finally the time in my life that they were coming to take me away? I had survived the river crossing. Was this it? I was going to be out-numbered and they had no respect for a Wyoming game warden. Heck the one guy was already a convicted felon. Who knew what the other two guys were capable of, hunting with a convicted felon! I was hoping they would show up to claim the elk sooner than later. I was also hoping a grizzly bear was not going to come along and try to kick me out of my cozy bed.

It seemed like I had lain there forever. I decided that maybe it was time to say a short prayer to my Lord. I folded my hands, closed my eyes, and looked into the heavens. I asked the Lord to protect me and be with me for what I was about to endure. I asked him to give me the faith and confidence that I was going to need to get through this situation. I told Him about the dream that I had had and asked Him if it was my time? I could feel tears starting to stream down my cheeks. What in the hell was I doing lying on top of a dead cow elk in the middle of nowhere, waiting for some crazy Missouri/Kansas douche bags to show up? I had no radio service, no cell service, and nobody in the world could have found me right now! I heard a noise. I opened my eyes and looked up. A Steller Blue Jay had just landed on a small branch less than five feet from my face. The bird looked at me and cocked his head back and forth slowly as he stared right into my eyes with its own tiny little black eyes. The Blue Jay started chirping at me like it was trying to tell me something?

I thought to myself, is this bird one of my angels? Is this bird my father who passed away while I was in high school? What is this bird trying to tell me? Is my father with me right now? The bird sang me a really nice song for just a minute and flew away. It became really quiet and was now getting dark. Was this just another Steller Blue Jay wanting a piece of elk meat? Or was it deeper than that? I became cold and considered building a fire, but they would never return for the elk if they saw a fire in the area or even smelled the smoke. About that time, I heard the sound of a truck approaching below. It actually sounded like two trucks with one of them being a diesel. I heard one truck shut off its engine, the other truck definitely sounded like a diesel as it idled for a few minutes before shutting off. I thought to myself, they are here and there are two trucks. This means they will arrive with more than three people. I reached into my backpack and grabbed my flashlight and put it in my left-hand coat pocket. I took my OC spray (people spray) out of the leather container and placed it in my right-hand coat pocket. I then took my portable radio out and tucked it in my inside coat pocket and clipped the mic on the collar of my coat in a visible manner. I pulled my pistol out of my holster and made sure it was locked and loaded and ready to go.

I hid behind a large rock that was located right next to the dead cow elk. This rock would provide me good cover if I needed it. I lay there in the dark very quietly and listened. Pretty quick I could hear voices coming up the hill below me. I could now see several rays of light bouncing from tree to tree as they headed up the hill. The first man was about twenty yards from me when I observed him stop and yell back behind him, "Where in the hell is this elk at?" The man below replied, "Its right there somewhere." The other man replied, "Is it a cow or a bull?" The man below stated that it was a cow elk. This told me that the man in the lead was not with them when the elk was actually killed. The man in the lead finally found the elk and was shining his flashlight on the elk right next to me hiding behind the rock. He yelled, "How many shots did you take and where did you hit it?" The man below said, "I took two shots, the first hit her behind the shoulder and the second one I shot her in the head to put her down." This told me that the second man coming up the hill was the shooter. Both men were now at the elk, and I could see several more people coming up through the trees towards us with flashlights.

The first man started removing the pine boughs from the covered dead elk. I heard him say, "Where is your license?" The second man said, "In my pocket." The first man said, "Why is it in your pocket, it's supposed to be on the elk?" The second man said, "I'm not going to tag it if I can get it out tonight without the game warden checking us." I felt the moment. I jumped up from my hiding place, turned on my flashlight and said, "Well, the game warden is here to check your license!" The first guy at the elk was so scared that he slipped and fell over backwards on the ground. He was the Kansas hunter wearing the cowboy boots in the snow. Both of the men had rifles slung over their shoulders. I wasn't sure why. They had already killed an elk and it was dark out. I walked over to the man who had killed the elk and shined my flashlight in his face. I said, "Oh you are the Missouri hunter that I checked earlier this morning. Where is your orange, BOY?" He replied, "I'm done hunting, so I don't have to wear any orange." I replied, "Aren't you worried about getting shot, BOY?" He replied, "Nope its dark outside and nobody can see me to shoot me, BOY!"

About that time three other hunters showed up. They all had rifles slung, which I thought was very interesting. Were they worried about a grizzly bear on the dead elk or a game warden? I asked the Missouri hunter why he hadn't tagged his elk before leaving the site of kill. He said, "I didn't think the tag needed to be on the elk while in transit? I said,

"You're exactly correct, except the elk is not in transit. It's lying up here in the middle of nowhere covered in pine boughs with no license on it." I then told the man that I had been wandering around the forest and found this elk un-tagged and covered in pine boughs. I didn't know who shot it, if it was going to be tagged or if anyone was coming back for it. That is why I was here right now! I then asked the man for his hunting license. He pulled it out of his front shirt pocket and handed it to me. I quickly looked at it with my flashlight. The license had not been filled out at all. I noticed his name on the license and tried to remember his name.

About that time, all the other hunters had surrounded me and had their rifles unslung and pointing towards the ground in front of them. I was soon walking in circles with my flashlight trying to keep an eye on all of them. They had me outnumbered and dead-to-rights if they really wanted to. I needed to think fast. I quickly grabbed my mic and said, "Pinedale GF-84 for your information, I'm currently on Pinion Ridge with Gary Benson from Jefferson City, Missouri in reference to a big game violation. Please mark my exact GPS coordinates from my portable radio and give me frequent status checks, thank you!" I quickly clipped my mic back to the collar on my coat and started asking Mr. Benson some more questions. I had absolutely no signal on my portable radio and was talking to no one, but they didn't know that. I asked Mr. Benson for his driver's license which he handed over to me. I now had his hunting license and his driver's license.

I was surrounded by all the hunters with rifles. Mr. Benson looked me in the eye and said, "So are you going to help me drag this cow elk back to my truck, BOY?" I looked him in the eye and moved my face about three inches from his face and replied, "Nope, looks like you have plenty of help tonight BOY!" I told him that I would meet him down at the truck when they had the elk packed out. I then took off quickly through the trees and got the hell out of there. It took me forever to find my ATV in the night. I had it pretty well-hidden. I couldn't believe that I was still alive but the night wasn't over yet. I still needed to issue him a citation and have him sign it. I was also going to confiscate his elk since he was such an intimidating prick to me! He just didn't know that part yet. I started up my ATV and turned on the headlights. I had never written a ticket in my headlights before but it actually worked out pretty well. I felt much safer away from them in the dark and now I was able to communicate with SALECS again if need be.

I finally had the citation written out for fail to properly tag the elk. The bond amount was going to be $200.00. If Mr. Benson couldn't come up with the bond, I would need to arrest him and haul him out on my ATV back to the Green River Lakes patrol cabin and on to Pinedale in my Game and Fish truck. I was starting to think about the river crossing again in the night with a confiscated cow elk and an arrested man from Missouri on the back of my ATV. As I was waiting for all the men to get the cow elk packed off the hill, I noticed Mr. Adams sitting in his truck with the heater on. I walked over to his truck and banged on the window. I told Mr. Adams what had happened with his non-resident hunter. I also lied and told him that I had interviewed all the hunters involved and they had told me that he was indeed charging them for hunting and outfitting without a license. Mr. Adams smiled and said, "Sir, there is no money exchanging hands here, we are just good friends. I worked Mr. Adams over with everything I had and couldn't get him to admit to outfitting without license and I knew damn well that's exactly what was going on.

Pretty quick I could see all the hunters coming down through the trees with the cow elk. I was waiting for them at their truck with my ATV running. I told Mr. Benson that I needed to speak with him alone. I also told the other hunters to load the cow elk on the back of my ATV. Mr. Benson threw a fit and said, "You are not taking my elk!" I said, "Yes sir, I am, and I will need $200.00 bond for your violation." He replied, "Two hundred dollars! I don't have two hundred dollars!" I said, "Well, you better get together with your buddies and come up with it or I'm going to have to haul you to jail." He looked at my ATV and said, "On that damn thing?" I smiled and said, "I have done it before, BOY, and the river crossing isn't very fun!" I had him sign his citation in the headlights of my ATV, and he went back to visit with his friends and try and borrow some money from them. He returned with cash and handed it to me. I pulled him aside and said, "You know, I have known Mr. Adams for years. He is the best outfitter that I have ever met. How did you guys meet? He looked me in the eye and stated, "We are just friends, there is no money exchanging hands here, BOY!" Mr. Adams had them pretty educated on the whole system. I would then go back and interview each hunter in the group separately. Every one of them stated, "There is no money exchanging hands here, we are just friends!" I would plan on getting our covert investigative unit together on this man in future years. Don't ever call me, BOY, and don't ever threaten me!

I left there with $200 cash in my pocket and a dead cow elk on the back of my ATV. I was still alive-however, the day wasn't over with yet. I still needed to forge the river at night with a pretty heavy load. As I bounced down the road in the late night, I felt pretty good about what I had just done. These guys were absolute dirt balls, had no respect for law enforcement and they got caught red-handed in the middle of nowhere when they thought they could outsmart me. I laughed to myself when I thought about the guy from Kansas falling over backwards because the Wyoming game warden just happened to be hiding behind a rock next to a dead cow elk in the middle of the night. Who would have thought? You know they made a game plan to return in the night because there was no way they would ever get caught.

I soon came to the river crossing. I stopped and said a short prayer to the man upstairs. I prayed, "Dear Lord, please help me make it home safely. I'm almost there and this has been one heck of a long day." Please look over me as I cross this river again." I leaned back and gave it the onion. All I could see was water splashing over my handle bars and lots of it. I closed my eyes and held the throttle wide open. Pretty quick I hit land on the other side. I had safely made it one more time. I was soaking wet again and the rest of the ride to the patrol cabin was extremely cold. I arrived at the cabin, found the key, and made it inside the cabin. I quickly turned on all the propane lanterns to help warm up the cabin. I grabbed the plastic Gatorade cup and filled it with icicles. This time I poured the plastic container completely full of whiskey and added no water. I built a roaring fire in the wood stove and took my wet clothes off. My feet were all shriveled up from wearing wet boots all day. My legs were nearly frozen from having wet pants on most of the day. I was tired and hungry. I would need to get up early again and go look for more dead elk from the father and son shoot out. I would also need to figure out which two guys killed 9 elk.

I felt overwhelmed. I had a dead cow elk on my ATV that I would need to care for and donate to someone in need of meat. Where would I store it so that the grizzly bears didn't eat it first?

I sipped on my whiskey next to the wood stove and turned on the AM radio. Again, the music sounded like shit, but it was noise none the less. I dug through my backpack and ate a frozen peanut butter and jelly sandwich. The bread was wet from the river crossing and had become frozen. Which made me think more about the early morning river crossing. That could have been really bad. I also thought about being surrounded by the hunters in the heavy timber in the middle of nowhere. Lying on a dead cow elk for heat. I thought about the scanner and how much poaching was really going on out there. I also thought about the "Roundy on the Radio" talk show that I listened to first thing this morning over a fire trying to warm up. I looked over at the wind-up battery-operated clock on the window sill. It read 12:04 PM. I had survived the day. It was pretty nip and tuck at times but I had survived. What was the meaning of the dream? Was it real? Did it make me more aware of my surroundings to actually save my life that day? I guess I will never know but I survived another day as a Wyoming Game Warden and was very thankful for that.

I finished my whiskey, set my alarm for 4:00 AM and turned off the propane lights. POP, POP, POP was the sound as the lights went off. I lay there in bed. The only thing I could hear was the sound of mice crawling around in the walls and ceiling and the sound of my alarm clock going TICK, TICK, TICK. I thought about the knot and blood on the man's forehead from the calf elk kicking him between the eyes. I thought about the heavy-set man tumbling down the steep rock slide backwards and the calf elk running over the top of him as he lay face down. I thought about the young boy who tried to grab my pistol out of my holster and kill the calf elk. I thought about the brain splatter on the boy's forehead and cheek from me putting the calf elk down. I smiled and thought to myself, sometimes you just can't make this shit up. I should write a book someday." Good night!!

* *Thanks to my beautiful wife Kim for taking the front cover picture of this book. "Yes dear, the gun is un-loaded."*